Changing Rapture

𝓒

Other Books by Aliki Barnstone

POETRY

The Real Tin Flower
Windows in Providence
Madly in Love
Wild With It
Blue Earth

POETRY TRANSLATION

The Collected Poems of C. P. Cavafy: A New Translation

ANTHOLOGIES

A Book of Women Poets from Antiquity to Now
with Willis Barnstone

The Calvinist Roots of the Modern Era
with Michael Tomasek Manson and Carol J. Singley

The Shambhala Anthology of Women's Spiritual Poetry
(paperback edition of Voices of Light: Spiritual and Visionary Poems
by Women Around the World from Ancient Sumeria to Now)

EDITION

Trilogy by H.D.
Introduction and Readers' Notes by Aliki Barnstone

Changing Rapture

Emily Dickinson's Poetic Development

C

Aliki Barnstone

University Press of New England
Hanover and London

Published by University Press of New England,
One Court Street, Lebanon, NH 03766
www.upne.com

© 2006 by Aliki Barnstone
Printed in the United States of America
5 4 3 2 1

LIBRARY OF CONGRESS CATALOGING-IN-PUBLICATION DATA
Barnstone, Aliki.
Changing rapture : Emily Dickinson's poetic development / Aliki Barnstone.
p.   cm.
Includes bibliographical references and index.
ISBN-13: 978-1-58465-534-3 (cloth : alk. paper)
ISBN-10: 1-58465-534-8 (cloth : alk. paper)
1. Dickinson, Emily, 1830–1886 — Criticism and interpretation. I. Title.
PS1541.Z5B29 2006
811'.4—dc22   2006031293

 This book is printed on recycled paper that meets the minimum requirements of the Green Press Initiative.

To my "Preceptors,"
Barton Levi St. Armand, Robert Scholes,
and James E. B. Breslin (1935–1996),
each of whom profoundly changed—and change—
the rapture of my thought.

Rap·ture, n. [L *raptus, rapio.*]

1. A seizing by violence. [Little used.]

2. Transport; ecstasy; violence of a pleasing passion; extreme joy or pleasure.

   Music when thus applied, raises in the mind of the hearer great conceptions; it strengthens devotion and advances praise into rapture.

3. Rapidity with violence; a hurrying along with velocity; as rolling with torrent rapture.

4. Enthusiasm; uncommon heat of imagination.

   You grow correct, that once with rapture writ.

   —from Noah Webster's 1828 *American Dictionary*

CONTENTS

ACKNOWLEDGMENTS

I trace the beginnings of this book to Barton Levi St. Armand, whose astonishing graduate seminar decades ago at Brown University confirmed my devotion to the poet and her culture. His own beautiful work on the poet and his stated faith that I, too, could be an Emily Dickinson scholar have sustained me, and I thank him for being my mentor. Also crucial to me in those early days of my development were the appearance first of Adrienne Rich's "Vesuvius at Home" and then of Sandra M. Gilbert and Susan Gubar's *The Madwoman in the Attic*. These groundbreaking feminist works transformed me, gave me something to say and the urgency to say it. I feel immense gratitude to my father, Willis Barnstone, who read and reread each draft of this book, and who commented with a discerning editorial eye. My brother, Tony Barnstone, and my dear friends, Beth Binhammer, Cynthia Hogue, and Russell J. Reising, gave me their help in reading this work and making suggestions. Thanks are also due to Nancy Sherman, who provided me with friendship, encouragement, and a place to stay when I worked at the Robert Frost Library at Amherst College. I owe a debt of gratitude to Mitchell Robert Breitwieser, Mary P. Ryan, and the late James E. B. Breslin for their helpful comments; I acknowledge Mitch for his wonderful work on early American literature and thought, and for stimulating conversations about Emily Dickinson's development. I am grateful to the University of Nevada, Las Vegas, for awarding me time to work on this book through a Center For Advanced Research course reassignment. Thanks are also due my research assistant, Nicole Foreman, for her astute editing. I am lucky to have a family that is not only loving but interested in and enthusiastic about one another's work; I am immensely thankful to my mother, Elli Tzalopoulou-Barnstone, and my brother, Robert Barnstone. To my daughter, Zoë, I apologize for the afternoons I could not play, and I thank her for protest, born of love, so like the poet's bird stamping her foot, crying, "Give me."

Earlier versions of the chapter "Mastering the Master" appeared in *The Calvinist Roots of the Modern Era* (Hanover, N.H.: University Press of New England, 1998) and in *The Drunken Boat* (www.thedrunkenboat.com), 4, III–IV (Fall–Winter 2004): ISSN: 1530-7646.

ABBREVIATIONS

Fr Emily Dickinson, *The Poems of Emily Dickinson: Variorum Edition*. Edited by R. W. Franklin. 3 vols. Cambridge, Mass.: Harvard University Press, 1998.

J   Emily Dickinson, *The Poems of Emily Dickinson*. Edited by Thomas H. Johnson. 3 vols. Cambridge, Mass.: Harvard University Press, 1951, 1955.

L   Letter(s) from Emily Dickinson, *The Letters of Emily Dickinson*. Edited by Thomas H. Johnson and Theodora Ward. 3 vols. Cambridge, Mass.: Harvard University Press, 1958.

MB Emily Dickinson, *The Manuscript Books of Emily Dickinson*. Edited by R. W. Franklin. 2 vols. Cambridge, Mass.: Harvard University Press, 1981.

ML Emily Dickinson, *The Master Letters of Emily Dickinson*. Edited by R. W. Franklin. Amherst: Amherst College Press, 1986.

PF Prose fragment(s) from Emily Dickinson, *The Letters of Emily Dickinson*. Edited by Thomas H. Johnson and Theodora Ward. 3 vols. Cambridge, Mass.: Harvard University Press, 1958.

Changing Rapture

Introduction

&

Emily is called in Amherst "the myth." She has not been out of her house for fifteen years. One inevitably thinks of Miss Haversham in speaking of her. She writes the strangest poems, & very remarkable ones. She is in many respects a genius. She always wears white, & has her hair arranged as was the fashion fifteen years ago when she went into retirement.

— Mabel Loomis Todd

Life only avails, not the having lived. Power ceases in the instant of repose; it resides in the movement of transition from a past to a new state, in the shooting of the gulf, in the darting to an aim. This is one fact the world hates, that the soul *becomes*."

— Ralph Waldo Emerson

Every soul is immortal. For that which is ever moving is immortal; but that which moves something else or is moved by something else, when it ceases to move, ceases to live.

— Plato

Unchanging Myth

Emily Dickinson "the myth." She is a genius, who writes "the strangest poems" in complete seclusion. She always wears white, the color of virgins, brides, and mourning, and has never changed. In her appearance, which stands symbol for her work and spirit, she remains untouched by time or stuck in one particular year. Immortality, the focus of her poetry and philosophy, was conferred on her in life as a kind of changelessness, as if a poet who so thoroughly examined—and questioned—the truth of God must be, ironically, as immutable as the very truth she confronted in changing and often contentious ways. Even in death, she was regarded as unchanged. Upon seeing her in the casket, Thomas Wentworth Higginson perceived that death was "a wondrous restoration of youth—she is 54 [55] & looked 30, not a gray hair or wrinkle, and perfect peace on the perfect brow" (Leyda 2:475). Similarly, when Mabel Loomis Todd notes in her journal that Dickinson "has her hair arranged as was the fashion fifteen years ago when she went into retirement," she reveals that she sees through the lens created by myth. As Todd never laid eyes on her, the observation about the poet's hair must be part of the mythologizing—and self-mythologizing—of Emily Dickinson: that she dwelled in an eternal and spiritual state that was also a temporal stasis.

The myth of Emily Dickinson as unchanging in life extends to her poetry as well, which most critics claim did not develop. A serious problem arises from this misconception: to understand a poet's artistic and intellectual achievement, it is essential to understand how her vision develops and changes over time. We don't think of Ezra Pound or William Carlos Williams as poets whose work remained static. Both poets began as imagists and ended up as authors of epic poems that represented the culmination of their philosophies and poetics. If a poet's career in its entirety is not considered, then her reputation as a thinker is diminished. Consider H.D. Until the corrective studies by feminist critics, H.D. was almost universally regarded merely as an imagist, not as the radical theologian who in her later antiwar work *Trilogy* synthesized the ancient pagan religions and the Judeo-Christian tradition. Even now, this myth of H.D. as imagist pervades her reputation, as can be seen by the selections of her work in textbooks and anthologies. Though Dickinson, unlike the modernist poets I have mentioned here, did not write epic-length poems, her work develops in distinct ways as her philosophy changes.

The claim that Dickinson's poetry did not develop damages her stature; one way a reader evaluates a poet's oeuvre is to trace her growth as a thinker. Thomas J. Travisano, in his *Elizabeth Bishop: Her Artistic Development*, also sees this connection between the stature of a poet as a thinker and an understanding of her development: "The claim for [Bishop's] importance begins with her formal elegance, but it rests on the continuity and courage of her writing, its philosophical freshness, its moral complexity and soundness" (6–7).[1] A gender issue that should not go unacknowledged is that Emily Dickinson, H.D., and Elizabeth Bishop, three of America's exquisite, most influential and philosophically complex poets, have been known for a few individual, exceptional poems, rather than as poets whose large concepts and worldviews changed over time. Anne Bradstreet wittily points out in her "Prologue" that men write about big events and big ideas, which "for my mean pen are too superior things."

> Men can do best, and women know it well
> Preeminence in all and each is yours;
> Yet grant some small acknowledgment of ours.

Bradstreet writes poetry but promises to stay in her place. But she cleverly breaks her promise: she locates her poetry in the domestic sphere, as a woman should, and creates a profound metaphysics, which is a man's role. It is as if the later world had made Anne Bradstreet's covenant with women poets; namely, to give them a "*small* acknowledgment."

Yet assessing development is intimately related to *large* questions of literary and cultural influence. How has a writer responded to cultural events, be they religious, intellectual, or artistic movements, or economic or political changes? How has she been influenced by her literary forebears and her contemporaries? Critics who do not contemplate answers to these questions tend to regard Dickinson with condescension. Though the early critic Charles Anderson notes a movement in her wit from "badinage and nonsense" to "penetrating observation" to the epigrammatic, he fails to see these changes as signs of development. On the contrary, he argues, "There are no marked periods in her career, no significant curve of development in her artistic powers, no progressive concern with different genres, such as might furnish the central plan for a book on Milton or Yeats" (xii). Because Anderson sees no significant change in the work, he deems the majority of the 1,775 poems failures: "Her really fine poems do not seem to me to number more than one hundred, her great ones about twenty five" (xii). R. P. Blackmur sees development neither in the poetry of Dickinson nor of Whitman, but "great, repetitious wastes in both poets" (185). To the claim that she revolted against poetic tradition, he counters with an attack: "Emily Dickinson never knew anything about the craft of verse well enough to exemplify it, let alone revolt from it" (174).

Even more recent feminist critics succumb to the power of the myth of Emily Dickinson by claiming that the poet never grew up, and that she could neither face the harsh reality of the outside world nor write about it. Barbara Antonina Clarke Mossberg emphasizes that Dickinson's *"poems are not informed by adult experience"* and cannot move beyond the stasis of childhood: "there is no progressive development in her attitudes toward or depiction of love, death, immortality, or herself. She expresses herself in the end in essentially the same idiom she began with" (9). For Sharon Cameron as well the work is repetitive: "the same poem of pain or loss keeps writing itself over and over" (*Lyric Time* 14). Cameron persistently finds that Dickinson's poetry fails to meet the "rigors and exactions" of what for Cameron seem to be absolute poetical categories:

> The absence of development within the 1,775 poems is reflected in the resistance of many individual poems to the rigors and exactions of sequence and progression. For the words in Dickinson's poems often exist outside a situation and, more disturbing, seem to shrink from the necessity of creating one. (*Lyric Time* 14)

Both Cameron and Mossberg, who often do excellent local readings of the poems, tend to make banal psychological speculations about Dickinson and find failures in her psyche reflected in what they regard as failures in her corpus. These critics judge it a psychological failure that the poet withdrew from society. Because, in their view, the results of withdrawal are no development, no influence, no "situation" or grounding in "adult experience," they, like their cranky predecessor Blackmur, find the poetry repetitious, confusing, and ill-crafted.

Vivian Pollak has a more complex view of Dickinson's supposed lack of development. She assumes that the poet has a "feminist intelligence" (22) that subverts patriarchal culture by attempting to create the poetry of a "universal mind" (21). Dickinson, according to Pollak, believes "that the process of observation is culture-free" (20). Pollak mediates this assessment with the view that Dickinson, regardless of her strategy of withdrawal, cannot evade culture; yet she uses the poet's withdrawal as the basis of her assertion that she did not develop:

> [H]er ambivalence toward the possible identities her immediate environment afforded was so thoroughgoing as to preclude a comprehensive definition of the issues over which her battle for identity was joined. Hence, her art exhibits no clear-cut psychological development; she has no early, middle, and late manner. Instead, Dickinson achieved limited resolutions to limited conflicts by blocking out some of the competing

impulses that drove her. Because of her inability to integrate these reso-
lutions, each poem begins again as if anew. (22–23)

Although Pollak's terms are less negatively loaded than those of the critics
I have discussed above, she is nonetheless condescending since she argues
that Dickinson did not know which issues of identity her work challenged.
My position is precisely the opposite. Dickinson knew *exactly* which cultural, religious, and literary traditions she disputed, and the stages in her
development define the issues with which she was most concerned during
distinct periods in her life. As Dickinson's identity developed, so too did
her poetry.

Critics who argue that Dickinson's poetry did not develop assume her
notorious withdrawal from society was absolute, making her poetry timeless and untouched by the outside world. Dickinson was a recluse for much
of her adult life, yet her isolation was compromised by her family, her reading, her abundant correspondence, and by her poems, which appropriate
the materials of culture.[2] She could not have exempted herself from influence, even if she had willed it. Although Dickinson writes to Higginson,
"[I] never consciously touch a paint, mixed by another person" (L 271), her
distinctive paint — to continue her metaphor — may be mixed by her alone,
but she steals the pigments from the culture at large. Her deathbed words,
"Called Back," sent to her cousins in a letter (L 1046), were the title of a
sentimental novel by Hugh Conway and were carved into her tombstone.
In the context of her work, "Called Back," though it is wholly appropri-
ated from Conway's title, becomes thoroughly Dickinsonian: her shortest
poem, it calls the reader back to her and claims in stone-fixed words her
immortality in heaven and in literature. Dickinson's poetic power to transform the materials of culture into her own voice has blinded some of her
readers, even sympathetic ones, to her sources and influences.

The myth of Dickinson as the recluse, whose poetry didn't change because she chose her internal universe over the external one, fits paradoxically into the then prevalent myth of America; she herself was influenced
by nineteenth-century notions of individualism, self-reliance, and the
desire to be new and not unduly influenced by England or earlier writers. Emerson's famous assertion that "imitation is suicide" (138) resonated
for Dickinson. Ironically, when she claims she never "touch[es] a paint,
mixed by another" she imitates the precepts in Emerson's "Self-Reliance":

> Familiar as the voice of the mind is to each, the highest merit we as-
> cribe to Moses, Plato and Milton is that they set at naught books and

traditions, and spoke not what men but what *they* thought. A man should learn to detect and watch that gleam of light which flashes across his mind from within, more than the lustre of the firmament of bards and sages. (*Complete Writings* 138)

Emerson believed that a pure light could be "detected" from "within" the soul. While "the voice of the mind," as it is articulated by the "bards and sages" (Moses, Plato, and Milton), is universal, in order to see the light at all, one must allow one's own light to shine brighter than the most esteemed prophets, philosophers, and poets. Whitman, too, echoed Emerson's call for self-reliance in his famous lines from "Song of Myself":

> You shall no longer take things at second or third hand
> . . . nor look through the eyes of the dead . . . nor feed
> on the spectres in books,
> You shall not look through my eyes either, nor take
> things from me,
> You shall listen to all sides and filter them from yourself.
> (lines 27–29)

Thoreau, also taking his cue from Emerson, removed himself from society in a radical manner, asserted the originality of his thought, and scorned conventional ideas — perhaps even more adamantly than Dickinson did. Dickinson was not alone among nineteenth-century American writers in choosing to live self-reliantly by claiming originality and by being a recluse. Her withdrawal from society and her eschewal of literary influence were, paradoxically, part of a literary tradition.[3]

Four Changes

In the first period of her development Dickinson externalizes her argument with Calvinism through satire. In the early period Dickinson makes a clear distinction between her own language and the language of received ideas. The concern for strict boundaries between the voice of the self and the voices of culture is reflected in many of the poems' structures. She may begin these poems by presenting the sayings of others as a thesis, and then refuting the words of those others with her own antithesis. So one poem begins, "A science – So Savants say –" (Fr 147; 1860) and another, "In lands I never saw – they say / Immortal Alps look down – " (Fr 108; 1859). She may render these sayings ridiculous by testing them against her own or by mouthing them in a childish or singsong manner. She uses weapons similar to those William Blake employed in his child-centered "Poems of Innocence" where the rhythm and speech and offhand manner "innocently" tell devastating tales of suffering and death (as in "The Chimney Sweeper"). The kinship with early Blake is deep, whether or not there was direct influence. In the following poem, which is characteristic of the early satirical work, her speaker takes on the persona of a taunting child. The repetition serves as a device that distances the speaker from the idea of heaven as "home":

> "Houses" – so the Wise Men tell me –
> "Mansions"! Mansions must be warm!
> Mansions cannot let the tears in,
> Mansions must exclude the storm!
>
> "Many Mansions," by "his Father,"
> *I* don't know him; snugly built!
> Could the Children find the way there –
> Some, would even trudge tonight!
> (Fr 139; 1860)

Dickinson evokes the notion of heaven as an opulent place where houses are mansions that shelter their inhabitants from sadness and "exclude storms." The notion of heaven as a place that compensates for the suffering and poverty of earthly life would make "some" of "the Children" willing to die in order to find their way there. Because the children of God would "trudge" toward their heavenly home, the language of the last line belies that it is easy to die and to make the passage from life to reside forever in the mansions of the heavenly Father. From the beginning of her poetic career, she finds the notion of heavenly reward preposterous. In 1856 she wrote to Mrs. Holland:

My only sketch, profile, of Heaven is a large, blue sky, bluer and larger than the *biggest* I have seen in June, and in it are my friends — all of them — every one of them — those who are with me now, and those who were "parted" as we walked, and "snatched up to Heaven."

If roses had not faded, and frosts had never come, and one had not fallen here and there whom I could not waken, there were no need of other Heaven than the one below — and if God had been there this summer and seen the things *I* have seen — I guess He would think His Paradise superfluous. Don't tell Him, for the world, though, for after all

He's said about it, I should like to see what He *was* building for us, with
no hammer, and no stone, and no journeymen either. (L 185)

In this letter and in "Houses" Dickinson uses the voice of the child to
expose the folly of adult constructions of heaven. She asserts that were it
not for the sorrow of death "there were no need of other Heaven" than the
one here on earth. And if God could know the bliss of summertime and of
happy connections between friends, even He would see that His mansion
was "superfluous." In both the letter and the poem Dickinson distances
herself from God by italicizing the *I*. In "Houses," she pointedly declares,
"*I* don't know him," and emphatically separates the speaker of the poem
from the Lord and from those — "the Wise Men" and "the Children" —
who believe what they are told, who would claim to know the Father and
who hope to dwell in His mansions.

The prosody of the poem also contributes to the distinction between
the speaker and others. The first stanza's exact rhyme, "warm" and "storm,"
and its repetition give it a rollicking feel, so that what "the Wise Men tell"
the speaker sounds silly. In the second stanza, in which the speaker asserts her point of view, the off-rhyme ("built" and "tonight") is sobering,
as well befits children trudging to their deaths. In the first stanza, the persona of the child and the tone of the nursery rhyme disarm the reader; in
the second, the speaker manipulates the child's voice and establishes her
authority. This speaker regards the sayings of "the Wise Men" as external
to herself, and, by italicizing the *I*, draws a distinct slash between herself
and them.

In the second period of Dickinson's development, 1863 represents the
glorious culmination of Dickinson's poetic battle with Calvinism. I use
"the poems of 1863" as a category because close to four hundred of Dickinson's poems are dated 1863. This means that she was writing more than a
poem a day in that year or that she was making fair copy into fascicles and
letters at this prolific rate. Whether Dickinson actually composed these
poems in 1863 or whether she finished revising them in that year does not
matter for my purpose, which is to draw the large outline of her development. Two of the poems — "There's a certain Slant of light" (Fr 320) and "I
felt a Funeral, in my Brain" (Fr 340) — that I use as prototypes of her "self-
conversion" period are dated 1862. The astonishing number of poems pro-
duced in the period in and around the year 1863 shows that during this
time Dickinson was deeply preoccupied with an internal struggle with
Calvinism and with love. This love — whether of God or of another per-

son — is shaped by Calvinism's severity, its associations with loss and exclusion, and its power to overwhelm. I believe by writing so many poems in this period, Dickinson performed a kind of ritual mastery over the forces she felt could master her: religion, love, ecstatic experience.

I call the poems of 1863 poems of "self-conversion." The work in this second phase differs from that in the early phase because she has internalized her struggle with Calvinism. Though by this time she had chosen never to convert, in her *poetry* she passionately contended with the demands of Calvinist crisis conversion, with feeling excluded both by her loved ones and community, and by God who did not chose to save her. The predominant tones one finds in these poems are despair, anger, loss, numbness, and self-division, as in this well-known poem:

> After great pain, a formal feeling comes –
> The Nerves sit ceremonious, like Tombs –
> The stiff Heart questions 'was it He, that bore,'
> And 'Yesterday, or Centuries before'?
>
> The Feet, mechanical, go round –
> A Wooden way
> Of Ground, or Air, or Ought –
> Regardless grown,
> A Quartz contentment, like a stone –
>
> This is the Hour of Lead –
> Remembered, if outlived,
> As Freezing persons, recollect the Snow –
> First – Chill – then Stupor – then the letting Go –
> (Fr 372; 1863)

In contrast to "'Houses' – so the Wise Men tell me –," "After great pain" blurs the boundaries between the ideas of culture and the self. In addition to the vastly different tone, the shifting stance of the speaker in this poem represents a characteristic difference between poems of self-conversion, such as "After great pain," and the earlier satirical poems, such as "Houses." The point of view of the speaker can be seen as specific to its own self, as general to all "Freezing persons," and as referring to those *other* than itself. Although each stanza can be interpreted from any of these three positions, the meditations in the poem tend to become progressively more distant from the speaker. The first lines appear to be a description of the aftermath of pain told from an implied first-person speaker. The last stanza, with its "Freezing persons" seems to be speaking from the point of view of the third person. This elusive speaker — who at once represents her own self, the universal self, and selected (or elected) selves that are *not* herself — reveals that, in this second phase of her development, Dickinson has internalized the conflict she fought externally in the earlier poems.

This poem is frequently read in psychological terms as a breakdown, or even as evidence of psychosis.[4] Certainly, the poem describes psychological suffering, yet the poem is more complex; questions of culture and development intersect within it. My reading of "After great pain" is mediated by both its religious cultural context and the date — 1863 — of its composition. I prefer to think that the poem is an astounding account (one of many) of a chapter in the story of Dickinson's spiritual journey, which is also the story of her poetic journey. John Owen King observes that the Puritan conversion "journey" entailed "steps" or "conventions by which the saint could understand his trials and thereby make a sensible case out of his troubles of conscience. . . . These internal migrations entailed 'strangeness,' a sense of one's alienation from God that began when a person suddenly sensed his own destruction. . . . Given this terror or a conviction of sin, the person seeking salvation could easily enough look upon himself as entering into a wilderness" (14–15). King also traces the way in which the Puritan spiritual narrative evolved: "By the nineteenth century the Puritan's community of psychological revelation had fragmented into isolated spiritual texts. The Puritans' corporate case of conscience . . . had turned into the Victorians' individual psychopathological case" (17). This progression from communal spiritual struggle to personal psychopathology has perhaps made its way into readings of Dickinson. I look upon reductive psychobiography as too much of a narrowing of complex forces in her work. Yet equally I do not wish to focus my argument exclusively on her response to Puritanism. In the course of this book, I explore the ways in which Puritan orthodoxy was mitigated by religious and political changes that democratized and softened its harshness. On the one hand these new movements freed Dickinson to perform her dazzling poetic subversions of Calvinism. On the other, despite these theological revisions, she was impelled by the facts of her family's Puritan heritage, the wave of revivalism in her youth, and that she alone in her family did not convert. As Hyatt Waggoner writes of Amherst:

> To be religious in this village society was to experience a conviction of salvation, to become an active member of the church, and to profess publicly faith in its dogmas.

To be uncertain of any of the dogmas, in a church that held to "justi-fication by faith through grace" and that defined faith not as a motion of the heart but as giving assent to certain propositions was to give proof that one was not one of the Saints, the Elect, who would be saved. Emily began by not being certain she could believe the dogmas and ended by being certain she couldn't. . . . As late as 1862, more than a dozen years after she had discovered Emerson and other outlets in the New Thought for her religious emotions, Amherst's way of defining the issues of faith and unfaith was still assumed in her statement to T.W. Higginson about her family: "They are religious — except me." (184–185; 1984)

The first stanza of "After great pain" provides a stunning example of in-ternalized conflict in the poems of 1863. The stanza describes what could be a step in crisis conversion, since requisite steps in the conversion expe-rience were the painful recognition of sinfulness and the vanity of the self, the annihilation of the self, and the rebirth through Christ. "Melancholy, a physical malady," King writes, "foretells of spiritual awakening" (19). In his "Personal Narrative" of conversion, Jonathan Edwards describes the anguish of seeing his own sinfulness: "When I look into my heart and take a view of my wickedness, it looks like an abyss infinitely deeper than hell." Only grace can release him from his pain; only Christ can destroy the wicked self and sanctify him:

> The person of Christ appeared ineffably excellent with an excellency great enough to swallow up all thought and conception . . . which con-tinued as near as I can judge, about an hour; which kept me the greater part of the time in a flood of tears, and weeping aloud. I felt an ardency of soul to be, what I know not otherwise how to express, emptied and annihilated; to lie in the dust, and to be full of Christ alone; to love him with a holy and pure love; to trust in him; to live upon him; to serve and follow him; and to be perfectly sanctified and made pure, with a divine and heavenly purity. ("Personal Narrative")

Edwards passionately wants his selfhood "emptied and annihilated"; he wants to die, "to lie in the dust," so he can be "full of Christ." Like-wise in "After great pain," the self has been numbed and the "stiff Heart questions" whether Christ bore the suffering and sin of humanity, and whether, perhaps, he will fill her with his grace. This moment of ques-tioning is in quotation marks, as so many phrases are in the earlier satiri-cal poems. Yet these quotation marks do not create boundaries between the cultural script and the speaker, as they do in Dickinson's early phase.

Instead, because the Christian phrases are spoken by "the stiff Heart," that is, inside the consciousness (and the body) of the speaker, the marks serve to show that such boundaries between the interior and the exterior are permeable, illusory—if they can be established at all.

The first stanza could be the melancholy that is the antecedent to re-birth. Yet instead of the breakthrough and union with Christ that Edwards depicts, in the second and third stanzas the self grows "regardless," and "The feet, mechanical, go round" and choose a "Wooden" lifeless way, instead of the "narrow" way in Matthew 7.14 "which leadeth unto life." Fordyce R. Bennett, who connects the images of quartz and snow to Revelation, maintains that the "echoes" are ironic and that the poem creates "the face of the false apocalyptic, its potential unmeaning in stark contrast to the desired beatific vision" (82). In this "Hour of Lead," time has stopped, has actually become physically heavy, as though rather than the soul's rising to eternity, it sinks and becomes all matter. The self is in a "Stupor" before "the letting Go" into death, perhaps, or another realm of consciousness. This utter abjection can be seen as the "humilation" of the self, which is the precursor to grace. Yet, despite "the letting Go" at the end of the poem, there is no grace as seen in Edwards's narrative, no warm, light-filled union with Christ.

The poem follows the same path prosodically. Just as it begins as an attempt to follow the traditional morphology of conversion, so the poem begins with the traditional iambic pentameter line. A. R. C. Finch points out that this poem has "more pentameters than appear in any other Dickinson poem, except two. . . . The pain appears to have weakened the poet's resistance to the hypnotic, 'mechanical,' 'Wooden way' of the traditional meter" (173). The entire first stanza is in iambic pentameter. As Finch puts it:

> The resigned question asked by the stiff heart—"was it He, that bore?"—seems to refer on one level to Christ's suffering, using Christian imagery as Dickinson's pentameters commonly do. On another level, the question might refer to the burden of subjectivity and responsibility long borne by male poets. The poet seems to ask in resignation, why should their authority be questioned now, anymore than that carried by other patriarchal institutions? (173)

After the speaker confronts Christian doubt, the second stanza breaks down the iambic pentameter, but does not return to the "8s and 6s" of Dickinson's predominant hymnal stanza,[5] as if the meter of church songs, "regardless" of her having adopted it as her own in so many other poems, is too laden with the weight of submissive belief and predictability.

That the poem returns to iambic pentameter in the last two lines serves neither as an affirmation of the patriarchal church nor of the poetics associated with male poets. Finch writes that "as the meter of the past poets overtakes the poem, the poet uses iambic pentameter to present an image of helpless, frozen stupor" (173). I agree that the image of a "helpless, frozen stupor" is captured in pentameters, yet the return to the pentameter line signifies that having broken down the formal ceremony, as well as the religious ceremony, the poet has "let go" of regular form. By the time she returns to pentameters, the meter has been irreparably converted to her poetics. The adherence to the pentameter line, then its breakdown, is a metrical representation of Dickinson's effort to embrace orthodoxy, only to break form, to divide into heterodoxy, and to turn to her radical *conversion* of form. The "letting Go" in the last pentameter line returns the reader to the original meter in the first line: "After great pain, a *formal* feeling comes" in the writing of a poem. The poem is a conversion narrative that ends not in the grace of redemption through Jesus Christ, but in the grace of the human poet's Word.[6]

Dickinson, then, in the period of 1863 appropriates the conversion experience and transforms it into poetic process. In so doing, she has both internalized and challenged Calvinism. As she moves out of this crisis period, her poetry changes from its focus from Calvinism to Transcendentalism. Though Calvinist theology continues to inform Dickinson's poetry, the intensity of 1863 wanes. The drama of despair and self-division gives way to calm, philosophical speculation. Stormy lines such as "'Twas like a Maelstrom, with a notch / That nearer, every Day / Kept narrowing its boiling Wheel" (Fr 425; 1862) belong to the period of self-conversion. In the next period, which I call "the adventure of the self," she senses with what she calls in one poem "Pyramidal Nerve" (Fr 1011; 1865) and her poems, which translate extraordinary states of being, are characteristically potent distillations. She does not stop portraying pain or death or tragedy; during this third period, she writes the devastating poem that begins "The last Night that She lived" (Fr 1100; 1865). Yet, as if describing this new moment in her growth as an artist, she writes that "Affliction [is] but a speculation — and Woe / A Fallacy, a Figment, We knew" (Fr 997; 1865); she sees psychic pain as clearly as before and from a certain distance. In this stage of her development, the perceptions of "Pyramidal Nerve," whether ecstatic or painful, lead to the enlightenment

of the consciousness in solitude, and Dickinson accords them the highest
spiritual value:

> There is a Zone whose even Years
> No Solstice interrupt –
> Whose Sun constructs perpetual Noon
> Whose perfect Seasons wait –
>
> Whose Summer set in Summer, till
> The Centuries of June
> And Centuries of August cease
> And Consciousness – is Noon.
>
> (Fr 1020; 1865)

In this poem, as in the "After great pain," Dickinson explores a "Zone"
that the self-reliant consciousness might reach. As in "After great pain"
that state might be eternal. Yet the suffering, the self-division, and the
numbness in "After great pain" are absent in "There is a Zone." "Zone"
comes much closer to Emerson's ideal of the eternal soul. The soul, Emerson writes in "The Over-Soul" "abolishes time and space," and

> time and space are but inverse measures of the force of the soul. The
> spirit sports with time, —
> > 'Can crowd eternity into an hour,
> > or stretch an hour to eternity.' (207)

Likewise, in Dickinson's "Zone" the "Sun constructs perpetual Noon."
Noon, which is an immeasurable instant, becomes eternal. "And consciousness is—Noon," and by extension is eternal as well. Noon is the
apex of the sun's light, and it is the moment of enlightenment. As can be
seen in poems such as "There came a Day at Summer's full" (Fr 325) and
"Further in Summer than the birds" (Fr 895), in Dickinson's private mythology,[7] summer represents a time of loveliness and bounty when "Each
was to each The Sealed Church, / Permitted to commune" (Fr 325). As
Barton St. Armand observes, Dickinson worshipped nature and she "gave
the summer day a whole new liturgical significance. The earthly paradise supplied all of the High Church ritual, all of that sacerdotal wealth
of embroidered vestments, gleaming vessels, and heady incense, that Puritanism had denied her, reared as she was within the wintry confines of
the New England meetinghouse" (206). The "Zone" is the space where
summer, with its heat and natural opulence, and noon, with its intensity

of light, come together for an eternity and unite with consciousness. This is the moment of communion, conversion or grace that Dickinson could not achieve with the Calvinist God.

Yet this sublime moment is not without disturbance or doubt. "Consciousness is – Noon" when "The Centuries of June / And Centuries of August *cease*." That cessation implies that the apex of soul occurs at death, a notion that Emerson would reject: for him the eternal soul is always present, in life and in death; union is always possible for the earnest and idealistic seeker. Dickinson, by contrast, is ambivalent, as is revealed by the variants for the word "cease," which are "fuse –," "lapse –," and "blend." A fusion or a blending of the centuries of summer would constitute, perhaps, an intensification of eternal time, when consciousness would reach its eternal noon. Fusion does not imply that one kind of consciousness must end in order for another higher order of consciousness to begin.

This ambivalence is important; while Dickinson seeks out and admires ecstatic moments, she, unlike Emerson and her Calvinist contemporaries, believes that life on earth, communing with nature and loved ones, is paradise:

> Eden is that old-fashioned House
> We dwell in every day
> Without suspecting our abode
> Until we drive away.
> (Fr 1735)

Dickinson's ambivalence reveals on the one hand that she wants to reach the "Zone"; on the other, however, she doubts that communion with the eternal soul can occur among the living. She criticizes Calvinist grace because it is compensatory:

> Which is best? Heaven –
> Or only Heaven to come
> With that old Codicil of Doubt?
> I cannot help esteem
>
> The "Bird within the Hand"
> Superior to the one
> The "Bush" may yield me
> Or may not
> Too late to choose again.
> (Fr 1021)

Dickinson "esteem[s]" the heaven on earth "Superior" to the "Heaven to come." By the mid- to late 1860s, which I mark as the beginning of her "adventure of the self," Dickinson scarcely takes seriously the Calvinist cosmology that disregards earthly bliss:

> To die – without the Dying
> And live – without the Life
> This is the hardest Miracle
> Propounded to Belief.
> (Fr 1027)

Her worship of nature gives her the freedom to ignore the dictates of the Calvinist God who asks that his subjects give up as vanity their earthly joys "[a]nd live – without the Life" in exchange for life everlasting—for dying "without the dying." "By fully assuming control of the amazing graces of natural communion," St. Armand argues, "she put herself on an equal with footing the parsimonious deity himself" (192).

In her third phase of development Dickinson grapples instead with Emerson's transcendental connection with nature. He writes in "The Poet" that "the world is a temple whose walls are covered with the emblems, pictures, and commandments of the Deity . . . there is no fact in nature which does not carry the whole sense of nature" (*Complete Writings* 243). In his doctrine of correspondence, the law of the Deity will be revealed to the individual who sees nature and is one with the universal soul. Furthermore, it is the duty of the poet to create beauty and to thereby, "re-attach . . . things to nature and the Whole." Things are rendered ugly by the "dislocation and detachment from the life of God" (244). Nature as God's creation can lead a soul to Him, but because the moment of union is *transcendental* that union involves distance from the world.

Dickinson, by contrast with Emerson, has a more intimate relationship with nature. Recall for a moment, her letter to Mrs. Holland in which she jokes not to tell God that were it not for death, His heaven would be "superfluous." God, the "distant – stately Lover" (Fr 615), is not only unreachable through the natural world, in Dickinson's estimation, He is hardly welcome in earthly paradise. Though Dickinson is influenced and empowered by Emerson's idealism, she, like Melville, resents her whole life long the Calvinist god she rejects:

> Far from Love the Heavenly Father
> Leads the Chosen Child,

Oftener through Realm of Briar
Than the Meadow mild.

Oftener by the Claw of Dragon
Than the Hand of Friend
Guides the Little One predestined
To the Native Land.[8]

(Fr 1032; 1865)

In "Further in Summer than the Birds," Dickinson worships nature, but that worship does not mean that she achieves union with the Deity.

Further in Summer than the Birds
Pathetic from the Grass
A minor Nation celebrates
Its unobtrusive Mass

No Ordinance be seen
So gradual the Grace
A pensive Custom it becomes
Enlarging loneliness

Antiquest felt at Noon
When August burning low
Arise this spectral Canticle
Repose to typify

Remit as yet no Grace
No Furrow on the glow
Yet a Druidic Difference
Enhances Nature now

(Fr 895; 1865)

The religious language is balanced by the adjectives "pathetic," "minor," and "unobtrusive." The crickets'[9] mass is small, not grand, and it "Remit[s] as yet no Grace," meaning perhaps that their "spectral Canticle" does not have the power to raise the listener up to God. Since "Remit as yet no Grace" can be read as an imperative, perhaps that the listener does not want that kind of grace; she prefers the magic and the mystery of the "Druidic Difference" that "Enhances Nature now."

The focus of "Further in Summer than the Birds" is on the perception of the sound of crickets' ghostly canticle rising from the grass; it is a

celebration of a "minor Nation" whose power lies in its ability to alter perception. It is important that, as in "There is a Zone," Dickinson plays with
time: the crickets' song is "Antiquest felt at Noon." The effect of their song
on consciousness resembles that eternal "Zone" both because it occurs at
the same moment—at Noon, in August—and because it evokes an exhil-
arated and reverent state of consciousness. Though Dickinson worships
nature, she differs from Emerson in that she does not unite the perceiver
and the "Mass" of crickets to God. She prefers instead the "Difference," or
the enhancement of nature, that perception creates. In another poem, she
explores this metaphysical difference between the subjectivity of perception and union with "The Object Absolute":

> Perception of the Object costs
> Precise the Object's loss –
> Perception in itself a Gain
> Replying to its Price –
>
> The Object Absolute – is nought –
> Perception sets it fair
> And then upbraids a Perfectness
> That situates so far –
> (Fr 1103; 1865)

Dickinson asserts that the subjectivity of the speaker always alters the
object perceived. Thus, the object is lost in the projections of the seer.
To return to "Further in Summer," though the perception of the crickets'
song "remit[s] as yet no Grace"—or unity—the perception of it "enhances
Nature." In "Further in Summer," the perception of the poet makes the
metaphorical connection between the crickets and a visionary religious
moment. That is, while the crickets may be a mass of insects, the crickets
sing a "Mass" because they have been transformed by the creative power
of perception. Idiosyncratic as it may be, the potential of perception to
create its own magic is a "Gain" that replies to the "Price" of subjectivity.

Furthermore, Dickinson contends that "The Object Absolute – is
nought"; it does not exist; it is nothing. Yet the poet observes that "Perception sets it fair," a statement whose multiple meanings add up to the
value of perception: namely, perception makes the object beautiful and
clear. Regardless of price, perception is a reliable and fair measure of the
world. "Our perceptual grid of time and space prohibits a pure knowledge
of absolute realities," writes Robert Weisbuch of this poem, "yet that grid

is a trustworthy human reality which allows for a relationship to things-in-themselves" (161).[10] Perception is a gain not simply in-and-of itself but as a mode of relation. The "Perfectness" of the "Object Absolute," were it possible, creates a distance between the perceiver and the object; that ironically named "Perfectness" that collapses subject and object would "situate" the "Object Absolute" "far" away. By contrast, the subjectivity of the perceiver creates a relationship between the perceiver and the perceived, as in "Further in Summer than the Birds." Perception "upbraids" that distancing "Perfectness." "Upbraids" is a strong word, one that turns the tables on the point of view, whether Calvinist or transcendentalist, that earthly perception is — to continue Dickinson's metaphor — an inferior product not worth its price, no matter how cheap. While Emerson sees perception as the means of uniting with the infinite, Dickinson sees that union with heaven as too dear — and impossible — a price to pay. Significantly, the variant for the last line of "Perception" is "that 'tis so Heavenly far." So the perception of an object that would unite the seer with God's heaven is likewise "upbraided" by subjective perception.

I see "Perception of the Object" as a refutation of Emerson's belief in the unity of perception. Emerson writes in "The Over-Soul":

[M]an is the soul of the whole; the wise silence; the universal beauty, to which every part and particle is equally related; the eternal ONE. And this deep power in which we exist and whose beatitude is all accessible to us, is not only self-sufficient and perfect in every hour, but the act of seeing and the thing seen, the seer and the spectacle, the subject and the object, are one. We see the world piece by piece, as the sun, the moon, the animal, the tree; but the whole, of which these are the shining parts, is the soul. (*Complete Writings* 206)

In his effort to redeem the human soul, Emerson collapses the distinctions between subject and object, between the soul and God. Everything tends toward the "ONE"; every object perceived is "perfect" in that it enables the soul to transcend itself and join with God: "The soul gives itself, alone, original and pure, to the Lonely, Original and Pure, who on that condition, gladly inhabits, leads and speaks through it" (215). At the sublime moment, the human soul, no matter how self-reliant, idiosyncratic, or original, is overwhelmed by the God-soul, which "inhabits, leads, and speaks through it." Ironically, this union with God is a great deal like Calvinist crisis conversion, but Emerson's "universal beauty" and goodness replace Calvinist innate sinfulness.

In his essay "Experience," Emerson is troubled by precisely the philosophical problem that Dickinson puts forth in her "Perception of the Object." He despairs that there may indeed be no "Object Absolute," that the object is an illusion created by the perceiver: "Dream delivers us to dream, and there is no end to illusion. . . . Nature and books belong to the eyes that see them" (*Complete Writings* 253). Emerson also suspects that perception costs "the Object's loss" and that subjectivity creates the "colored and distorted lenses" through which we see, and whose "errors" we have no way of ascertaining: "We have learned that we do not see directly but mediately, and that we have no means of correcting these colored and distorted lenses which we are, or of computing the amount of their errors. Perhaps these subject lenses have a creative power; perhaps there are no objects" (261). Emerson's experience of the death of his son forces him to struggle with his own idealism, though he tries to reassure himself that "Grief too will make us idealists" (253). For Dickinson, death breaks down faith irreparably; for Emerson, losing his son temporarily fragments the unity of his vision.

In earlier essays, Emerson asserts that there is unity in diversity; although the soul's creative expression is self-reliant and idiosyncratic, expression nonetheless is like water flowing from the same source of holiness, from the same truth. In "Experience," he fears that diversity leads to fragmentation rather than unity: "I know better than to claim any completeness for my picture. I am a fragment and this is a fragment of me" (264). Yet in the end he reasserts his doctrine of self-reliance: "We cannot say too little of our constitutional necessity of seeing things under private aspects, or saturated with our humors. . . . That need makes in morals the capital virtue of self-trust. . . . It is the main lesson of wisdom to know your own from another's" (263). Emerson returns to his view that the human soul, untainted by misperceptions of society, will connect with the universal soul. In "Experience," he allows that differentiating between one's own vision and that of others is a difficult path. His own experience has taken him into the worlds that most challenge his idealism, yet he believes there is "victory yet" and retracts his skepticism:

> I know that the world I converse with in the city and in the farms is not the world I *think*. I observe that difference, and shall observe it. One day I shall know the value and law of this discrepance. . . . in the solitude to which every man is always returning, he has a sanity and revelations which in his passage into new worlds he will carry with him.

Never mind the ridicule, never mind the defeat; up again, old heart! — it seems to say — there is victory yet for all justice; and the true romance which the world exists to realize will be the transformation of genius into practical power. (264)

Though these words have a bravado that leaves the reader a bit incredulous, Emerson returns to that solitude where "sanity and revelations" will create victory, and individual genius reattaches the world to God.

In the third phase of her development, Dickinson embraces the subjectivity of perception and the possibility of relatedness that subjectivity creates. She maintains her love of the earth, and rejects the notion that ecstatic moments must mean viewing the pleasures of earthly life as vanity. She extends her criticism of Calvinism to Emersonian transcendentalism because, in trying to unite with God, both cosmologies create distance between the self and its earthly attachments. The poems in the third phase of Dickinson's development, however, are not dramatic accounts of despair and doubt. Even those poems evoking Calvinism and its torments do so from a different, less conflicted point of view. The voices of culture, which she satirized in the first phase of her development and which she internalized in the second, have been incorporated into her poetics and philosophy. Dickinson responded to Calvinist theology as a formidable foe; Emerson, by contrast, served as a playful sparring partner for her. His work from the beginning had been an inspiration, and she shares affinities with his idealistic philosophy, even as she argues with it. The poems in this third phase crystallize her philosophical concerns in shorter, more epigrammatic poems whose tone is one of meditative calm. In these poems, the battle is over, and she has achieved closure.

In these pages, I have shown ways to read Emily Dickinson by considering her poems in the context of her development. In the last years of her life, however, the question of how to read Dickinson is complicated by the fact that her writing process changed. And this change in process was radical. In the period around 1876, she virtually stopped making fair copies of her poems and organizing them into fascicles and sets. The fascicles represent poems in fair copy that she sewed together at the spine and bound into forty booklets. The sets are poems that were arranged in the same manner, but that she did not bind. The poems we have from this fourth period of her life are gathered from letters and from scraps found among her papers. In the last years of her life, Dickinson's texts reveal — with immense implications — that she no longer categorized her writing into the distinct genres of "poems" and "letters." Throughout her life, Dickinson sent her poems to others in letters, but in those last years, virtually all the "poems" we have from this period are those portions of her letters, working drafts, and scraps of paper that her editors deemed "poems."

When Dickinson's readers read her late work divided into "poems," "letters," and "prose fragments," it is essential to know that these categories were determined by her editors.[11] Paula Bennett writes that because Dickinson did not publish, "textual authority for the poetry resides in the holographs alone. *All* published versions of Dickinson's poems, even those in critical text such as this, represent editorial revisions" (*Emily Dickinson* xvii). Those editorial revisions become even more problematic in the late period when the editors could not base their decisions on Dickinson's fair copies. In determining whether or not a text is a poem, Johnson[12] generally regards literary language in regular rhyme and meter as "poems," and literary language that deviates as "letters" or "prose fragments." I maintain that the decisions made are often idiosyncratic. In the first place, Dickinson's poetry deviates from strict rhyme and meter. Second, and paradoxically, most of her writing, including the letters, is metrical and contains at least off-rhyme or other sound devices. Johnson is inconsistent in his criteria. Sometimes he categorizes work as "poetry" that does not contain regular prosody. Two such short examples in his editions are the following poems, which contain no rhyme at all: "Is Immortality a bane / That men are so oppressed?" (Fr 1757; undated) and "A Letter is a joy of Earth – / It is denied the Gods –" (Fr 1672; 1885). Yet this poetic fragment below is not, in his view, a poem, though it is metrically similar to the two above:

> My Family
> of Apparitions
> is select,
> though dim.[13]

He classifies as "letters" work that is more conventionally written. In contrast to the two rhymeless examples above that he classifies as "poems," this "letter" is as regular in rhyme and meter as many of Dickinson's late poems, and is more so than those above:

> Dear Kendall,
>   I send
> you a Blossom
> with my love –

Spend it as
you will –
The woods
are too deep
for your little Feet to
grope for
Evergreen –
    Your friend
    Emily
        (L 1027)[14]

Although this piece may not appear to be lineated (as one would expect a poem by Dickinson to be), in fact, in manuscript, many of her poems — especially those in the later period — look like this. The handwriting is large, and frequently there are only two or three words to a line. The "letter" quoted here resembles others that contain lines that were excerpted and deemed poems:

Sweet foot,
that comes
when we call
it!
I can go
but a step
a century
now –
How slow the
Wind – how slow
the Sea – how
late their Feathers
be!
    Lovingly,
    Emily
        (L 832)

In Johnson's and Franklin's editions, there appears the following poem:

How slow the Wind –
how slow the sea –
how late their Feathers be!
    (J 1571; Fr 1607; 1883)

This editorial decision to excise portions of letters in order to create poems raises several issues. First, if one is going to lineate poetic language, why lineate portions of a piece and not others? Why not include the whole letter-poem? Here I have lineated the entire letter-poem using Johnson's criteria:

> Sweet foot,
> that comes when we call it!
> I can go
> but a step a century now.
> How slow the Wind –
> How slow the Sea –
> How late their Feathers be!

Johnson might argue that only those lines that rhyme can be considered part of the poem, yet "wind" doesn't rhyme with "sea" or "be." "Century," which he omits and is the line-ending in manuscript, does rhyme. Furthermore, in the context of Dickinson's prosody, which makes use of much off-rhyme, it would not be unusual for her to rhyme "foot" and "it" and "go" and "now." In the letter-poem to Kendall Emerson, "deep," "feet," and "evergreen" do rhyme. If the same criterion of rhyme were used for all Dickinson's manuscripts, there would be a lineated version that would read:

> The woods are too deep
> for your little feet
> to grope for Evergreen –

In reading the letter-poem, "Sweet Foot," the first two sentences are crucial. This is a letter-poem, after all, written in 1883, at the end of her life. So when the poet writes, "I can go / but a Step / a Century / now," she refers to her own frailty. The "Sweet Foot / that comes / when we call / it!" may refer to a person who draws near to the person in ill-health. Or it may refer to her younger self, whose body responded as she commanded it. Or perhaps it refers to the metrical foot, to poetic language that comes easily, on the wind or on the sea, and gives the poet wings. If death is considered a return to nature, the sea and the wind are slow in taking her; the feathers of redemption are late in coming. Characteristically, Dickinson plays with time. The speaker has slowed down so much, she can "go but a Step a Century." As in the poem "There is a Zone," in which consciousness is both "Noon" and an eternity, a "Step" becomes a "Century," and perception likewise lengthens the time of the wind and the sea. Without the first two sentences, however, poem 1571 is intriguing, but slight. The poem deprived of the first two sentences is dominated by the trite rhyme "sea" and "be," and loses its pathos, its personal resonance, its metaphysics, and its speaker.

The greeting and the closing of the letter-poems are also crucial. Throughout her career — not just in letter-poems, but in the poems sewn into the fascicles — one of Dickinson's characteristic voices directly addresses the reader. As Erika Scheurer points out, "The rhetorical intent . . . Dickinson's textual voice achieves — engaging the reader in dialogue — permeates Dickinson's poems as much as her letters" (87). Though she is generally thought of as poet whose themes — love, death, nature, immortality — are so vast that they transcend the particular, Dickinson does involve the reader in her personal relationships. In the poem, "Dying! Dying in the Night!" (Fr 222), the speaker calls out to her friend "Dollie." (Dollie was a pet name for Emily's dear friend and sister-in-law, Susan Dickinson.) Likewise in the poem "Why make it doubt – it hurts so –," Dickinson's invocation of "Master" creates a devastating interaction between the poet and her reader: "Oh, Master, This is Misery –" (Fr 697). Dickinson makes frequent use of the second person in order to entice the reader with nearness and bring her into the poem, as in the following earlier poems:

> You see I cannot see – your lifetime – / I must guess – (Fr 313)
> You know that Portrait in the Moon – / So tell me who 'tis like –
> (Fr 676)
> You'll know Her – by Her Foot (Fr 604)
> Let Us play Yesterday – / I – the Girl at school – / You – and Eternity –
> the untold Tale – (Fr 754)
> You taught me Waiting with Myself – (Fr 774)
> You said that I "was Great" – one Day – (Fr 736)

This kind of opening throws into question the notion that the poem is self-contained and that the reader is outside the poem, overhearing the meditations of the poem's speaker. The use of the second person in poems is a seduction and betrayal in that it simultaneously may have two contrary yet related effects: it may include the reader who identifies herself as the second person or exclude the reader who identifies the second person as other than herself. In either case, these opening lines immediately engage the reader with their intimacy.

The late letter-poems represent a further development and intensification of—to use Dickinson's own word—her "confiding" voice. When the poet signs "Sweet foot," "Lovingly, / Emily," her signature continues the prosody of the lines above. "Lovingly" and "Emily" lullingly rhyme with "century," "sea," and "be" and serve to echo onomatopoetically the slowness and persistence of the sea and the wind and the sweet footsteps of the passage of time. The signature itself insists that the letter-poem not end, but continue to resonate. When Dickinson wrote her letter-poems, she transformed the genre of the letter into poetic language, so the salutations and the signatures become thematically inextricable from her epistolary poetics.

The late poems must be read in the context of a poet who in her last years gave the majority of her fair copy manuscripts to friends in letters. She developed a radically relational poetics that was connected with the world, a world of specific readers. This last phase of her development in which the genres of poetry, fragments, and letters become indistinguishable is her final stylistic statement about communication and her lifelong refusal to reject her earthly attachments in order to gain entrance into God's heaven. She refutes the notion that the poem is an immortal and sacred artifact separate from the writer and her readers. By making her last writings epistles to those earthly beings whom she loved, she revises poetic immortality, enlarging it to an intimate gesture between friends. In her last poetry, she creates an immortal union with her readers in letters, and transforms the popular nineteenth-century belief that those who died rejoined their loved ones in their heavenly home. Throughout her career, as I have shown, Dickinson asserted that heaven was on earth; her last poems create an intimate, earthly unbroken circle.

Though it is a critical commonplace that Dickinson went beyond nineteenth-century conventional poetics, her editors edited her work using nineteenth-century standards. As a result of this editorial revision of Dickinson's innovations, many of her most intriguing poems are read as non-poems or excised from the whole. The question of how to establish a reader's edition of Dickinson's poems is the subject of a great deal of debate; in her late period this question is particularly vexed, as I have indicated here and explore more deeply in chapter 4. To read in manuscript Dickinson's beautifully laid out late fragments and letter-poems is exhilarating; her distinctive calligraphy creates moving pictograms of her words. But these manuscripts are not readily available to any but those who go to the archives to find them. To read the same poems—I believe they are poems — in print in the Johnson and Franklin editions is simply devastating. These fragmentary poetic works, deprived of their line breaks, become mere aphorisms. Susan Howe writes: "As a poet, I cannot assert that Dickinson . . . was careless about line breaks. In the precinct of Poetry, a word, the space around a word, each letter, every mark, silence, or sound volatizes an inner law of form — moves on a rigorous line" (*Birth mark* 145). Because these late works are not prose, but innovative poetic language, they need their line breaks, their spaces, their greetings and signatures. While not everyone may wish to read Dickinson in manuscript (though I highly recommend it) everyone should be able to read these works in their entirety and with the line breaks Dickinson chose.[15]

If Dickinson's poetry does not develop, she becomes a literary aberration rather than a revolutionary. She is forever a child, feminine and dressed in white, innocent of tradition, unaware of or untouched by history or current events, indifferent to society. Her work does not represent stages in an important poet's ideas. Rather, as Blackmur puts it, "the bulk of her verse is not representative but mere fragmentary indicative notation" (195). Because her poems' radical idiosyncrasies challenge cultural categories, Dickinson's poetry may seem to some to lack development and to exist apart from cultural influence. But the poems do not, as Cameron claims, "shrink from the necessity of creating" (*Lyric Time* 14) a cultural situation; on the contrary, they strive to turn the cultural situation on its head and to rename it. When Dickinson writes, "The Soul selects her own Society – / Then – shuts the Door –" (Fr 409), she does not, as some assume, shut out all society. She makes a *selection*. I concentrate on the selection Dickinson makes and how she transforms it over time. By establishing taxonomies for her work along the lines of her development, I hope that readers will read her poems in a more complex way, with an awareness of Dickinson's intellectual concerns at the time of their composition. I also hope that other readers will be able to develop the stages I have delineated even further.[16]

For the most part, Dickinson scholars have not challenged the early critical assessment that her work did not develop, as if that early perception of the poet's work were such a powerful component of Dickinson mythmaking that it became an inviolate truth.[17] In describing the nature of myth, Richard Slotkin observes that "[r]eference to . . . [a] myth or to things associated with it — as in religious ritual — evokes in people the sense of life inherent in the myth and all but compels belief in the vision of reality and divinity implicit in it" (6). Perhaps it is a testament to the power of and the human need for myth that a century of Dickinson's critics have accepted and advanced the counterintuitive notion that a poet did not develop. Yet, how, after all, is it possible for any artist *not* to develop, even if it is to fall into decline or fraily to imitate his or her own earlier achievements? Of course, if an artist dies young or stops practicing her art, there may be little development to observe, but Emily Dickinson's first poem is dated in 1850, when she was twenty, and she continued to write until her death in 1886, when she was fifty-five.[18] When Dickinson was named "The Myth" by her community in Amherst, the name both conferred the power of the genius upon her *and* a limited perception of her; as Slotkin observes, myth "reduces both experience and vision to a paradigm" (6). "The mythopoeic mode of consciousness," Slotkin continues, "comprehends the world through . . . a process of reasoning-by-metaphor in which direct statement and logical analysis are replaced by figurative or poetic statement" (7). While I do not wish to overprivilege "direct statement and logical analysis," it might be helpful to think about how "reasoning-by-metaphor" has shaped and perpetuated the myth of Emily Dickinson.

Dickinson herself engaged in a great deal of self-mythologizing.[19] As I initially suggested, her wearing white is a case in point. White is the symbol of purity, of brides, angels, virgins, innocence, mourning, ghosts, and the white light of Dickinson's visionary "Noon." Judith Farr writes that her

> white clothes may indicate her vision of herself as one with those who overcome tribulation (as cited in scriptural passages as Revelation 3:5). . . . [It] verifies Dickinson's right to be counted among the elect. Her white raiment, the sign of her integrity . . . is also that of a soul "at the White Heat": one who has earned heaven by the full exercise of God-given artistic powers. (220)

By wearing white, Dickinson sets herself apart and asserts her self-reliance. She is virgin in the sense that she remains true to herself and her own vision, even at the expense of suffering. And like Christ's, her vision is redeemed through suffering. Her white dress is a sign of her poetic power, and stands for those aspects associated with the romantic genius: innocence, timelessness, purity. When she speaks in the voices of the child, the daisy, the bird, the small one, she extends the metaphor of pure vision. Dickinson, who asks, "Dare you see a Soul *at the White Heat?*" (Fr 401), challenges the reader to look into the blaze of her mythological genius.

The associations of Dickinson with the myth of the genius, as I have shown, fit into the myth of America, the New World in which each person can create selfhood, can be unique, self-reliant, free of the past, of what Emerson calls "the corpse . . . of memory" (*Complete Writings* 141). The drive for self-creation endures and speaks to a human need. In her solitude, Emily Dickinson "select[ed] her own Society / . . . / and shut the door" (Fr 409), and she took her cue from Emerson, who wrote "on the lintels of the door-post, *Whim*" (*Complete Writings* 140). As a mythological figure, Dickinson serves as a model of one who would follow her whim and whose genius is timeless. Susan Howe says in an interview: "I think that when you write a poem you use sounds and words outside time. You use timeless articulations. I mean the mystery of language is something . . . it's just . . . it's like earth from the astronauts' view — that little blue film, a line floating around space sheltering all of us" (*Birth-mark* 172). While I have questioned here the limited view that Dickinson wrote in a vacuum and never developed, I do not wish to destroy the vast, sheltering, and empowering possibilities of poetic language. When I read Sappho, as when I read Dickinson, I do not doubt that poetry is timeless, that its power to awe continues beyond the lives of the poets, or my own life. My work is anti-mythological only to the extent that the myth of Emily Dickinson is reductive, that it limits how her work can be read, and that it diminishes her stature. I hope that in delineating the development of Dickinson's work I may show the genius of her transformations, and that her readers will stand, as I do, "amazed before the change":

> The Thrill came slowly like a Boon for
> Centuries delayed
> It's fitness growing like the Flood
> In Sumptuous solitude –
> The desolation only missed
> While Rapture changed it's Dress
> And stood amazed before the Change
> In ravished Holiness –
>
> (Fr 1528; 1880)

~1~

"Burglar! Banker – Father!"

Renaming God through Satire

𝓬

My friend attacks my friend!
Oh Battle picturesque!
Then I turn Soldier too,
And he turns satirist!
How martial is this place!
Had I mighty gun
I think I'd shoot the human race
And then to glory run!

—Emily Dickinson

You only have to look at the Medusa straight on to see her. And she's not deadly. She's beautiful and she's laughing.

—Hélène Cixous

Her efforts at lightness are distressing.

—Yvor Winters

Analysts have had their go at humor, and I have read some of this interpretative literature, but without being greatly instructed. Humor can be dissected, as a frog can, but the thing dies in the process and the innards are discouraging to any but the pure scientific mind.

—E. B. White

Burglar! Banker – Father!

Emily Dickinson's early satirical work is a primer for later developments in her thinking.[1] Out of her satirical voice comes her mature idiosyncratic lexicon. Through satire she distinguishes her own voice from the voices she has been schooled to hear; she writes:

> I shall know why – when Time is over –
> And I have ceased to wonder why –
> Christ will explain each separate anguish
> In the fair schoolroom of the sky –
> (Fr 215; 1861)

The ironic tone of "the fair schoolroom of the sky" reveals that the speaker of the poem finds the religious teachings that "explain" earthly anguish inadequate. Only when she "has ceased to wonder why," when she is dead and cannot question, will those conventional explanations suffice.

Dickinson takes on God — and orthodox constructions of God — in a battle of wit in the early poems. In these poems, she claims her territory most often through humor. Humor is a way of liberating vision and achieving dominion over received ideas. Nancy A. Walker explains that "[b]ecause the humorist adopts at least the *stance* of superiority, claiming the freedom to point out incongruity or absurdity in a world that others are accustomed to accepting on its own terms, he or she works from a position of privileged insight" (25). If Dickinson could through her cleverness prove the world framed by orthodoxy to be ridiculous, then she might also free herself from its mandates. Humor is a powerful tool, a method of differentiating one's own perception from the conventional view. "Most humor theorists agree," Walker points out, "that the creation of humor requires the ability to 'stand apart' from the reality of one's own existence and to view that existence with detachment and objectivity. The ultimate logic of that detachment is the creation of a separate reality" (23). So Dickinson in her struggle with God tries through words to alter the world.[2]

The speaker in the early poems is often a pugilist[3] "A little East of Jordan" retells the story of Jacob wrestling with the angel for divine notice:

> A little East of Jordan,
> Evangelists record,
> A Gymnast and an Angel
> Did wrestle long and hard –

> Till morning touching mountain –
> And Jacob, waxing strong,
> The Angel begged permission
> To Breakfast – to return –
>
> Not so, said cunning Jacob!
> "I will not let thee go
> Except thou bless me" – Stranger!
> The which acceded to –
>
> Light swung the silver fleeces
> "Peniel" Hills beyond,
> And the bewildered Gymnast
> Found he had worsted God!
>
> (Fr 145; 1860)

At the end of the poem, "the bewildered Gymnast / found he had worsted God!" This is likewise the poet's wish: through her use of language to get the better of God, from whose kingdom she feels excluded. Cynthia Griffin Wolff stresses the importance in the poem of "the transition that took place at Peniel: God concealed His face and gave a *word* in its place—humankind's first tragic fall into language" (152). Dickinson turns this story around. She feels that God not only conceals Himself but regards her as invisible; in retaliation, she takes His word and uses it against Him. For the poet, who does not count herself among the elect, the word is her greatest weapon; it is her way of achieving mastery over a cosmology that leaves her unblessed and deprived of eternal life in God's heaven. Through her poetry, she mocks, she teases, and she is unafraid to take on God's sovereignty, for poetry has the power to create its own ascendancy and eternity.[4]

In the poem "A little East of Jordan," it is crucial that Jacob wrestles the angel in order receive a blessing: "'I will not let thee go / Except thou Bless me' – Stranger!" He fights for entrance into the eternal kingdom of heaven, for a sign of God's love and approval. Because Dickinson never converted, like Jacob she feels unblessed, excluded by God and by the faithful. In her early letters, especially around the time she attended Mount Holyoke Female Seminary, she still contends with the social pressure to "become a Christian." She writes to Abiah Root from school: "There is a great deal of religious interest here and many are flocking to the ark of safety. I have not yet given up to the claims of Christ, but trust I am not entirely thoughtless on so important & serious a subject" (L 20). Because Abiah is born-again, Dickinson presents a more devout face than she does in her letters to her brother Austin, for example. She represents the process of becoming a Christian as "giving up" to Christ, a notion of surrender that is fundamental to conversion. Yet her tone emphasizes the martial connotation of "surrender" and belies her hostile confrontation with God. She is angry that He ignores her; she has not "worsted God" and remains "unblessed."

Dickinson notices that the majority have "religious interest" and that there is safety in numbers. The others climb aboard "the ark of safety," which will take them to eternal life in heaven. God approves of them, loves and blesses them; likewise, they feel safe in their common belief that their destiny will be happy. As Dickinson will point out often in her poems, salvation and the heavenly afterlife are social constructions: in her satirical rendition, there is "a schoolroom in the sky" just as there are schoolrooms on earth. In another poem, she imagines the cruelty of children who taunt those who do not conform to the current trend:

> Perhaps the "Kingdom of Heaven's" changed –
> I hope the "Children" there
> Wont be "new fashioned" when I come –
> And laugh at me – and stare –
>
> (Fr 117; 1859)

The "children" of God in heaven, the speaker worries, will be like His intolerant followers in life.

Similarly, in "What is "Paradise," the childlike speaker wonders if questions of loneliness, alienation, and class will persist in heaven:

> What is – "Paradise" –
> Who live there –
> Are they "Farmers" –
> Do they "hoe" –
> Do they know that this is "Amherst" –
> And that I – am coming – too –
>
> Do they wear "new shoes" – in "Eden" –
> Is it always pleasant – there –
> Wont they scold us – when we're hungry –
> Or tell God – how cross we are –
>
> You are sure there's such a person
> As "a Father" – in the sky –

So if I get lost – there – ever –
Or do what the Nurse calls "die" –
I shan't walk the "Jasper" – barefoot –
Ransomed folks – won't laugh at me –
Maybe – "Eden" a'nt so lonesome
As New England used to be!
(Fr 241, 1861)

The persona here speaks in one of Dickinson's characteristic voices, that of a small child who is innocent yet whose questions reveal piercing, unconcealed skepticism. In this case, the child is learning the world of "Farmers" who "hoe," "Amherst," "new shoes," and "a Father" in "Paradise" through the words and explanations of adults. The speaker asks if the names for the world in what she's been taught is "Amherst" will translate in heaven when she "do[es] what the Nurse calls 'die.'" Ronald Wallace observes that this child persona is "vulnerable, deprived, powerless, naive" (81) and proposes that in "What is 'Paradise,'" "The question of heaven isn't something to believe or doubt, it is just a matter of childlike wonderment and curiosity. Paradise is a given for the child; she merely wants to hear more about it. The questions themselves are their own answers, embracing the affirmative premise from the outset" (82). Yet the poem is not as benign as Wallace asserts it is. The child persona enables the poet to use the posture of being "vulnerable, deprived, powerless, naive" in order to achieve power and knowledge. Through the pose of naïveté, she asks ironic, subversive, and even blasphemous questions: "You are sure there's such a person," this speaker asks innocently, "As 'a Father' – in the sky –." In effect, she confronts the unspeakable, fundamental question: she doubts the existence of God. At the very least, through her feigned ignorance she shows "how unlikely" (as Elizabeth Bishop says in her child-voice) it is that God exists as a man much like an earthly father overseeing a domestic paradise.[5] The posture in the poem of the child asking why serves a satirical purpose. As with the child who points out that the emperor wears no clothes, the unschooled child voice shows conventional assumptions to be arbitrary and false.

In "What is Paradise" and in many other early satirical poems, Dickinson argues with an exclusionary understanding of God by excluding the language of election from her own. The way she shapes her language confirms her rejection of God as He is presented in the teaching; she differentiates her voice from those other voices by enclosing them in quotation marks, underlining them, showing their absurdity through a predominance of exclamation marks. Often in her satirical poems, Dickinson plays with the economics of redemption, especially with the paradigm of feminine and masculine "spheres," in which the masculine is associated with the market and corruption. She frequently associates God, who is seen as male, with the brutality of the market, and those seeking entrance into the kingdom of heaven with beggars, as in "I never lost as much as twice" (Fr 39; 1858), which I discuss at length later in this chapter, and in other poems as well.[6]

Implicitly, the economic metaphors in these poems raise the issue of class as well.[7] The satire of God as ungenerous and inhospitable would not work were it not for Dickinson's condemnation of the earthly suffering of the poor at the hands of the upper classes. When the child in "What is Paradise" asks if they'll have "new shoes" in Eden and if they'll be scolded "when we're hungry – / Or tell God – how cross we are –," she plays on Dickens's Oliver Twist asking for "more" food.[8] God—whom she names "Burglar! Banker! – Father!" (Fr 39; 1858) and "Necromancer! Landlord!" (Fr 100; 1859)—is elitist and lacking in compassion. As the omnipotent, He is to blame for refusing admission to the beggars at the gates of heaven, as well for the fact of their poverty on earth; after all, good and evil, life and death are his will.[9] In the poem beginning "I have a King, who does not speak—," the child persona refuses to pray "God's will be done," for it would be a lie:

> And I omit to pray
> 'Father, thy will be done' today
> For my will goes the other way,
> And it were perjury!
> (Fr 157; 1860)

In the following poem, which is replete with devices to distinguish the speaker from the words of others, she satirically posits that entrance into paradise is "costly":

> You're right – "the way *is* narrow" –
> And "difficult the Gate" –
> And "few there be" – Correct again –
> That "enter in – thereat" –
>
> 'Tis Costly – So are *purples!*
> 'Tis just the price of *Breath* –

With but the "Discount" of *the Grave* –
Termed by the *Brokers* – *"Death"*

And after *that* – there's Heaven –
The *Good* Man's – *"Dividend"* –
And *Bad* men – "go to Jail" –
I guess –

(Fr 249; 1861)

This poem is a wonderful example of Dickinson's playful, complex and thrillingly clever wit (though it is not her strongest, and was placed among her unfinished poems). It also shows the how the poet used her influences, the materials of popular and literary culture, in what her descendant, Marianne Moore, called "a hybrid method of composition."[10] The first stanza of the poem comes from Matthew 7.14. Jesus says, "strait *is* the gate, and narrow *is* the way, which leadeth unto life, and few there be that find it."[11] The eternal life is "Costly"; you have to pay with your life. You get a little "discount" on the grave (or, the poem puns, your life is discounted by the grave). The brokers — perhaps the clergy or the angels — call the price death. The good man's "dividend" is heaven, paid out by the big boss-man of the company, God. The bad men, like the good ones, pay with their lives as well, but for the price exacted receive eternal "Jail" or hell.

The tantalizing question in the poem is, From whose point of view is it spoken? The tone of poem is light; its speaker is a seeming innocent following a simple logic to an outrageous conclusion, the way children so often do. Yet the poem is informed by the adult poet's learned thought.[12] The innocent is responding to, perhaps, the religious teachings of her parents or the church. Or, perhaps, the second person in the poem is Jesus himself, whose Word is between quotation marks. The poem takes the question of judgment to task: in Matthew, the first sentence of the chapter in which Jesus warns that the "way *is* narrow," he also admonishes his followers, "Judge not that ye be not judged." This question of who is deemed good and who bad coupled with the ruling metaphor in the poem of the stock market leads to Emerson's famous adage in "Self-Reliance": "Society is a joint-stock company." Let us look at the saying in context:

> Society is a joint-stock company, in which the members agree, for the better securing of his bread to each shareholder, to surrender the liberty and culture of the eater. The virtue in most request is conformity. Self-reliance is its aversion. It loves not realities and creators, but names and customs.

Whoso would be a man, must be a nonconformist. He who would gather immortal palms must not be hindered by the name of goodness. Nothing is at last sacred but the integrity of your own mind. . . . a valued advisor . . . was wont to importune me with dear old doctrines of the church. On my saying, "What have I to do with the sacredness of traditions, if I live wholly from within?" my friend suggested, — "But these impulses may be from below, not from above. I replied, "They do not seem to me to be such, but if I am the Devil's child, I will live then from the Devil." (*Complete Writings* 138)

Dickinson has revisioned two texts with great cultural importance — one sacred, one so revered and influential as to be nearly sacred[13] — and her juxtaposition throws the tenets of both into question. Yet at the same time, the truths of the sayings of Jesus and Emerson are reinforced by the poet's social critique, by her showing the ways in which conventional thought misreads them. "He who would gather immortal palms," Emerson professes, "must not be hindered by the name of goodness." In society's joint-stock company, "the virtue in most request is conformity." So the person who is "named" good by the company is believed to get the "dividend" of heaven after death. The bad men, those whom the company names the "Devil's children," will "go to Jail." That Dickinson sets the phrase "go to Jail" between quotation marks is important because the punctuation indicates this judgment is separate from the speaker of the poem, and may be the voice of society at large whose courts decide guilt or innocence. It is also important that she does not say hell but "jail," the punishment to which those named "bad" are sentenced on earth.[14]

Read with Emerson in mind, the poem makes fun of those who believe that by conforming to social standards one gains entrance to the kingdom of heaven.[15] Emerson advocates living within, and surmises that those who are nonconformists will be seen as the children of the devil. In her poem, "You're right the way is narrow," Dickinson follows the antinomian tendency seen in Emerson. She asserts that for those who "live within" the way *is* narrow, for they cannot be diverted from their individual paths, not even when threatened with jail.[16] "You're right" serves as a rehearsal for one of Dickinson's strongest proclamations about the risks of self-reliance:[17]

Much Madness is divinest Sense –
To a discerning Eye –
Much sense – the starkest Madness –

> 'Tis the Majority
> In this, as all, prevail –
> Assent – and you are sane –
> Demur – you're straightway dangerous –
> And handled with a Chain.
>
> (Fr 620; 1863)

Both "You're right" and "Much madness" express the difficult choice faced by those who choose the narrow path, who "live within": persecution may be the price of the nonconformist's "divinest Sense." In "You're right" the speaker exclaims, the way is "costly – So are *purples!*" In the Bible "purples," associated with royalty, are also expensive. Before Jesus is crucified, the soldiers mock him:

> And they clothed him with purple, and platted a crown of thorns, and put it on his *head,*
> And began to salute him, Hail, King of the Jews!
> And they smote him on the head with a reed, and did spit on him, and bowing *their* knees worshipped him.
> And when they had mocked him, they took off the purple from him, and put his own clothes on him, and led him out to crucify him.
> (Mark 15.17–20)

Later Jesus will say from the cross "My god, my god, why hast thou forsaken me." Is the poet chiding God for "forsaking" his Son? Or for forsaking the poor masses, the unelect who will not enter through the "difficult Gate" of heaven? Or is she saying that those who are mocked by the crowd are akin to Jesus? We cannot know the answer, yet the poem has cunningly asked these vexing questions. Each of these positions is subversive, yet her rhetorical strategy seduces the reader into this dangerous territory. She begins the poem, "You're right," a position that will make anyone listen. And she ends the poem with the pose of naïveté, "I guess." The poet is the Devil's child (or at least the Devil's advocate) in that she puts forth ideas in an ingenuous manner that many would find shocking or sacrilegious.[18]

Through her satire Dickinson breaks free of conventional poetics and hears her own innovative inner voice. Emerson proclaimed, "Whoso would be a man, must be a nonconformist"; if Emily Dickinson wished to be a woman, Hélène Cixous might say, she would have to "explode" the masculine literary tradition. Cixous writes:

If woman has always functioned "within" the discourse of man, a signifier that has always referred back to the opposite signifier which annihilates its specific energy and diminishes or stifles its very different
sound, it is time for her to dislocate this "within," to explode it, turn it
around, and seize it; to make it hers, containing it, taking it from her
own mouth, biting that tongue with her very own teeth to invent for
herself a language to get inside of. (257)

Dickinson keeps "the discourse of man" separate from herself, questioning
it and ridiculing it. This is an externalized battle, not the kind of internalized battle in which Dickinson engages later in her career. In these earlier
poems she renames God and develops her divergent theology, her lexicon, her unique way of loving—all of which culminate in the next phase
of her development, which, in chapter 2, I call her "self-conversion."

As a means of combating society's eye that would scrutinize and silence her, through her singular voice Dickinson confronts and rejects
what Dana Crowley Jack calls the "Over-Eye" (in order to encounter and
unite with the "Over-Soul").[19] Jack, like Dickinson—and Emerson—before her, identifies two competing voices: the voice of inner life and the
voice of culture. The difference is that Jack argues that socialization silences women because of the expectation that they serve others selflessly
at the expense of self-development. She differentiates between the voice of
the "Over-Eye," which enunciates the imperatives of culture and the voice
of the "Authentic Self," which women frequently suppress in order to gain
approval from significant others and society:

I will call this third person voice the Over-Eye, because of its surveil-
lance, vigilant, definitively moral quality.
The Over-Eye carries a decided patriarchal flavor, both in its collective viewpoint about what is "good" and "right" for a woman and in its
willingness to condemn her feelings when they depart from expected
"shoulds." The Over-Eye persistently pronounces harsh judgment on
most aspects of a woman's authentic strivings, including her wish to
express herself freely in relationship, her creativity, and her spirituality.
Because the judgments of the Over-Eye include a cultural consensus
about feminine goodness, truth, and value, they have the power to over-
ride the authentic self's viewpoint. (94)

Dickinson reveals in her poems and letters that she hears the voice of
the Over-Eye, and that she refutes it. In the early poems she silences the

Over-Eye through satire in order to give voice to the authentic self. Her "business is circumference" (L 268) and through her innovative writing and complex ideas she expands the limits:

> and I alone –
> A speck opon a Ball –
> Went out opon a Circumference –
> Beyond the Dip of Bell –
> (Fr 633; 1863)

In her wild explorations beyond the boundaries, Dickinson is unmistakably unlike most nineteenth-century American women writers whose subject matter was limited to propagating the values of woman's "sphere," of selflessness as wife and mother, religious devotion, and unfailing virtue. Paula Bennett explains, "For the majority [of women writers] — the homebound women whose poems on love, duty, nature and God, filled local newspapers and magazines — writing was little more than an extension of the values they held most dear" (*Emily Dickinson* 2). Dickinson, who was influenced by — and perhaps even empowered by — aspects of sentimentality, gave the subjects of "love, duty, nature and God" different meanings; she gave them a twist and whole new dimensions. Significantly, Dickinson's subjects as they traditionally have been delineated are similar to the sentimentalists' list; they are, as St. Armand puts it, "those enduring yet disturbing categories into which Dickinson's first editors parceled her art: 'Life,' 'Love,' 'Nature,' and 'Time and Eternity'" (15). These taxonomies are more useful, and perhaps less disturbing, if they are seen contextually, as Dickinson's revisions of cultural tropes.

In the nineteenth century, the polarization of gender roles into "spheres" emphasized woman as unconditionally loving and compassionate, the purveyor of religious truth. God likewise was transformed from the angry, punishing Father of orthodox Calvinism to the sentimental, understanding, feminized Christ the Bridegroom. In the harsher, earlier Calvinist understanding of salvation, God is the elitist who inscrutably elects the privileged few to join him in his heavenly home. By contrast, the figure of the nurturing Christ democratizes salvation, making it available to all who would join the flock. Sentimentalism dispenses with the problem of evil.[20] God is, as Bennett observes, "fully exonerated for the misfortunes besetting humanity. . . . Heaven has become the recompense for every ill. . . . Never, perhaps, in the history of Christianity was the promise of life-after-death employed so cavalierly or so popularly to deny the reality of pain, the intractable Being-ness of suffering, evil and loss" (*Emily Dickinson* 57). Feminized Christ could serve as a mirror to women, who like Him could count on redemption through suffering.

Although God's transformation from the fierce and vengeful God to the nurturing and compassionate Christ made Christianity appealing to many, Dickinson cannot exonerate the Calvinist God because the world, his glorious creation, is forever burdened with his punishments, with evil and death. While she appropriates both understandings of God, she finds neither suffices. She would like to love God, but resents him because He is all-loving and terrible at the same time. Throughout her career her thought is informed by religious movements that attempt to soften the terror of the Calvinist God and to democratize salvation — most notably by the Sentimental Love Religion and by transcendentalism.[21] Yet in spite of the theological revisions that engage her imagination, and in spite of her appropriations of them, she circles back to her conflict with the un-sentimentalized, jealous Calvinist God.

He powerfully moves her and she wishes to reach Him, even though, as she writes in 1863, He responds as "a distant – stately Lover" (Fr 615). She cannot forgive God for being "Burglar! Banker – Father!," for taking away those she loves through death, and for excluding her forever from hope of heavenly reunion:

> I never lost as much but twice –
> And that was in the sod.
> Twice have I stood a beggar
> Before the door of God!
>
> Angels – twice descending
> Reimbursed my store –
> Burglar! Banker – Father!
> I am poor once more!
> (Fr 39; 1858)

This God does not resemble sweet Christ of the Sentimental Love Religion, though Dickinson plays on sentimental tropes. "Like her Puritan forbears—" Bennett notes, "and distinctly unlike many of her own contemporaries—Dickinson was prepared to look God's 'evil' squarely in the face" (*Emily Dickinson* 62). The beggar in this poem stands, like one of Dickens's destitute characters, "Before the door of God!" But God is a Scrooge who never learns the lesson of generosity. On the contrary, He is the supernatural masculine figure of the marketplace so maligned by the sentimentalists, who regarded the man's world of money and commercialism as corrupt, the antithesis of woman's sphere of spirituality and virtue. In the division of spheres, the world of the market is inevitably corrupt, so that a banker necessarily becomes a burglar. Dickinson puns on the monetary meaning of redemption, making God the Father a loan shark who assesses a value for human life, and hoards His wealth without compassion for one who begs for mercy. "The capricious economy of scarcity that willed the allotment of grace in the New England theology," writes St. Armand, "implied that if God was not a miser he had to be a monster" (91). He lends out life to His children only to steal them away, making the speaker, who loves them, "poor once more!"

In "I never lost" Dickinson plays on the sentimental trope of the child seeking shelter and solace from the heavenly Father. However, Dickinson does not articulate the child's vulnerability, smallness, deprivation, and powerlessness with either acceptance or submission, as might the sentimental writers (Harriet Beecher Stowe, for example) who were her contemporaries. In their depiction of the weak and lowly, the child would be anything but ironic and skeptically humorous about salvation. Stowe, as Jane Tompkins argues in "Sentimental Power: *Uncle Tom's Cabin* and the Politics of Literary History," gives the "lowly" (women, slaves, and children) power by identifying them with Christ: "the pure and the powerless die to save the powerful and corrupt, and thereby show themselves more powerful than those they save" (23). In the Sentimental Love Religion[22] the suffering of the powerless is redeemed through their exemplary virtue, which ensures them a place in heaven and which also has the power to save others. The child who has not yet been corrupted by the world knows paradise instinctively through faith. Tompkins elaborates:

> In a sketch entitled "Children," published the year after *Uncle Tom's Cabin* came out, Stowe writes: "Woudst thou know, o parent, what is that faith which unlocks heaven? Go not to wrangling polemics, or creeds and forms of theology, but draw to thy bosom thy little one, and read in that trusting eye the lesson of eternal life." If children because of their purity and innocence can lead adults to God while living, their spiritual power when they are dead is greater still. . . . When the spiritual power of death is combined with the natural sanctity of childhood, the child becomes an angel endowed with salvific force. (24)

In such poems as "What is Paradise?" Dickinson refutes the idea that the child has innate knowledge of what Stowe calls "the lesson of eternal life." She, in this instance, falls on the side of nurture rather than nature. As the child was a focal point for the nineteenth-century sentimentalists' evangelism, Dickinson's clever and accurate portrayal slyly uses sentimental rhetoric to point out the silliness of that version of heaven.

In another poem, although Dickinson adopts a sentimental tone, she makes God a stern Calvinist who excludes children from heaven:

> Some, too fragile for winter winds
> The thoughtful grave encloses –
> Tenderly tucking them in from frost
> Before their feet are cold –
>
> Never the treasures in her nest
> The cautious grave exposes,
> Building where schoolboy dare not look,
> And sportsman is not bold.
>
> This covert have all the children
> Early aged, and often cold,
> Sparrows, unnoticed by the Father –
> Lambs for whom time had not a fold.
>
> (Fr 91; 1859)

As I noted earlier in the introduction, Dickinson in her satirical poems employs techniques that are similar to William Blake's. Her "Some, too fragile" particularly recalls Blake's "The Chimney Sweeper":

> A Little black thing among the snow,
> Crying "'weep! 'weep!" in notes of woe!
> "Where are thy mother & father? say?"
> "They are both gone up to the church to pray.
>
> "Because I was happy on the heath,
> And smil'd among the winter's snow,
> They clothed me in the clothes of death,
> And taught me to sing the notes of woe.
>
> "And because I am happy & dance & sing,
> They think they have done me no injury,
> And are gone to praise God & his Priest & King,
> Who make up a heaven of our misery."

Both Dickinson and Blake use kind language to make a fierce attack on God's and heaven's heartlessness in stealing the lives of young children. In Dickinson the grave "Tenderly tuck[s] them in from the frost / Before their feet are cold." In Blake "the clothes of death" shelters the boy from "the winter's snow." Both poets expose the cruelty of a theology that asserts that heaven compensates for human suffering. Those who believe "make up a heaven of our misery"; that is, they create heaven out of the misery of the helpless. Both poets also use the family as a means of intensifying their satirical refutation of salvation. The parents in Blake's poem have abandoned their child in order to praise God for the suffering He has inflicted on their boy. Likewise, in Dickinson's poem, the grave takes on trite maternal characteristics: it is "thoughtful," "tenderly tucking" in the "fragile" children. In this grotesque transformation of Victorian family roles, the motherly grave attends to those "sparrows" and "lambs" "unnoticed by the Father."[23]

In "Some, too fragile for winter winds," as in "What is Paradise," Dickinson employs sentimental rhetoric in order to refute its ideology. St. Armand writes that the sentimental "gospel of consolation" developed "its own set of uplifting responses to sudden death" (46), particularly to the deaths of children:

> [I]nfant salvation replaced a Calvinistic emphasis on infant damnation, and justification by death and suffering overcame the capriciousness of justification by grace. . . . The concept of the sinless child countered orthodox ideas of natural depravity and was gradually extended to include all Christian adults who struggled valiantly with disease and against the brutal embraces of "The Spoiler," death. Since human nature was now seen as basically angelic rather than demonic, the doctrine of eventual reunion in heaven became a logical corollary of the gospel of consolation. . . . the family circle was never really broken, even by death. (45–46)

Dickinson's poem, in contrast, reinstates the cruel God who tears the family apart forever through death and by damning innocent children, whose only sins are their frailty and their early graves. Rather than democratize salvation, as do the sentimentalists, Dickinson democratizes death, as does the Calvinist doctrine of election: "This covert have *all* the children." Dickinson satirizes both models of God: she makes the grave the embodiment of the maternal figure of God while God the Father is fatally negligent and absent. She speaks the language of the Sentimental Love Religion almost without an accent, so the poem's deceptively sad, pitiful tone masks its wicked irony. The grave is a formidable shelter for birds and lambs from the horrors of death by the hands of mischievous schoolboys and murderous sportsmen; it protects the weak from cold, from illness, and ultimately from itself, from the crude realities of death. In short, these fragile creatures are protected from death by being dead. This poem plays on the sentimental trope of death as a release from earthly suffering, but it does not grant its children a home in heaven. These children are "unnoticed by the Father" and the members of their family are refigured not in loving, heavenly reunion, but in the eternal exile of death. Furthermore, the children in this poem do not possess the "salvific force" that they have in Tompkins's account of nineteenth-century sentimentalism. Their fragility does not translate into power. They convert no one through their deaths; they neither save nor are saved. Later, in 1863, in the poem beginning, "Of course – I prayed – / And did God Care?" with lucid anger and bitterness she transforms the sparrows of this early poem into herself, her own "unnoticed" Bird, her unsaved self: "He cared as much as on the Air / A Bird – had stamped her foot – / And cried "Give Me" – (Fr 581; 1863).

God is the stonefaced figure of connection thwarted; he will neither love nor allow others to love. In the mythology about Emily Dickinson, the eccentric poet, disappointed in love, wrote "the Soul selects her own Society" (Fr 409; 1862), and withdrew to a society of one, to her own solitude and poetic vision. From 1891 when the first edition of Dickinson's poems was published until now, critics and gossips have tried to uncover the secret of her unrequited love and to theorize how that love affected her poetry and psychology. To me, it is a happy occasion to read Lavinia Dickinson's corrective letter to a newspaper writer:

> Emily never had any love disaster; she had the choicest friendships among the rarest men and women all her life, and was cut to the heart when death robbed her again and again. . . . Emily had a joyous nature, yet full of pathos, and her power of language was unlike any one who ever lived. She fascinated every one she saw. Her intense verses were no more personal experiences than Shakespeare's tragedies, or Mrs. Browning's minor-key pictures. There has been an endeavor to invent and enforce a reason for Emily's peculiar and wonderful genius. (153; quoted in Sewall)[24]

Lavinia's letter is revealing because while she refutes the notion that Emily had a "love disaster," she does expose a specific source of anguish: "she had the choicest friendships among the rarest men and women all her life, and was cut to the heart when death robbed her again and again." Throughout her life she felt inconsolable pain over the death of loved ones. In her early work, she is furious at God for "robbing" of her friends, as Lavinia puts it, and as Dickinson herself wrote in "I never lost as much but twice." Later in the poems of around 1863, her response is despair. In the last years it is pure elegiac grief. This letter is refreshing because it asks Emily Dickinson's readers to notice that "her power of language was unlike any one who ever lived," to concentrate on the development of the poet's thought and linguistic innovation, and to abandon the impossible task of determining whom she loved and whether or not it propelled her into poetic genius.

Of course, there *was* a love disaster—or several of them, or it happened in stages.[25] (There was also happiness in love later in Dickinson's life, when she and Judge Otis Phillips Lord fell in love and nearly married.) The importance of Dickinson's disappointment, in my reading, is not related to specifics, to a desired person, but to something cataclysmic, all-encompassing, which makes the circumference of love far wider than that of conventional romantic love. Her disaster led her to a new epistemology, to "a different dawn" (Fr 13; 1858). Her belief, as it unfolds in her poems and letters, that she could not love conventionally, though it may have been by her choice and her perception, left her with a profound sense of alienation and exile that extended to human love and God's love. As has often been observed, it is often difficult to tell in Dickinson's poems whether she is addressing a person or God.[26] Her anger, evident in her early poems and letters, and in her satirical voice, is a response to the imperative that women stay silent. Her feeling of being rejected is not simply the result of unrequited love, but of a cultural dynamic that rejects the goals of feminine self to be heard, one in which women are objectified, socialized to behave according to limiting norms, and are effectively invisible while the subjectivity of men is privileged.

Dickinson's satirical anger serves as a way to expose cultural stereotypes and create a different reality. As an assertion of the self, anger creates the possibility of relationships in which each person is equally visible. Jack explains: "Anger is aroused when a significant relationship is threatened, and its goal is to promote, not to disrupt, the relationship. Anger [in a relational context] has the goals of removing obstacles to a reunion and discouraging further separation" (41). Dickinson's satire is likewise a way of promoting relationship because it creates a self capable of mutuality;

satire is a way of creating a self apart from cultural imperatives that discourage women from self-expression. As Jack writes, "From the relational viewpoint, the self (in both women and men) is part of a fundamentally social experience. . . . Relational theory considers attainment of a sense of basic human connectedness to be the goal of development" (10). For Dickinson, the whole relational field is threatened by the ways in which God is imagined by her culture and by the rigid role that women are expected to play in relationship to the Lord and others.

In the nineteenth century, a woman's function was severely restricted to the role of giving to others. The strivings of the Authentic Self for self-expression ran contrary to the prescription that a woman's role was to serve selflessly as a model of virtue. "Throughout the ante-bellum and Civil War period, liberal ministers were preoccupied with establishing and fixing the correct feminine role," writes Ann Douglas in *The Feminization of American Culture*. Horace Bushnell, she recounts, "instructed his daughter to have no needs, almost no character of her own . . . she should be 'above all . . . unselfish. . . . We demand . . . that she shall seem to have alighted here for the world's comfort and blessing . . . all the ways of selfishness are at variance with her beautiful errand'" (50–51). Historian Nancy F. Cott writes that while married women provided spiritual compensation to their husbands, they did so by sacrificing selfhood and economic freedom:

> Recoiling from the spirit of self-interest and self-aggrandizement they saw in the marketplace, rhetoricians of domesticity looked to the home for a sanctuary of "disinterested" love. . . . Because their property and earnings belonged to their husbands, married women could not operate as economic individuals. Wives lacked the means and motive for self-seeking. . . . Beyond equating wives' economic dependence with disinterestedness, the canon of domesticity went a further step and prescribed women's appropriate attitude to be selflessness. The conventional cliché [was] "that women were to live for others" . . . for only by giving up all self-interest did women achieve the purity of motive that enabled them to establish moral reference points in the home. Thus women's self-renunciation was called upon to remedy men's self-alienation. (70–71)

A woman's role as a Christian, following Paul's dicta in 2 Corinthians, was complete effacement of the self in the service of others and in the service of a feminine ideal. In its selflessness, this role resembles the process of conversion, which requires self-annihilation. So in her relation both to the divine and to earthly others, woman was to make herself into nothing. For the writer, who is a maker, this is an untenable situation. The interdiction against exploring one's inner life, if obeyed, makes creativity impossible.

My Little Force Explodes

Several recent critics, including Jane Tompkins, have argued that sentimental writers served to empower women of the nineteenth century. In *Beneath the American Renaissance: The Subversive Imagination in the Age of Emerson and Melville*, David S. Reynolds delineates "types of American womanhood"; like Tompkins, he makes an impressive argument for the ways in which sentimental women writers fueled reform. If women were to provide a sanctuary from the selfishness and aggression of the masculine marketplace, they also could (and did) create alternative worlds in their writing.[27] Reynolds sees Dickinson's work as the creative culmination of women authors' rebellion against the masculine tradition:

> If other women authors attempted to gain freedom by freely exploring dark philosophical realms, her poetic radical democracy led her to proclaim: "My country is Truth. . . . It is a very free Democracy." If their effort for freedom led to breaches of literary decorum, she could explain her "spasmodic" style to Higginson in radical-democratic terms: "I had no Monarch in my life, and cannot rule myself, and when I try to organize — my little Force explodes — and leaves me bare and charred — " (L 271). She had no monarch because she *chose* to have no monarch, and her little Force constantly exploded because she allowed it to. Emily Dickinson — not Fanny Fern — was the *real* 'little Bunker Hill,' the American woman who militantly asserted her creativity through ingenious metaphorical play and through brash imaginings of gender-free literary reality. (421)

The other women writers of the period exploited female stereotypes in order to undercut them; as Reynolds observes: "The female moral exemplar became a chief means of reconstructing moral value in a world of devalued, amoral males. That is why many ante-bellum domestic novels, despite their religious intention, lack clergymen characters — the female moral exemplar takes the place of the male clergyman" (342). Yet it is also true that these writers did a great deal to firmly establish those stereotypes. The power that women writers gave their sex as "moral exemplar" also disempowered them by entrenching what Jack calls "the collective viewpoint about what is 'good' and 'right' for a woman." They firmly established "the Angel in the House." The internalized stereotype serves as the Over-Eye, silencing the Authentic Self—or, in Dickinson's terms, the Over-Eye becomes the Monarch who censors the explosions of the "little Force."

These stereotypes preclude the possibility of relation or exchange because they severely restrict self-expression. Unlike a male writer who assumes an audience for his particular subjectivity, for what might lie beyond the stereotype, the female writer who would break the mold, risks not only the loss of audience, but becoming monstrous. Cixous writes in "The Laugh of Medusa":

> Who, surprised and horrified by the tumult of her drives (for she was made to believe that a well-adjusted normal woman has a . . . divine composure), hasn't accused herself of being a monster? Who, feeling a funny desire stirring inside her (to sing, to write, to dare to speak, in short, to bring out something new), hasn't thought she was sick? Well, her shameful sickness is that she resists death, that she makes trouble. (246)

Cixous refers to a "divine composure" similar to the one Horace Bushnell prescribed for women, that "beautiful errand" to nothingness, that death that writing, as the antithesis of selflessness, "resists." Cixous imagines a more relational—and expansive—model of reading and writing: "In the beginning are our differences. The new love dares for the other, wants the other, makes dizzying, precipitous flights between knowledge and invention. The woman arriving over and over again does not stand still; she's everywhere, she exchanges, she is the desire-that-gives" (263). Reading the other becomes a creative act. And creating, while "wanting the other," becomes a "flight between knowledge and invention." This creative exchange in which each person maintains selfhood is the opposite of a creative process in which the autonomous artist narcissistically objectifies the other.

Emily Dickinson anticipated these feminist concerns about expression. She saw that the feminine ideals of selflessness and of goodness as servitude, if taken seriously, could spell the death of a writer.[28] And she saw the need for a relational mode of writing in which "love dares for the other." In 1851 (about the time her earliest poems are dated), Emily wrote a characteristically funny letter to Austin in which she deals with the assumption that she might write in a "simple style," as did other women of her day. She is at odds with her brother for several reasons:

> I feel quite like retiring, in the presence of one so grand, and casting my lot among small birds, and fishes — you say you dont comprehend me, you want a simpler style. *Gratitude* indeed for all my fine philosophy! I strove to be exalted thinking I might reach *you* and while I pant and struggle and climb the nearest cloud, you walk out very leisurely in your slippers from Empyrean, and without the *slightest* notice request me to get down! As *simple* as you please, the *simplest* sort of simple — I'll be a little ninny — a little pussy catty, a little Red Riding Hood, I'll wear a Bee in my Bonnet, and a Rose bud in my hair, and what remains to do you shall be told hereafter. (L 45)

This letter shows, as do so many, that Emily is serious about her writing and her ideas. She proves her worth through humor, as Walker suggests: she takes the position of a person with "privileged insight." She self-consciously affirms the worth not only of her own philosophy and independence but of her obscurities and her linguistic innovations. The letter openly competes with her brother's literary wit, in fact, opens with a challenge — and with irony: "At my old stand again Dear Austin, and happy as a queen to know that while I speak those whom I love are listening, and I am happier still if I shall make *them* happy." *She* is writing, and is "happy as a queen" to be doing so, particularly knowing that "those whom I love are listening." She plays on the notion of the woman making "those she loves happy," but the implication is that she wants to make those whom she loves happy through her exalted creations. This is the kind of exchange that is "desire-that-gives," a relational and connective understanding of writing in which the fullest expressions of the self, those "dizzying, precipitous flights between knowledge and invention," are gifts to the other.

Austin has apparently asked that Emily simplify her style so he can understand. She returns that perhaps he, whom she loves, isn't listening as carefully as he might, especially considering how "grand" he is. Austin's letters are so highly regarded by the family that Emily taunts him in a later letter: "Father says your letters are altogether before Shakespeare, and he will have them published to put in our library" (L 46). The poet is annoyed that her effort "to reach" Austin through "fine philosophy" has resulted in his asking her to "get down" from her exalted cloud. So, through her wit, she defends her gift of words and philosophy, outdoing her brother, whom, she chides as the *son*, is given the place of Shakespeare.

Dickinson, as is her tendency, plays with the question of who's on top and who's on the bottom. She had hoped, she points out, that responding with philosophy and wit equal to his own would please him. But her effort fell beneath his regard: "without the *slightest* notice" he "request[s she] get down!" Perhaps in order to receive recognition from him she will have to resort to being stereotypically feminine, and silly: "I'll be a little ninny—a little pussy catty, a little Red Riding Hood, I'll wear a Bee in my Bonnet, and a Rose bud in my hair." She repeats the word "little" three times in her list of foolish feminine things she could be, but she includes in her list the figure of anger, wearing a bee in her bonnet. She suggests that the seemingly nonthreatening "little ninny" or the seductive woman with a rosebud in her hair also wears the buzzing bee of fury. She is ambivalent toward Austin. She loves him, wants to reach him. Yet she resents his inability to read her, to see fully—and to be pleased by—the expressions of her authentic self. This ambivalence, which is the result of inequality, is a paradigm for Dickinson's relationship to the masculine, including the masculine God.

Dickinson satirizes the roles of men and women often, but particularly economically and comically in the following poem:

> Over the fence –
> Strawberries – grow –
> Over the fence –
> I could climb – if I tried, I know –
> Berries are nice!
>
> But – if I stained my Apron –
> God would certainly scold!
> Oh, dear, – I guess if He were a Boy –
> He'd – climb – if He could!
>
> (Fr 271; 1861)

As in her letter to Austin, Dickinson uses the metaphor of climbing in "Over the fence." And the speaker in the poem—as in the letter—shows that she regards the limitations set upon her as gender-specific. The speaker "knows" she could climb the fence, but her socialization builds internal blocks, fences her in with the threat that "God would certainly scold!" She aligns the voices of culture with the voice of God, just as social thinkers such as Horace Bushnell align their notions of proper Christian behavior for women with those of divine truth. Dickinson, while imagining that God would scold for a stained apron, also puts God up in the sky in the position of a girl on earth who can't do what boys can do, but for different reasons. As God is the ultimate authority, He can't play as a boy would — but like the girl He would if He could. Through humor, the girl's voice in this poem takes a position, as Walker would say, of "superiority" through her "privileged insight" (25) that even God would like permission to get dirty and explore and eat sweet fruit. "Berries are nice!" the speaker exclaims, not only because they are tasty, tempting fruit, but because the journey getting to them is forbidden. The speaker also wants to gather berries by her own action. After all, God would "climb — if He could!" In these earthly social adventures even God loses His omnipotence to share a woman's limitations.[29]

The poem shows how the Over-Eye instructs that a woman should not "climb an exalted cloud" and give voice to the experience of her exalted thinking; nor should she have character, nor be an agent nor a quester. Dickinson wrote to Jane Humphries:

> The halt — the lame — the blind — the old — the infirm — the bed-ridden — and superannuated — the ugly, and disagreeable — the perfectly hateful to me — all *these* to see — and be seen by — an opportunity rare for cultivating meekness — and patience — and submission — and for turning my back on this very sinful, and wicked world. Somehow or other I incline to other things — and Satan covers them up with flowers, and I reach out to pick them. The path of duty looks very ugly indeed — and the place I want to go more amiable — a great deal — it is so much easier to do wrong than right — so much pleasanter to be evil than good, I dont wonder that good angels weep — and bad ones sing songs. (L 30)

Dickinson writes that the less fortunate whom she enumerates give her "an opportunity rare for cultivating" those prescriptive characteristics of woman, that selflessness that Horace Bushnell advocated. Dickinson refutes the notion that women by nature are "meek, patient and submissive" by using the language of masculine achievement, that is, calling the sight of the less fortunate an opportunity for cultivation. Just as a man might cultivate the characteristics of determination, enterprise, self-reliance, innovation, and ambition, so Dickinson implies that submission and selflessness require conscious — and perhaps opportunistic — shaping of the self. She pokes fun at the notion that these qualities arise naturally from the emotive feminine self.

In this letter and in others, she places her path in the realm of Satan, not because she believes she is evil, but because society regards those who deviate from the norm as children of the devil. (Anne Hutchison exemplifies this designation.) She humorously says she can only be her own self; in Emerson's words; "if I am the Devil's child, I will live from the Devil." She is in the tradition of Milton and Blake in her outrageous reversals, in creating her own mythology, in making the evil "amiable" and the good "ugly." She, like her precursors, associates Satan with creativity, wit, rebellion, freedom, joy, and, above all, with writing. Just as Blake imagines priests "binding with briars my joys and desires," so Dickinson imagines the prescriptions of Christian duty keeping her from "other things," from an "amiable" path covered with flowers. She would rather sing songs than weep, would rather be bad than good. "Good angels weep" for others and, perhaps, for their own dutiful selves. "Bad ones sing songs" because they unbind their joys and desires and take the freedom to sing, to make songs, and to make poetry.[30]

Through her satire, Dickinson clears the briars from the path of poetry; she, as Cixous says, "break[s] up the 'truth' with laughter" (258). In this stage of her development, too, she works her way through the dominance of her satirical voice, though she retains elements of it throughout her career. Because she separates the conventional voice from her own by mocking it, she frees herself to focus on her own voice. She is no longer in danger of surrendering to the role of the weak and submissive woman, so the necessity of satirizing that role diminishes. Significantly, when Dickinson comes into her own, her language resembles that of her descendent, Cixous: both bad angels sing in the language of volcanoes, storms, dizzying flight, explosions, bombs. This voice reaches its wildest, most idiosyncratic pitch around 1863 when she writes some of best-known poems: "I felt a funeral in my brain" (Fr 340; 1862), "The Soul has bandaged moments" (Fr 360; 1862), "There is a languor in the life" (Fr 552; 1862), "He fumbles at your soul" (Fr 477; 1862), "Before I got my eye put out" (Fr 336; 1862), "After great pain a formal feeling comes" (Fr 372; 1862), "I heard a fly buzz when I died" (Fr 591; 1863), "Dare you see a soul *at the white heat?*" (Fr 401; 1862). These poems often define the canon of Dickinson's work, not necessarily because her voice is limited, but because they are uniquely, painfully, and explosively hers; they represent the culminating moment when the poet "sees the soul *at the white heat*" — free, dangerous, ready to face the fierce light of the self.

~2~

Mastering the Master

Appropriations of Crisis Conversion in the Poems of 1863

Č

Every unconverted man properly belongs to hell.

— Jonathan Edwards

Let Emily sing for you because she cannot pray.

— Emily Dickinson

The old words are *numb* — and there *a'nt* any *new* ones — Brooks — are useless — in *Freshet-time* —

— Emily Dickinson

I cannot tell when I first became aware that she had *elected* her own way of life.

— Martha Dickinson Bianchi

The Old Words Are Numb

On the outskirts of the city of Madison, Wisconsin, where I once lived, a sign in front of a farm reads: *All the world guilty before God.* The Puritan tradition of guilt and original sin, familiar to Emily Dickinson, has sustained its power for a long time.

In Calvinism the world is vanity and the human soul lowly and despicable, but at least the individual has direct access to the Lord — without papal intermediary. Dickinson found the hierarchical relationship with the divinity (wherein the abject soul is unequal) suspect and even intolerable. While she maintained an agonizing discourse with the Master, whom she believed had excluded her from the circle of the elect, she never granted him mastery by accepting a humble and condemned state. Indeed, to the Wisconsin farmer who proclaims, "All the world guilty before God," she might dare ask if God himself is the guilty party: "Whether Deity's guiltless / My business is, to find!" (Fr 175). So Emily Dickinson talked with the Master but rejected the orthodox premise for the conversation. This intense dialogue, on her terms and in her guiltless lexicon, became her poetry. Because Dickinson invents a language beyond orthodoxy and tradition, one that relies on heterodoxy, ambiguity, and fragmentation, her work, like that of her contemporary, Walt Whitman, marks the beginning of American modernism.

Dickinson is a religious poet and an appropriator of religious language, who paradoxically excludes the vocabulary of sin from her work. Like Emerson, Dickinson rejects the tenet of original sin, as shown by the virtual absence in her poetry of the words "evil," "sin," and "guilt." When she uses them, she does so satirically, informing the reader that they pertain to others, not to her. In the late poem beginning "The Bible is an antique Volume – / Written by faded men," she mockingly writes that sin is "a distinguished Precipice / Others must resist" (Fr 1577; 1882).[1]

By excluding sin from her vocabulary, however, Dickinson excludes herself from the faith of her family and community. Though each of her family members converted, entering the First Congregational Church through professions of faith, Emily never did. To have joined the faith would have meant having a crisis conversion wherein the self sees its own absolute sinfulness. In this crisis the self is annihilated and submits to divine will. But Dickinson maintained her worldliness, as when she writes: "The mysteries of human nature surpass the 'mysteries of redemption.'" She was an outsider, resisting the religious revivals of her time and her education at the evangelical Mount Holyoke Seminary:

How lonely this world is growing, something so desolate creeps over the spirit and we don't know it's [sic] name, and it won't go away, either Heaven is seeming greater, or Earth a great deal more small, or God is more "Our Father," and we feel our need increased. Christ is calling everyone here, all my companions have answered. . . . I cant tell you *what* they have found, but *they* think it is something precious. I wonder if it *is*? How strange is this sanctification, that works such a marvelous change, that sows in such corruption, and rises in golden glory, that brings Christ down, and shews him, and lets him select his friends! (L 35)

The letter asserts that she has chosen not to join the flock. She is skeptical about what her companions have found, and that skepticism leads to satire. Dickinson makes fun of the notions of status and size, casting perception into doubt. Heaven *seems* greater and earth smaller. God is a greater father while humanity feels its need increased in the face of its own lowliness. The people around her think they have found "something precious," but Dickinson questions the value of their truth, pointing out that the hierarchy is perceived by some but not by others; she casts her uncertainty in the telling understatement: "I wonder if it *is*." Yet her friends' perception of Christ's ascendancy gives Him His power and "lets him select his friends" (while presumably excluding the unelect). The letter also reveals Dickinson's loneliness. That her friends and family converted gave her a double sorrow, for she was shut out of love in two ways: Christ did not come down and "select" her for a friend, and her earthly friends who stood with Christ abandoned her; they, with the other elect, would be together on the other side. Conversion became something "desolate that creeps over the spirit." Through satire Dickinson contends with this desolation, with election's pain-inflicting companions: loss and exclusion.

The tone of the above 1850 letter (also the year her first poem is dated) combines satirical whimsy with lament. And in the poems written in this first stage of her career, she similarly satirizes election from the vantage of her own exclusion. Fighting off her cultural inheritance, an outsider, she sets her language apart from the voices she mocks, frequently framing the mocked voices in quotation marks, as in these humorous lines at the end of the poem beginning "'Arcturus' is his other name / I'd rather call him 'Star'":

> Perhaps the "Kingdon of Heaven's" changed
> I hope the "Children" there
> Won't be "new fashioned" when I come –
> And laugh at me – and stare –
>
> I hope the Father in the skies
> Will lift his little girl –

> Old fashioned – naughty – everything –
> Over the stile of "Pearl."
> (Fr 117; 1859)

In this poem, as in many early poems, she throws into doubt conventional, theological, and even scientific naming. By taking the position of the "naughty" girl, she makes fun of those who imagine the mystery of an afterlife in the terms of familiar social categories.

In another early poem, she transforms prayer into a jesting nursery rhyme:

> Papa above!
> Regard a mouse
> O'erpowered by the Cat!
> Reserve within thy kingdom
> A "Mansion" for the Rat!
> (Fr 151; 1860)

The tone of the line, "A 'Mansion' for the Rat!" mixes outrage with the ominous and even the grotesque. This stanza lowers the reverent diction of "Our father who art in heaven" to the familiar and rather taunting, "Papa above!" For the lowly mouse, who asks the overpowering cat for notice and a place in the kingdom of mansions, election is not only exclusionary and hierarchical, but predatory. St. Armand writes that "Dickinson . . . assumed the role of victim, toyed with by an aloof cat-god who possessed the power of imparting or withholding sanctifying grace" (166). Since she is the victim and he the cat-god persecutor, he remains outside herself; she can wittily dismiss him and repay him for his exclusion with exclusion. As she says in another poem beginning, "Going to Heaven" (Fr 128; 1859), "I'm glad I don't believe it." As these poems show, Dickinson is able in her early poems to set her language apart from the voices she satirizes; she is engaged in an externalized battle with her cultural inheritance.

These early satirical poems culminate around 1863, when she internalizes the battle and begins the second period of her career.[2] She has what one might call a grand intertextual experience. When she writes, "The Brain is wider than the Sky / . . . / The one the other will contain / With ease – and You – beside –" (Fr 598; 1863) she observes that the text of the world forms the text of her mind. Dickinson, always critical of hierarchy, recognized that the masculine dominates both the religious and the literary traditions. Accordingly, her "Master," whether man or God (there is much critical speculation) also becomes an internal problem. Now, rather than regarding Calvinism as a foe she can control with satire, she acknowledges the potentials of her faith and that she must subdue the internal imperative to convert. By transforming the critical religious experience of crisis conversion into poetic practice, she achieves mastery over the Calvinist forces in herself. She emerges from this ecstatic visionary encounter not with prayer but poems. In a letter she affirms her conversion to poetry: "Let Emily sing for you because she cannot pray"(L 278). Susan Howe puts it succinctly: "Emily Dickinson's religion was Poetry" (*My Emily* 48).

As a consequence of her internal combat with her religious and cultural inheritance, in the second phase of her poetic development, *numbness* emerges as one of Dickinson's primary poetic modes. So much internalization inevitably leads to self-division. The pain is so great that the self dislocates from itself or it stands as two or more selves or it dies inside itself. In the poems I call the "numb" poems, she appropriates the self-exiling theology of crisis conversion. In conversion the self must be numb to its own sensations and to its attraction to the vanity of the world. This numbness is a kind of dissolution because the self must separate from its sensory parts. Thus, Dickinson observes that the saved man "hath endured / The dissolution – in Himself" (Fr 659). Internal forces rage, paining her, overwhelming, dividing, and ultimately numbing her. This numbing is frequently an inner death. Or the self is dislocated or multiple. She depicts this self-division relentlessly, as the first lines of these famous poems show:

> I felt a Funeral, in my Brain (Fr 340)
> I got so I could take his name / Without Tremendous gain / That Stop-
> sensation – on my Soul (Fr 292)
> After great pain, a formal feeling comes (Fr 372)
> I felt my life with both my hands / To see if it was there (Fr 357)
> There's a Languor in the life / More imminent than Pain (Fr 552)
> The Soul has Bandaged moments – (Fr 360)
> Pain – has an Element of Blank – (Fr 760)

In these numb poems, as in conversion, the self is numb to itself. Because Dickinson contains the self-exiling theology of crisis conversion in the poems, they are a form of mastery—a mastery of containment through language.[3]

The numb poems follow the pattern of Calvinist crisis conversion, in which the self is annihilated to be reborn in God, but they do so with a twist: they achieve self-conversion as opposed to Christian conversion. Dickinson's mastery means annihilating the self to transform it into art. By mastering the text of orthodoxy, she outwits the Word who is God, and she is reborn into the Words of Poetry. Because Dickinson internalizes the visionary religious experience of crisis conversion but does not enter the faith, she converts the language of orthodoxy and the language of the genre. The failure for her of religious orthodoxy also leads to the failure of conventional form and to her triumph of poetic innovation. Her language exceeds conventional boundaries because, as she writes in a letter to Thomas Wentworth Higginson, she is not the subject of a ruler; she has annihilated the governing language of sin and abjectness: "I had no Monarch in my life, and cannot rule myself, and when I try to organize — my little Force explodes — and leaves me bare and charred — " (L 271).[4] Sixty years before Eliot's *Waste Land*, Emily Dickinson, in a numb desolation in which no Monarch prevails, creates an intensely personal idiolect and radical poetics, all of which bloom in her own proto-modernism.

In the second stage of her career, Dickinson's work portrays the boundaries of the self as fluid. Her famous statement, "My business is circumference" (L 268), refers to the necessity and difficulty of delineating the self. The cultural inheritance that she so caustically fought, she now perceives is contained inside herself. The battle continues internally. Accordingly, in this David and Goliath allegory, she regards her earlier assaults as self-destructive:

> I took my Power in my Hand –
> And went against the World –
>
> . . . .
>
> I aimed my Pebble – but Myself
> Was all the one that fell –
> (Fr 660; 1863)

To hold in so many internal forces causes pain, overwhelms, and ultimately numbs her. In the poems, this numbing is frequently an inner death. In this second period in her poetry, her crucial concern is the business of circumference, which is the business of finding the boundaries of the self, with all its attendant pain and numbness. The poems that recount pain — with this wavering circumference and the deadening of that pain — frequently have a male figure as the source of the soul's dilemma. For example, in "I got so I could take his name" (which plays on "taking the Lord's name in vain"), it is a "He" who causes "That Stop-sensation—on my Soul." In some numb poems, there are two internal male figures—one godly, one demonic—vying to conquer the soul. In "The Soul has Bandaged Moments—" a personified thought, "a Goblin," accosts another personified thought, the "Lover," who is "a Theme so fair." In "'Twas like a Maelstrom, with a notch," the masculine figures are more specifically godly and demonic:

> And not a Sinew – stirred – could help,
> And Sense was setting numb –
> When God – remembered – and the Fiend –
> Let go, then, Overcome –
>
> (Fr 425; 1863)

This vast and embattled self has particular significance for Calvin-ist election. First, even though Dickinson may have chosen not to heed Christ's call, she reveals that the internal imperative to do so remains. Second, this self with its compromised boundaries corresponds to what the soul must endure in the conversion process. The Calvinist self, like the self in Dickinson's numb poems, will be divided, self-annihilated, and overwhelmed. Crisis conversion, as Mitchell Breitwieser writes in his dis-cussion of Cotton Mather, begins with a "severe trauma" in which the self discovers it continues "only by the arbitrary kindness of God. . . . Mather repeatedly calls it a kind of dying. . . . A part of thought would step out of self and look upon it. It would see two things: sin, that is the baseness and vanity of self; and its inability to correct error" (28–29). Once the self is annihilated and thereby utterly submissive to divine will, "the law can be seen clearly" and "the mind can rise to survey the whole pattern in which it has accepted its part" (30).

Cotton Mather strives to give himself to God by abasing conscious-ness. Thus, in his diary he writes, "There is nothing of more Consequence to my Safety and Welfare, than a constant strain, of the most self abas-ing Humility. Wherefore I would constantly chase all vain Thoughts, and Vainglorious Ones out of my Mind, with the greatest Abhorrence of them" (quoted in Breitwieser 32). This hunt in which the self is prey is itself a form of consciousness in that it drives out what Dickinson might call "Fiendish" thoughts. By implication, one must focus unwaveringly on God, so that, in Dickinson's terms, God will "remember" and the "Fiend / Let go, then, Overcome."

The Puritan always must be vigilant; even those who achieve a crisis conversion are not assured of salvation. A perfect assurance, in fact, is considered a sign of the unelect. Calvin cautioned against assurance because, as Perry Miller explains, "predestination takes place in the inmost recesses of divine wisdom," and to enter there is to "'enter a labyrinth from which he shall find no way to depart.' To him it seemed unreasonable that men should scrutinize what the Lord had hidden in Himself" (370). Edmund S. Morgan, in a further complication of the labyrinth, writes, "This was the constant message of Puritan preachers: in order to be sure one must be unsure" (70).

Dickinson's doubt goes beyond orthodox uncertainty. She internalizes the conflict — and its attendant doubt — that before was externalized. The numb poems fight dual internal battles: one the Calvinist battle against the self and the other against a cultural inheritance urging just such conversion. The enigmatic poem, "Me from Myself – to banish –" (Fr 709; 1863) is a model for Dickinson's transformation of crisis conversion into poetry; it can be read both as a prayer for the self-banishment of conversion and as a description of Dickinson's poetics. The poem, as in the Bible, proceeds by logical parallelism and speaks in riddles. In the Gospel of Mark, when the Twelve ask Jesus why he speaks in parables he answers that it is to keep the unelect outside, "That seeing they may see, and not perceive; and hearing they may hear, and not understand; lest at any time they should be converted, and *their* sins should be forgiven them" (4.12). In this poem, as in so many others, Dickinson the outsider adopts the strategy of Jesus' parables, in which, as Frank Kermode puts it, "The riddle remains dark, so does the gospel" (47). Thus, "Me from Myself – to Banish –" poses a riddle that with each line is complicated and questioned, recomplicated and requestioned; with each articulation, the darkness is intensified, but, as in one of Mark Rothko's dark canvases, there is much to see in the blackness:

> Me from Myself – to banish –
> Had I Art –
> Impregnable my Fortress
> Unto all Heart –
>
> But since Myself – assault Me –
> How have I peace
> Except by subjugating
> Consciousness?

> And since We're mutual Monarch
> How this be
> Except Abdication –
> Me – of Me?
>
> (Fr 709; 1863)

On the one hand, this poem employs the language of Calvinism and expresses Dickinson's desire to convert. On the other, the poem turns Calvinist language against itself. Thus, if the questions asked in Dickinson's poem are answered affirmatively, then the poem rehearses the anguish of conversion and advocates banishment, subjugation, and abdication of the self—just as would the Puritan seeking to give herself to God. The assaulted self in Dickinson's poem wants "peace / . . . by subjugating / Consciousness"; in Mather's terms, it must "constantly chase all vain Thoughts" out of mind. Likewise, the self must abdicate its position as ruler in order to be subject to God.

Because one can never be assured of salvation, it is fitting that a Calvinist reading of "Me from Myself – to banish –" is equivocal. The poem resists theology with its doubting structure in the way each line questions the previous line. David Porter's observation that Dickinson's poems move "from belief to questioning and disjunction" (91) is true of the structure of "Me from Myself," which moves from an assertion in the first stanza to two questions in the second and third stanzas. The disjunction occurs within, when the self disjoins from itself and, as Dickinson writes in another poem, when there is "internal difference / Where the Meanings, are" (Fr 320). That is to say, the first stanza states that the exaction of conversion is self-banishment and that the desired result is to be invincible to the temptations of the heart. To shut out the self that cherishes corrupt worldly love would make the speaker free to accept Christ's love. However, although the poem's language of conversion theology implies, it does not mention God (and, as Marianne Moore observes, "Omissions are not accidents").[5] By omitting God, Dickinson circles back to the "Fortress" that is "Myself." In this alternative reading, the double meaning of the pivotal line, "Had I Art," moves away from the more humble, "had I means," toward the more self-reflexive, "had I Poetry." The self wishes to shut out the love of God, to construct a fortress of the self that would be impregnable to God's invasive Word. In the fortress that she constructs with her own human word, God's intrusive divine Word will not penetrate. In the same moment that the poem seems to assert faith, it likewise asserts the disjunction in the self-annihilating requirements of Calvinist conversion. That disjunction turns the poem toward self-conversion, which is to say, her conversion to art.

The poem's disjunctive structure is typical of Dickinson's poetic strategy. Martha Dickinson Bianchi says that the Puritan's "shadows hung over" (76) the poet, even after she saw the "fictional quality" (76) of their theology. Karl Keller writes that Dickinson cannot escape the very religious vision she protests: "She stamps her foot at what she stands on. She yells at the voice she yells with. Like the Brahma, it is with Puritan wings that she has the power to flee the Puritan past" (67–68). Seen in this way, the assaulted self in the second stanza is the one who is attacked by its cultural inheritance; she achieves peace by "subjugating" the consciousness that contains that inheritance. The poem, then, may be seeking to banish not the self that resists conversion, but the self that is infused with conversion's self-banishing theology.

Once that inheritance has become "subject," however, which self has achieved ascendancy? The "Me" in the last stanza is a "mutual Monarch," who contains all the selves it wishes to "subjugate." The phrase "mutual Monarch" contains a double dichotomy of four monarchs. The first two are the ones the poem explicitly names, "Me" and "Me." The second two are the two immortal masculine forces to which the "Me" might yield: Lucifer, Prince of Darkness and, as Milton names Him, the "Omnipotent, / Immutable, Immortal, Infinite, / Eternal King . . . Author of all being" (*Paradise Lost* III: 372–74). "Mutual Monarch" works to hold each of the monarchs in a horizontal line. Since each monarch is contained in the phrase, no one of them can rise or abdicate. The rhetorical question at the end of the poem throws mastery and hierarchical categories into question.

Because the poem ends with a question, it emphasizes the impossibility of resolution. "Abdication – / Me – of Me" is a formula that mocks the logic of Calvinist self-annihilation, for to subtract me from me equals zero. How, after all, can a zero either be saved by the Lord or submit to Him? Thus, the poem addresses the problem of the split self by suggesting that each self is so integrally related to the other that abdication is impossible. If one returns to the first stanza, one can see that the poem's impossible formula of self-banishment hinges on the subjunctive: "Had I Art." Art compromises the formula in which self-banishment equals zero and zero equals numbness. Since the poem is art, it suggests that art is the path through self-banishment. And since art, not Calvinism, is the result of this numbness, numbness is the path to art. The poem is the banished self, an "Invincible . . . Fortress," that by "subjugating / Consciousness" has made consciousness its subject. The "Mutual Monarchs," "Me" and "Me," are the author and the Calvinist text, each subject to the other, and each author of the other's being.

The poem, then, takes the reader through the steps of a conversion experience that sincerely searches for the Deity, but ends in union with poetry rather than with Christ. The self annihilates itself—or attempts to—but Christ fails to call on the prepared self. Of God, who does not respond to her fervent supplication, Dickinson bitterly writes in another poem:

> Of course – I prayed –
> And did God Care?
> He cared as much as on the Air
> A Bird – had stamped her foot –
> And cried "Give Me" –
> My Reason – Life –
> I had not had – but for Yourself –
> 'Twere better Charity
> To leave me in the Atom's Tomb –
> Merry, and Nought, and gay, and numb –
> Than this smart Misery
>
> (Fr 581; 1863)

God's indifference triggers Dickinson's experience of self-banishment, numbness, self-conversion, and art. Numb poems, such as "Me from Myself – to banish" and the one above describe a religious and artistic practice. Again and again they record a self-banishment that ends not in conversion, but in poetry. These poems, like the experience of crisis conversion, can be regarded as ecstatic, for *ekstasis* in its Greek etymology is to be "put out of place," that is to say, to stand outside oneself. The self is moved to some other state. In Dickinson's case, when the self stands outside, its boundaries can be filled (or expanded) by God or art. Thus, in Dickinson's lines of numbness ("Pain – has an element of Blank –" and "After great pain, a formal feeling comes –" for example) the ecstatic religious experience of conversion is an analogy for ecstatic artistic experience. It is Dickinson's art—and not God—that elects her to immortality. I call this practice "self-conversion."

"Me from Myself – to banish" questions the hierarchy of orthodox conversion in which the self must be utterly abased before God's higher Power. The poem also regards love, a crucial component of conversion, as hierarchical, for love is a conquest. Thus, the speaker in the poem wishes to be "Invincible . . . / To all Heart." Like romantic love, the kind of love experienced in conversion could mean an absolute union. But that union is not reciprocal; the self must be so overwhelmed with love that it desires subjugation, even if it means self-extinction. "Conversion," as Susan Howe writes, "is a sort of Death, a falling into Love's powerful attraction" (*My Emily* 79). As Cynthia Griffin Wolff points out, conversion was popularly regarded as just such "a falling into Love's powerful attraction": "For the women especially, this Christ Who came to call for them so importunately—offering himself as the 'Bridegroom' of salvation and beseeching them to become 'Brides of Christ' by accepting faith—could be a compelling Suitor" (103). Dickinson makes these connections between conversion and both kinds of love, profane and holy. Since she is always turning toward self-conversion, she, too, is evangelical in the sense that she wants the reader to convert to her. In the following poem, she proclaims that "The Saints" will remember her:

> My Holiday, shall be
> That They – remember me –
> My Paradise – the fame
> That They – pronounce my name –
> (Fr 389; 1862)

These lines turn the tables on conversion. As in "Me from Myself – to banish," the words simultaneously refer both to salvation and to poetry. The poem, in one reading, is humble; it seeks no other fame than to be able to join the saints in heaven. In an alternative reading, the poem seems to substitute literary recognition for divine salvation. She may ask for the union of divinity and her subjugate self, but will settle for the union of the reader and her poem. She will be elected to immortality not by God but by the readers who pronounce her name and who make her poems live.

Mastering the Master

For all her criticism, Dickinson is not cynical about conversion or love. If conversion were reciprocal, it would indeed be a divine love, a mutual reading in which both selves ecstatically stood aside for the other. One can see this hope in one of Dickinson's most despairing pieces of writing, the second "Master Letter," which was written in the same period as most of the numb poems. Wolff writes that in this letter, "the microcosm of the lovers assumes the same tragic configuration as the macrocosm that is ruled by God: it is a world desolated by wounding and by the loss of face-to-face communication" (408). Yet, in spite of failed communication, we hear Dickinson implore the Master to *believe* — or, to put it a bit differently — to love her, to convert to her, to *read* her:[6]

> Master.
> If you saw a bullet
> hit a Bird – and he told you
> he was'nt shot – you might weep
> at his courtesy, but you would
> certainly doubt his word.
> One drop more from the gash
> that stains your Daisy's
> bosom – then would you *believe*?
> Thomas' faith in Anatomy, was
> stronger than his faith in faith.
> God made me – ~~Sir~~ Master – I did'nt
> be – myself. ~~He~~ I dont know how
> it was done. He built the
> heart in me – Bye and bye
> it outgrew me – and like
> the little mother – with the
> big child – I got tired
> holding him. I heard of a
> thing called "Redemption" – which
> rested on men and women.
> You remember I asked you
> for it – you gave me something
> else. I forgot the Redemption
> ~~in the Redeemed – and I did'nt~~
> ~~tell you for a long time, but~~
> ~~I knew you had altered me –~~
> I was tired – no more ~~– so dear~~
> ~~did this stranger become that~~
> ~~were it, or my breath – the~~

~~Alternative — I had tossed~~
~~the fellow away with a smile.~~
I am older – tonight, – Master
but love is the same –
so are the moon and the
crescent — If it had been
God's will that I might
breathe where you breathed –
and find the place – myself –
       can
at night – if I never forget
that I am not with you –
and that sorrow and frost
are never than I – if I wish
with a might I cannot
repress – that mine were the
Queen's place – the love of
the – Plantagenet is my only
apology – to come nearer
than Presbyteries – and nearer than
the new coat – that the Tailor
made – the prank of the Heart
at play on the Heart – in holy
Holiday – is forbidden me –
You make me say it over –
I fear you laugh – when I do
not see – ~~but~~ "Chillon" is not
funny. Have you the Heart in
your breast – Sir – is it set
like mine – a little to the left –
has it the misgiving – if it
wake in the night – perchance
itself to it – a timbrel is it –
itself to it a tune?
These things are ~~reverent~~ holy, sir,
I touch them ~~reverently~~ hallowed, but
Persons who pray – dare remark
~~our~~ "Father!" You say I do
not tell you all – Daisy "confessed –

and denied not."
Vesuvius don't talk – Etna –

    2   1

~~They~~ said a syllable – one of them
a thousand years ago, and
Pompeii heard it, and hid
Forever – She could'nt look the
World in the face, afterward –
"Tell you of the ant" – you
know what a leech is, don't

    ~~remember that~~

you – and Daisy's arm is small
and you have felt the Horizon –
hav'nt you – and did the

    n

sea – ever come so close as
to make you dance?
I dont know what you can
do for it – thank you – Master –
– but if I had the Beard on

    like you –

my cheek – and you – had Daisy's
petals – and you cared so for me –
what would become of you?

    me

Could you forget in fight, or
Flight – or the foreign land?
Could'nt Carlo, and you and I
walk in the meadows an hour –
and nobody care but the Bobolink –
and his – a silver scruple?
I used to think when I died –
I could see you – so I died
as fast as I could – but the

    Heaven

"Corporation: are going too so ~~Eternity~~

    now

wont be sequestered ~~at all~~
Say I may wait for you –

say I need go with no stranger
fold
to the to me – untried ~~country~~
I waited a long time – Master –
But I can wait more – wait
Till my hazel hair is dappled –
and you carry the cane –
then I can look at my
watch – and if the Day is
too far declined – we can take
for
the chances ~~of~~ Heaven –
What would do with me
if I came "in white"?
Have you the little chest to
Put the alive – in?
I want to see you more – Sir –
than all I wish for in
this world – and the wish –
altered a little – will be my
only one – for the skies –
Could you come to New England –
would
this summer – could you come
to Amherst – Would you like
to come – Master?
~~Would it do harm   yet we both~~
~~Fear God~~ – Would Daisy disappoint
You – no – she would'nt – Sir –
It were comfort forever – just
to look in your face, while
You looked in mine – then I
could play in the woods – till
Dark – till you take me
where sundown cannot find
us – and the true keep
coming – till the town is full
~~Will you tell me if you will?~~

.   .   .

> I did'nt think to tell you
> did'nt come to me "in white" –
> Nor ever told me why
>
> +No Rose, yet felt myself
> a'bloom,
> No Bird – yet rose in Ether –

Critics have been trying for years to identify the Master. I, for one, am glad we know neither who the Master was nor the circumstances under which Dickinson wrote the Master letters. The uncertain identity of the Master allows us to slip with the constant slippage of identity in this letter. We can treat the Master as a figure, as Dickinson does. "The prank of the Heart at play on the Heart" may be "forbidden," but she plays anyway. Each self stands outside itself; each self is linguistically fused with the other, only to be cast aside again.

This letter is despairing and full of loneliness, yet it contains instructions to the Master-reader, who, even as he acts on the letter in order to read it, must stand outside himself to make way for the text. Dickinson teaches belief and doubt: "If you saw a bullet hit a Bird – and he told you he was'nt shot – you might weep at his courtesy, but you would certainly doubt his word." This injunction, which might be summarized as "believe not words, but what you see" is followed by a fervent request for the Master to believe "not what you see, but words." He is to believe a metaphor: that the words on the page are a drop of blood from the wound on "Daisy's bosom."[7] Just as the Jesus is a "Word made Flesh," so the writer wants her words to become the gashed flesh she wants the Master to see.

The structure of the letter constantly questions and affirms what the reader can infer either from words or from the phenomenological world. That is to say, the letter vacillates between doubt and faith, words and phenomena. Thus, after asking the Master to have faith in her metaphorical wound, in the depth and pain of her love, she undercuts the notion of belief: "Thomas' faith in Anatomy, was stronger than his faith in faith." But to what kind of anatomy is she referring? The sentences preceding and succeeding the adage about Thomas refer to the anatomy of the soul, to Daisy's wounded bosom with its self made by God and its heart built by God, the heart that outgrows its boundaries and "– like the little mother – with the big child –" becomes tiring and stands outside as a "him."

This anatomy of the soul is also the anatomy of the "thing called 'Redemption' which rested on men and women." In exchange for standing aside for God, Dickinson would receive absolute union and rest, that is, entrance into the Kingdom of Heaven. But redemption won't rest on her. She asks the Master for "it" and he gives "something else." She is "tired – no more" when she forgets "the Redemption." But that Redemption is replaced by another kind of redemption that alters her and is so precious that she would choose "it" over her own "breath"; she seemingly would face self-extinction "with a smile." This redemption, like the other, does not rest but multiplies "Alternatives" so quickly that it is hard to tell what is "it" and what is "something else": "so dear did this stranger become that were it, or my breath – the Alternative – I had tossed the fellow away with a smile." Which "fellow" is it who would be tossed away "with a smile"? Breath, Redemption, the stranger, the heart "built by God," the him, the her, or the *it*?

The letter reenacts the conversion experience by making identity slip away from itself in the same moment that words slip from their meanings. Dickinson speaks both in the first person and in the third person as Daisy; to say "God made me . . . I did'nt be – myself" is to say "I didn't become myself by my own volition," "I didn't have being," and "I didn't have being by my own volition." This kind of "prank of the Heart" points to no absolute redemption by words and meaning.

Dickinson is committed to redemption, but she is aware that her pursuit is through language, through the *Word* of God or the word of poetry. She suspects language can invent what she desires. No sooner is redemption part of her vocabulary than it slips away into doubt, not only religious doubt but also epistemological and linguistic doubt. She is left in the place where "We must meet apart," with her art, wit, the blankness of doubt, and "that White Sustenance / Despair" (Fr 706, 1863).

Yet even as the letter shows the impossibility of redemption through love, it asserts its possibility by asking the Master for empathy. If the Master would *believe*, he would convert. He would become a woman: "but if I had the Beard on my cheek – like you – and you – had Daisy's petals – and you cared so for me—what would become of you?" Of course, this moment of faith, too, will be undercut by doubt, but the words carry with them the hope that this uncertain territory can be mastered. Dickinson wants "to wait," rather than to go alone with the self that is a "stranger." Such an alternative can hardly be articulated; the pain is so utter that it nearly results in syntactical breakdown: "Say I may wait for you – say I need go with no stranger to the to me – untried [country] fold." If the words are to cross the realms between spirit and flesh, Daisy and Master, writer and reader, it will be between the lines, in "the gash" (or gap) between Master and Daisy, in "internal difference / Where the Meanings, are."

By the end of this letter, Dickinson has nullified the category of self by constantly positing "Alternatives." She reinvents redemption; it is no longer doctrinal salvation, but the transforming redemption of "something else" redeemed by something else. This alternative redemption tends to level the hierarchy between the masculine master and his feminine subject. Margaret Homans writes that in manipulating "language to reverse its ordinary meanings," Dickinson uses "linguistic power first to reverse the ordinary direction of power between the feminine self and a masculine other, and then . . . uses it to discard the idea of dominance altogether" (201). Dickinson undoes "the idea of dominance" by transforming the contending identities: Daisy has "the Beard" on her "cheek" and Master has "Daisy's petals." Like "Me from Myself – to banish –," the letter follows the pattern of "belief . . . questioning and disjunction" to the extreme place where Dickinson establishes linguistic categories only to undo them.

Dickinson's linguistic transformations have particular implications for reading, conversion, and authority. Reading, as Norman Pettit points out, was crucial to the process of conversion. "Grace came not from God as a removed creator but through a personal experience of the direct operation of His Spirit" (10) as one read the Bible or wrote about the conversion experience. Even the Puritans questioned whether their understanding of the Word was God's absolute meaning or a product of fancy. Dickinson goes farther than doubting whether her perception is true. She takes pleasure in multiplicity and even declares, "the Object Absolute is Nought."[8] Although she appropriates religious discourse, she equivocates. Her poems, as Mutlu Konuk Blasing writes, "[rule] out any authoritative reading" (178). The poem "There's a certain Slant of light" invites this sort of equivocating slant on God:

> There's a certain Slant of light
> Winter Afternoons –
> That oppresses, like the Heft
> Of Cathedral Tunes –
>
> Heavenly Hurt, it gives us –
> We can find no scar,
> But internal difference
> Where the Meanings, are –

None may teach it – Any –
'Tis the Seal Despair –
An imperial affliction
Sent us of the Air –

When it comes, the Landscape listens –
Shadows hold their breath –
When it goes, 'tis like the Distance
On the look of Death –

(Fr 320; 1862)

One reading of the poem is that an afflicting light oppresses the soul with the knowledge of its unworthiness in the sight of the Lord. Such a realization in an orthodox interpretation would be a prelude to conversion.[9] The phrase "the Seal Despair," a play on the seals of the Revelation, unveils not the crisis leading to rebirth but "the Distance / on the look of Death." The sinner foresees not the heavenly afterlife but the death of the soul. The poem as a cautionary tale is undermined because the poem overtly invites multiple readings. She *should* read the Scriptures and find the one absolute meaning in the Word. But she turns to poetry and finds "internal difference" in such terms as "Cathedral Tunes," "Affliction," "Heavenly Hurt," and "the Seal Despair"; she subverts their Calvinist meanings and transforms them into her own multivalent poem.

As in "Me from Myself – to banish," "There's a certain Slant of light" does not mention God, but nevertheless undercuts His Supreme Authority. In "Slant," which deals with oppression, despair, hurt, and affliction, Dickinson undoes the orthodox notion that God inflicts pain for didactic purposes. Dickinson's Puritan predecessors, Mary Rowlandson and Anne Bradstreet, upheld the tenet of affliction as a good lesson. Rowlandson makes her captivity narrative public "for the Benefit of the Afflicted" (317). Rowlandson affirms her faith in God's love when she writes that the Scriptures teach that "For whom the Lord loveth he chastenth" (Hebrews 12.6). He will help the loved and afflicted "and make them see, and say they have been gainers thereby. And I hope I can say as David did, *It is good that I have been afflicted*. The Lord hathe shown me the vanity of these outward things" (266). Through affliction the Calvinist sees the vanity of the world. Seeing that vanity helps prepare her for turning toward God by turning her away from the self that clings to such worldliness. Similarly, Anne Bradstreet, like Rowlandson a seventeenth-century Puritan, writes in her "Verses upon the Burning of Our House, July 10, 1666":

> Farewell, my pelf; farewell, my store;
> The world no longer let me love.
> My hope and treasure lie above.

For all the ambivalence in their work, both women ultimately bless the Lord for His difficult lesson.

Unlike Rowlandson and Bradstreet, Dickinson is not reassured that affliction is the sign of God's Paternal Omnipresence. Rather, affliction is the sign of His absence and His inscrutability. Whatever sign the Lord may appear to send only further obscures knowledge of Him, thereby intensifying the affliction. In "There's a certain Slant of light," Dickinson appropriates God's signs and fills them with empty despair. The poem compares the "Slant of light, / . . . That oppresses" to "Cathedral Tunes" and alludes to the worship of the God with the irreverence of "Tunes" rather than with the reverence of hymns. The grandeur of a cathedral, a monument to the Lord, is juxtaposed not with hymnal songs of praise, but ironically with tunes, which are the melodies without the words. "Imperial affliction," too, has been emptied of its ordinary meaning. While the poem links affliction with teaching ("None may teach it – any –"), this religious justification is mocking, since it is "Sent us of the Air." Whether "the Air" is the air we breathe or is an "air" (meaning one of those "Cathedral Tunes"), the satirical tone suggests a blankness: tunes without words, light without revelation, affliction without reason."[10]

This blankness throws affliction's "imperial" modification into question. Affliction seems to come out of nowhere, out of "the air"; it has no sign ("We can find no scar") and no significance ("But internal difference / Where the meanings, are"). Even light, God's emissary, is merely the object of a preposition, not worthy of being a subject nor of being capitalized. It is the light's "Slant" that is subject and capitalized. And that slant seems to hit each word at a different angle. The first pronoun — "it" — seems clearly to refer to the "Slant." Thereafter, with each reiteration, "its" referents multiply. By the end of the poem, "it" could be the Slant, Heavenly Hurt, internal difference, the Seal Despair, an imperial affliction, and/or the listening Landscape. The slant is also Dickinson's oblique self receiving orthodox messages.

Even the speaker is multiple since the poem is written in the first person plural. She includes the reader among those who are afflicted, but at the end neither speaker nor reader is present. Distant, we (who are both the readers and the implied speakers) no longer hurt because we no longer perceive: "When it comes, the Landscape listens." For all the pain the "Slant of light" inflicts, the landscape is animated by it: "the landscape listens – / Shadows hold their breath." "When it goes," the landscape looks distant and dead. The poem's end is filled with loss: the loss of the light and the loss of the speaker and the reader as they exit the poem. Like the landscape, we have lost our animation. We are like the excluded unelect in the Gospel of Mark: "That seeing they may see, and not perceive; and hearing they may hear, and not understand; lest at any time they should be converted, and *their* sins should be forgiven them" (4.12). The light that was the sign of "affliction" now has the detached "look of Death." It has not taught the vanity of the world and the hope of another. We have been neither converted nor forgiven.

If the poem refutes the lesson of afflicting light, it paradoxically "listens" to it and reverses the meanings again. The "Slant of light," in all its variety, refracts infinitely in each facet of the "it" that it illuminates. The light, God's sign, is multiple, not absolute. Thus, the "internal difference / Where the meanings, are" undoes religious doctrine and posits a protomodern religious pluralism and a relativity of meaning. Dickinson releases the signs from their ordinary meanings and points her reader to an alternative, "slanted" signification. Paradoxically, by refuting religious doctrine, she restores God's unknowability and thereby asserts a fundamental tenet of Puritanism. In her doubt, she is a most pure Puritan. Unlike her religious forebears, however, she accepts faith not through Calvinist crisis conversion but through self-conversion. She annihilates both the self that has internalized a conventional god and the theology associated with him.

In that blankness is Emily Dickinson's poetry, a poetry devoted to the unknowable. In her ambiguity of meaning, her fragmented form, her doubt and parody of tradition and God, in her finding her home in the wasteland of self-division, and in her transference of meaning from God to poetry, Dickinson anticipated the concerns and techniques of the modernists. Her doubt and revisionary theology of self-conversion provide her with the language of negation, the tongue of blankness, and the slanted faith of her protomodernist poetry. Brilliant, innovative, *it* is her Faith.

~3~

The Adventure of the Self

Transforming Calvinism and Emerson's Transcendentalism

C

Adventure most unto itself
The Soul condemned to be –
Attended by a single Hound
Its own identity.

—Emily Dickinson

Undoing Calvinism

In 1857 Emerson lectured in Amherst and was a guest of Emily Dickinson's brother and sister-in-law, Austin and Sue. Sue wrote of the sage philosopher, "I remember very little of the lecture except a fine glow of enthusiasm on my own part. . . . I felt strangely elated to take his transcendental arm afterward and walk leisurely home" (Sewall, 115 n).[1] Unlike Emily, Sue was born-again and a member of the First Congregational Church, yet she elatedly accepts Emerson's spirituality. Emerson's transcendentalism contradicted the orthodox religious beliefs of Sue and the whole Dickinson family, yet they were transported by the vision in his lecture. In the mid–nineteenth century, transcendental romanticism and the other religious movements of the day attenuated the power of orthodox Calvinism. This cohabitation of belief systems is reflected in Emily Dickinson's poetry, which develops from a rewriting of Calvinist self-annihilation and despair to a rewriting of the romantic, exalted discovery of the self.

As I argued in chapter 2, the poems in the second phase of Dickinson's development, which I call the poems of self-conversion, frequently appropriate Calvinist crisis conversion by recounting the process in which the self, seeing its sinfulness and lowliness before the Lord, is annihilated in order to be reborn in Christ. However, because Dickinson never converted, the despair in these poems lies in failing to have the kind of faith that leads to redemption; for a faith in self-annihilation is the key to divine rebirth. On the contrary, her self-annihilation is a decisive turning point resulting not in union with God, but in alienation from Him and His select society. In her version of Calvinist self-annihilation, Dickinson empowers herself to write a poem by ritually nullifying the orthodox self and, in so doing, achieves literary election. In the next phase of her development, her adventure of the self, she sees her exclusion from the society of the Calvinist elect as an opportunity for self-exploration. In this chapter, I delineate the change in Dickinson's theology by focusing on two poems in which the speaker anticipates her death and speaks as though she were experiencing the moment the self passes out of this world. Taking my cue from the poet — who writes — "O Necromancy sweet —," I call these poems "necromantic."[2] I use "I felt a Funeral in my Brain" (Fr 340; dated 1862) as a prototype for Dickinson's transformation of Calvinism and "This consciousness that is aware" (Fr 817; dated 1864) as a prototype for her transformation of Emersonian romanticism. By speaking in the necromantic voice, both poems put a theological system to the test, for how the afterlife is constituted — who is admitted and who is excluded at the gates of heaven, and whether there *is* a heaven — helps define the relationship of the self to others and to earthly existence. As Roland Hagenbuchle points out: "[T]he 'Tomb' . . . is for Dickinson the place *par excellence* from which man looks in two directions, toward finitude and toward infinity. That 'Death sets a Thing significant' is an insight that Emerson would have found difficult to understand. . . . Not the emblematic potential of nature but the otherness of things is [Dickinson's] focal point" (144). The necromantic position in the poems is a device through which Dickinson disperses the typological connections of Puritanism or the natural emblems of transcendentalism. Death is "But Gravity – and Expectation – and Fear / A tremor just, that all's not sure" (Fr 543). That

ubiquitous uncertainty plays itself out in "I felt a Funeral," in which the
psyche of the speaker imagines a posthumous scene in the Puritan the-
ater of Hell and the ultimate exclusion of the unsaved; the reader sees
her captured midfall into the abyss, like one of Jonathan Edwards's "Sinners in the Hands of an Angry God." However, Dickinson employs a
rhetoric in "Funeral" that sets up expectations of Calvinist conversion,
salvation, or damnation and descent into Hell, only to thwart them.
Similarly, "This Consciousness that is Aware" employs language that creates the expectation of transcendence, but the poem defies the logic of
transcendentalism.

While both poems speak from a necromantic position, the difference
in tone is revealing. "I felt a Funeral in my Brain" is gothic. Its nightmarish mourners "treading – treading" and drum "beating – beating" are
reminiscent of Edgar Allan Poe's throbbing "Tell-tale Heart." Her speaker
is downtrodden, anguished, "wrecked, solitary." The movement in the
poem is downward, as it rehearses a long, dizzying fall. In contrast, the
movement of "This Consciousness that is aware" is forward. The poem
employs the language of the enlightening quest; the speaker looks ahead
to the "most profound experiment," to "discovery" and "adventure." Her
consciousness, which "is aware / Of Neighbors and the Sun," asserts that
her experience is commonly shared, since it is "Appointed unto Men." But
the consciousness in "Funeral" shares no such connection with others;
it reduces those who mourn her to an oppressive synecdoche: they are
"Boots of Lead" that "creak across [her] Soul." "Funeral" ends with blank
ambiguity while "Consciousness" ends with "Identity." While "I felt a Funeral in my Brain" does not leave much hope for a differentiated self or for
"Its own identity," it paradoxically clears a space in which the self in later
poems will adventure:[3]

I felt a Funeral, in my Brain	I felt a funeral, in my brain
And Mourners to and fro	And Mourners to and fro
Kept treading – treading – till	Kept treading – treading – till it
it seemed	seemed
That Sense was breaking through –	That Sense was breaking through –
And when they all were seated,	And when they all were seated,
A Service, like a Drum –	A Service, like a Drum –
Kept beating – beating – till	Kept beating – beating – till I
I thought	thought
My mind was going numb –	My mind was going numb

And then I heard them
lift a Box
And creak across my ~~Brain~~
Soul
With those same Boots of
Lead, again,
Then Space – began to toll,

As all the Heavens were
a Bell,
And I, and Silence, some
strange Race
Wrecked, solitary here –
Strange Race
Wrecked, solitary, here –

And·then, a Plank in
Reason, broke,
And I dropt down, and
down –
And hit a World, at every
+plunge,
Crash – +Got through –

And then I heard them lift a Box
And creak across my Soul
With those same Boots of Lead,
    again,
Then Space – began to toll,

As all the Heavens were a Bell,
And Being, but an Ear,
And I, and Silence, some strange
    Race
Wrecked, solitary, here –

And then a Plank in Reason, broke,
And I dropped down, and down –
And hit a World, at every plunge,
And finished knowing – then –
                    (Fr 340; 1862)

This poem is simultaneously a revision of Calvinist funeral customs and a kind of funeral for those customs, a rite of passage into another way of thought. In the most obvious reading of "Funeral," the poem describes the unbeliever's nightmarish descent into oblivion; R. Jackson Wilson writes that Dickinson "picture[s] dying a limitless fall into mere nothing, and the terminal consciousness of the dead as no more than a chilling realization of that intolerable truth" (263). The poem is not so single-minded, however, although many readers do attempt to limit it by saying "I felt a Funeral" is about a story of some particular event. So for Judith Farr the poem is a "story of a fainting spell" (90); for Sharon Cameron it "is about knowledge and the consequences of its repression" (*Lyric Time* 96–97) — a proposition with which I might concur, if Cameron did not come to a conclusion that gives credence to the idea that "[a]s J. V. Cunningham remarks, the poem is a representation of a 'psychotic episode' at the end of which the speaker passes out" (*Lyric Time* 97). I propose instead that the poem recounts a fall away from the very notion of single-mindedness.

Not limited to creating the sensations of a dying, fainting, or psychotic consciousness, "I felt a Funeral" takes on religious debates of Dickinson's day, from the orthodox position of the Congregationalists to the romantic position of the transcendentalists. The poem reveals a consciousness falling away from these cosmologies, that is, a consciousness in the process of freeing itself from the prescriptions of these belief systems.

My reading of "I felt a Funeral" hinges on the moment when the world constructed by "Reason" gives way to "Worlds" once a crucial Plank breaks. There are multiple levels of irony here, since Reason has several theological significances. Reason, in the latter-day Puritan theology of Emily Dickinson's family, is a delusional path away from the truth. In her reading of "I Felt a Funeral," Wolff reproduces from Holmes and Barber's *Religious Allegories* (1848) an emblem entitled "WALKING BY FAITH." Commonly used for didactic purposes in the nineteenth century, it illustrates the religious adage asserting that the soul reaches heaven not through reason but through blind faith. The emblem depicts a man at the edge of a precipice and walking across a narrow plank labeled FAITH that spans a gulf between the land and clouds that conceal the radiant heavenly city. The man does not look where he is going but down at the Bible in his hand since faith in the word of God, not reliance on his own sensations, will lead him to the kingdom of heaven: "[O]nly the plank of 'FAITH' can provide transport — so this emblem asserts. Yet having renounced faith, Dickinson substitutes 'a Plank in Reason,' which breaks because no rational explanation can be adequate to bridge the abyss between earth and Heaven" (230). From the perspective taught by the Holmes and Barber emblem, the "Plank in Reason" must break, for reason is a construction of the human mind, which cannot have knowledge of God.

In Emerson and Coleridge, reason is the path to the one truth; Dickinson's poem suggests a failure of visionary romanticism, as the "Plank in Reason" breaks, then gives way to a plurality of worlds. Emerson writes in "Nature" that reason is the "universal soul" and though it, the world's diversity is united:

> This universal soul [man] calls Reason: it is not mine, or thine, or his, but we are its; we are its property and men. And the blue sky in which the private earth is buried, the sky with its eternal calm and full of everlasting orbs, is the type of Reason. . . .
>
> If the Reason be stimulated to more earnest vision, outlines and surfaces become transparent, and are no longer seen; causes and spirits are

seen through them. The best moments of life are these delicious awak-
enings of the higher power, and the reverential withdrawing of nature
before God.[4] (*Collected Writings* 8–15)

Emerson's famous transparency reveals the essential truth that dwells in
the material universe. His concept of "reason as imagination and intuition," writes Amy Schrager Lang, suggests that "self-reliance as the key to
truth and the source of cosmic unity" (118). In Dickinson's "Funeral," self-
reliance leads to alienation (the speaker is "Wrecked, solitary") and to a
collapse of cosmic unity (she "hits a world at every plunge"). Reason does
not serve as a transcendental unifier in which, as Kenneth Burke puts it,
"a realm HERE is being talked about *in terms of* ELSEWHERE — and there
is a terminology designed to *bridge* these disparate realms" (29). Instead,
Dickinson's language breaks down that terminology ("And then a Plank in
Reason, broke, / And I dropped down, and down").

Significantly, in the manuscript of the poem, the terminological bridge
"crashes" at the variant ending. In Johnson's and Franklin's versions, the
last line is "And finished knowing – then." Because "then" is between
dashes — an ambiguous notation — it is not clear whether the speaker finishes knowing then, at a particular moment, or if "then" is a narrative
marker for something else to follow that happens in the blankness of the
page, something unarticulated after the poem breaks off at the dash. In
her work on Dickinson's manuscripts, Susan Howe advocates reading the
poetry as the poet laid it out on the page, and she does not consider any
word a variant, as Johnson and Franklin do. Read in this way, the words
"Crash – +Got through" are variants for "plunge" and "And finished knowing – then –," so the text might read "And hit a World, at every / Crash, /
And Got through – then." "Crash – Got through" can also be read as the
last line. If "Crash – +Got through" is the last line of the poem, finishing
knowing doesn't end knowing; rather it is a kind of barrier through which
the speaker may "crash" and "get through" to a different, as yet undefined,
epistemology. Yet the ambiguity of "And finished knowing – then" doesn't
rely on the variant (or other) ending, "Crash – +Got through." The variant serves as confirmation of the suspicion that "And – finished knowing
– then" is a death in the poem from which as Hagenbuchle says, one can
look "in two directions, toward finitude and toward infinity" (144).

Whether conceived in Calvinist terms or in transcendental terms, reason leads not to a single truth, but to uncertain plurality. Even the way
reason is posited evokes rival epistemologies, throwing them into doubt,

into a downward spiral in which each word is a plank that gives way to a fall in which one "hits a World at every plunge." Those "worlds" could be levels of the cosmos (like Dante's levels of Hell, Purgatory, and Heaven) or they could represent multiple perspectives from which the absolute categories of Calvinism and transcendentalism break down—a device typical of Dickinson's poetics. Though initially it does read as a fairly straightforward (for Dickinson) narrative of a fall into oblivion, "I felt a Funeral" poses epistemological questions through contradiction and inversion. There is much narrative action in the poem. Place markers such as "And when" and "And then" create the illusion of chronology. And the richness in sensation serves as local sound and color. But this seeming security in time and space intensifies the poem's extreme dislocations. Death undoes time and space. The way the poem "tells its story"—its surface narrative structure and texture—is reassuringly ordinary (given its horrifying subject). Yet its premise—"I felt a Funeral in my Brain"—is extraordinary: this very first line thwarts the normal expectation that literal and figurative levels can be distinguished.

At each moment when the poem creates the expectation of a chronological unfolding, a narrative rupture occurs. At each "and then" or "and when" the reader must contend with a contradiction that challenges conventional epistemological understandings; like the speaker, the reader "hit[s] a world, at every / plunge" as she reads down the page. For example, in the third stanza, the mourners lift the box containing the deceased speaker and simultaneously "creak across" her soul with "Boots of Lead." In another inversion, the mourners seem both to be burying her (that is, confining her), and to be opening for her a vision of endless "Space" and "all the Heavens." She is as alienated in her cosmic vision as she is by physical burial because it is not a vision of connection. Presumably, the speaker has left her body but instead of reaching heaven and joining the elect on the other side, she is oppressed by those who mourn her, and then finds herself utterly "Wrecked, solitary," and surrounded by tolling space. Ironically, while space objectively tolls, the "Heavens" are in the subjunctive mood: space tolls *as if* "all the Heavens were / a Bell." In the space between the stanzas lies the difference between the objectivity of infinite space and the subjunctivity of the eternal heavens, which are hypothetically infused with religious spirit. Hence, when Dickinson uses seemingly synonymous expressions—Brain, Mind, and Soul, a funereal feeling and numbness—she accentuates the differences between the meanings rather than their similarities.

Though Dickinson questions heaven through her use of language, she doesn't question the soul. In fact, she introduces the more scientific, physical "Brain" in the first stanza and transforms it into the "Soul" in the third stanza. She even initially writes "Brain" then crosses it out and replaces it with "Soul." As one reads down the page the notion of the brain is progressively transformed from the scientific to cerebral to spiritual nomenclature; that is, from "Brain" to "Mind" to "Soul." Because heaven is subjunctive and therefore questioned, the movement of the language suggests that one can question heaven and still have a soul. Herein lies a hint of Dickinson's later critique of transcendental self-reliance. Since the self in "Funeral" is finally "wrecked" and "solitary," self-reliance in the poem becomes a lonely thing when one imagines the soul without heaven and without the possibility of ultimate connection.

As I have been showing, there is no single narrative or literal path through "Funeral." Rather, "Funeral," as Dickinson says in another poem, "dwells in Possibility" (Fr 466). What can "I felt a Funeral, in my Brain" mean? The line suggests two possibilities: first, a psychological state in which the speaker experiences a death of the self and, second, a physical state in which the dead speaker's voice comes from beyond the grave. In asking her readers to decode this complex intertwining of the conceptual and the physical, Dickinson creates a reading process that reenacts the epistemological transformations the poem performs. The funeral is not *observed* by the mind but *felt* by the brain, as if the brain were a physical stage on which the nightmare of the funeral unfolds. "Feeling the funeral" conveys both feeling death itself and feeling the observation of death. Perhaps the line *can* literally mean that the speaker felt a funeral service internally. But this understanding of the line again challenges literal and figurative categories; it asks the reader to transform the physical *brain* into the more ephemeral notion of *the mind*. By making the brain at once a physical, literal place to feel action and metonymically a mind to observe it, Dickinson blurs the boundaries between subject and object, consciousness and action, and, in so doing, allows a dialectic between those two polarities. This dialectic, which continues throughout the poem, works to undermine a conventional understanding of death, particularly a Calvinist one. The movement of language in Dickinson's work, Hagenbuchle observes, removes the "Center" and replaces it with "Circumference," so that while she invokes Calvinist ideas, her poetry releases them into a self-reflexive poetic orbit.[5]

To feel a funeral in one's brain can be read as an essential part of crisis conversion, since conversion requires a virtual death of the self. The price exacted for enlightenment is to allow the overwhelming light of God to blank out one's own vision. Calvinist faith meant the sacrifice of one's individual identity and of the world (considered "vanity") because absolute submission and obedience to the Lord demanded it. Dickinson found it impossible to make such a renunciation and to relinquish the self and the world. As a young woman in the late 1840s — years of revivalism in which she struggled to convert — Dickinson repeatedly laments that her love of the world moves her more than her love of God or her fear that she won't be saved from hell. In an early letter she compares the world to a tempting siren, whose appeal is greater than God's truth:

> the world allured me & in an unguarded moment I listened to her syren [sic] voice. From that moment I seemed to lose my interest in heavenly things by degrees. . . . I felt my danger & was alarmed in view of it, but I had rambled too far to return & ever since my heart has been growing harder and more distant from the truth. . . . (L 11)

Dickinson's referring to God's truth as "the truth" reveals her characteristic dilemma: paradoxically, she has faith and lacks it (she walks the plank and breaks it). The letter, accordingly, creates two realms. One is heavenly and "true"; the other is tempting, dangerous, and represented by the beautiful siren "voice" of the world, which by making her lose her faith will conduct her to extinction. It is important that Dickinson invokes the myth of the sirens as a counterpoint to patriarchal Christianity. The world and knowledge of it, traditionally represented as negative and irresistible, is feminine. Her temptations — embodied in the sirens, Circe, Pandora, and Eve — lead inevitably to death because every earthly thing must die. Yet for Dickinson the world's siren voice engenders and collaborates with her own — a far cry from adhering to the Lord's will and silencing the self, that ultimate extinction. When she later writes, "Let Emily sing for you since she cannot pray" (L 278), she suggests that she has chosen to sing with the world rather than to pray prostrate to the Lord. Instead of faith in "heavenly things" she chooses a transformative faith in the world, which like herself is feminine, and a different singing form of immortality. In the world (or in many worlds) and in her own truth, she "rambles far," and the further she rambles, the more God's truth becomes distant and unapprehendable. She believes enough in religious doctrine to describe it in this early letter as the supreme, single order; yet her own truth is convincing enough, despite the "danger," to lure her away and make her "lose interest in heavenly things."

Dickinson's early disposition against "giv[ing] up all for Christ," then, is part of her continual effort to frame her own vision, even of death. "Mine – here – in Vision – and in Veto!" she asserts in this often quoted poem:

> Mine – by the Right of the White Election!
> Mine – by the Royal Seal!
> Mine by the Sign in the Scarlet prison –
> Bars – cannot conceal!
>
> Mine – here – in Vision and in Veto!
> Mine – by the Grave's repeal –
> Titled – Confirmed –
> Delirious Charter!
> Mine – long as Ages steal!
>
> (Fr 411; 1862)

Each of the line's elements—separated by dashes—is crucial. She is entitled to her vision; it is her vision; it is "here" in the world; and she has arrived at her vision, in part, by selection or "Veto." Significantly, because the American president has "veto power," the word "veto" transforms "election" from orthodox to democratic language, suggesting a voice that can raise singular opposition. A basic principle of democracy is that each person, including the president, is entitled to a say or a vision. Earthly democracy incorporates heterodoxy, while God the King's monarchy requires orthodoxy and a relinquishing of the self in the service of that orthodoxy.

By claiming her own power in vision and veto, the speaker undoes the hierarchy of religious orthodoxy. The poem uses the language of the Bible and of conversion in order to glorify the poet's own visionary battle against God. Dickinson transforms religious doctrine into legal doctrine, and the poem echoes earthly documents of the political state, which grant entitlements and rights. This is a bill of rights that usurps the language of another patriarch, her own father (who was an attorney and congressman), in order to assert her personal/political vision against a collective religious imperative. Accordingly, she combines the speech of church and state to proclaim that she is "Titled – Confirmed." Here is her poetic constitution, her "Delirious Charter" which, like the constitution of the government, is eternal, outlasting the framers: "Mine – long as Ages Steal!"

Her title and her rights are granted by the "Right of the White Election," which is distinct from orthodox election. In her own religion of poetry, she elects herself through poetic vision, symbolized by whiteness.[6] White is part of her self-mythologizing: it is well known that Dickinson wore a white dress through much of her adulthood; less well known is that she left instructions to be buried in a white casket.[7] In her poem, "Dare you see a Soul *at the White Heat?*" (Fr 401; 1862), the whiteness of the blacksmith's flame "stands symbol" for the internal energy of the creative act. In "Publication — is the Auction / Of the Mind of Man" (Fr 788; 1863), she refers to herself as "White" and her poems as "snow": "We – would rather / From our Garret go / White – unto the White Creator." Whiteness, associated with purity, brides, death, snow, and the blazing light of noon, links opposites; as Jane Donahue Eberwein points out, "[t]his 'colorless all-color' of Ishmael's meditation leads Dickinson's critics, like Melville's, to the heart of ambiguity" (*Dickinson: Strategies* 34). Dickinson's white at once appropriates the shadowless, absolute light of God, "the White Creator," and inscribes it with the poet's ambiguity. This ambiguity mimics God who is unknowable but who demands perfect submission to his one truth. The words describing her vision are often paradoxical in order to reveal her bold opposition to that conventional sight which would make her blind to herself and the world. Her poetic vision, her entitlement, is her "White Election" precisely because she has vetoed the traditional Calvinist election that requires her to veto herself.[8]

Dickinson suggests that the "alarm" she feels at having "lost interest in heavenly things," arises from the loss of a Calvinist — that is, a compensatory — attitude toward death in which a renunciation of the world might lead to a heavenly afterlife. In another early letter she again affirms her attachment to the world while questioning the price Christ exacts for salvation. "The world holds a predominant place in my affections," she writes, "I do not feel I could give up all for Christ, were I called to die" (L 13). Dickinson's use of the subjunctive "were" is odd, as death is the one certainty in life. Perhaps the subjunctive questions whether Christ comes "calling" at death and perhaps it questions the cultural tropes associated with conversion and dying. In this system of rewards and punishments, "giving up all" means renouncing as vanity everything that "holds a predominant place in [one's] affections." Furthermore, this traditional system means feeling grateful not only for one's own death but for the deaths of loved ones and the loss of the loved things of the world. So Anne Bradstreet writes in her "Verses upon the Burning of Our House, July 10 1666":

Then straight I gin my heart to chide.
And did thy wealth on earth abide?
Didst fix thy hope on mold'ring dust?
The arm of flesh didst make thy trust?
Raise up thy thoughts above the sky
That dunghill mist away may fly.

Especially in Dickinson's time, the death of a loved one could induce the mourner, frequently prompted by the clergyman, to convert. Calvinism in its nineteenth-century sentimental incarnation was empathic, as Karen Haltteunen points out, and mourning manuals advised their readers: "'The religion of Christ . . . is eminently the religion of the heart'" (129). In this later poem, Dickinson plays on the notion of empathic deathbed conversion when she writes:

I never hear that one is dead
Without the chance of Life
Afresh annihilating me,
That mightiest Belief,
            (Fr 1325; 1874)

Here Dickinson leaves ambiguous whether she means life everlasting in heaven or life on earth, the self-annihilation of converting or the annihilation of not converting (and therefore facing the extinction of the grave). From a conventional nineteenth-century point of view, empathizing with the dying loved one might force the bereaved to feel one's own death, which in turn might precipitate a crisis and a conversion. Death, furthermore, might shock the mourner to relinquish her affection for the world: "[o]ut of the mourner's grief came a deep sense of the vanity of earthly happiness" (Haltteunen 129). Hence, the death of the self means that, at least in the heart of the believer, the world also dies. When Dickinson brilliantly writes, "Looking at death, is dying" (Fr 341; 1862), she refers both to that empathic experience of death and to conversion's requisite death of the self and of its earthly attachments. Dickinson's earthly attachment and the anguished tone of these lines, however, expose the cruelty of a jealous god who both demands that those who love Him "give up all" for Him and grants the power of empathy only to intensify the pain of the loss He requires.

Conversion also might come about at the eleventh hour, on the deathbed. It was seen as a sign of election if the dying were "willing to die."

Customarily, the bereaved seeking consolation would write the clergy-man to ask if the deceased had gone to death willingly (Dickinson wrote such letters).[9] In another necromantic poem, a poem of fearful whimsy, "I heard a Fly buzz – when I died –," those in the deathbed scene wait for just such a revelation of elect status, "for that last Onset – when the King / be witnessed – in the room":

> I heard a Fly buzz – when I died –
> The Stillness in the Room
> Was like the Stillness in the Air –
> Between the Heaves of Storm –
>
> The Eyes around – had wrung them dry –
> And breaths were gathering firm
> For that last Onset – when the King
> Be witnessed – in the Room –
>
> I willed my Keepsakes – Signed away
> What portion of me be
> Assignable – and then it was
> There interposed a Fly –
>
> With Blue – uncertain – stumbling Buzz –
> Between the light – and me –
> And then the Windows failed – and then
> I could not see to see –
>
> (Fr 591; 1863)

By putting death in the subjunctive in this poem and in the letter above, Dickinson questions the cultural construction in which the experience of death might be an occasion to meet the Lord. In fact, in "I heard a Fly," the King is witnessed neither by the mourners nor by the deceased whom He presumably would carry to heaven. The poem verges on blasphemy by replacing Christ's call with a fly's buzz. Rather than imagining the soul's continuing life in heaven, Dickinson stresses physical death with the fly buzzing around the corpse. This grotesque physicality undermines the sentimental notion of an angelic and beautiful death.[10] The speaker has no revelation at death; on the contrary, her physical faculties shut down with-out compensatory vision or flight. The fly, representative of the physical universe, is "interposed" between the speaker and "the light." And what that light represents, the eternal light of God or the failing light of earthly existence, is left "uncertain."

In "I heard a Fly," then, Dickinson rewrites sentimental nineteenth-century deathbed customs. The "Eyes around" the bed are "wrung . . . dry" from weeping and the dying one has "Signed away" her "Keepsakes." Comparing the scene to Harriet Beecher Stowe's Little Eva distributing "her golden curls on her deathbed in Uncle Tom's Cabin," St. Armand writes that "the expected vision of a delivering Christ and the 'commendations and intercessions' of friends are frustrated, even ironically undercut, by the loud buzzing of the fly, and a final confession of faith is never achieved. A perfect and holy dying is spoiled" (61). Not only is the ritual spoiled by the interposition of an uncouth fly, both the ritual and the understanding of death as the moment the soul crosses into the kingdom of heaven has been rendered meaningless: the fly's "uncertain stumbling Buzz" transforms faith into "uncertainty," converts the walk on the path with Christ into "stumbling," and reduces holy words and signs into mere "buzzing."

"I felt a Funeral," like "I heard a Fly" invokes nineteenth-century mourning rituals that seek to jolt the unbeliever into professing faith; just as "Fly" rewrites deathbed rituals, so "I felt a Funeral in my Brain" rewrites the funeral service. In these poems — as in so much of her work — Dickinson posits alternative death scenes in order to reveal that one's epistemology is framed by what one imagines, or is taught to imagine, might happen at death. In "Funeral," the persistent treading of the mourners raises the faint hope "That Sense was breaking through," that perhaps consciousness is reawakening, and that the poem will tell the story of holy deliverance. But in the second stanza the service, which keeps "beating – beating," and the mourners, who keep "treading – treading," make the speaker numb instead of pushing her to a conversion breakthrough. The poem creates the expectation of a causal relationship between the treading and the beating and what happens next, but what happens next is a tautological return to the first line of the poem: "I thought / My mind was going numb." Because feeling a funeral can be construed as synonymous with thinking one's mind is going numb, what happens next in the poem is seemingly the same as what happens at the beginning: a death of the mind. The variation, however, between feeling a funeral and feeling numb underscores ways in which the two phrases differ in meaning; these differences establish the prevailing feeling in the poem of opposition between the speaker and the others, between the individual self and the religious custom represented by the mourners and their service.

It is not death, but the funeral service, in which the clergyman recites

Calvinist doctrine regarding death and the soul, that *numbs* the speaker's mind: "A Service, like a Drum – / Kept beating – beating – till I thought / My Mind was going numb." By making the service dull the mind of the speaker, Dickinson inverts the self-annihilating Calvinist notion that in the service of doctrine one's mind must be insensitive to itself. In this stanza not only is the speaker numb to herself, but to doctrine. The moment when the "Sense" of doctrine might break though becomes instead mere deadening sensation. The words of the funeral service, which would generally be regarded as more profound than other kinds of discourse, have no significance whatsoever; they are mere sound ("like a drum beating – beating") and that sound is numbing, erasing meaning rather than creating it. This movement in the poem, in which noise obliterates religious meaning, is akin to the moment in "I heard a Fly" when a pronouncement of faith is blocked by a fly and its "uncertain stumbling Buzz."

In both poems the failure of religious custom is accompanied by an alienation from other people. Dickinson employs two devices in order to intensify the speaker's exclusion: synesthesia and synecdoche. People are indeed solitary and wrecked when they are represented as fragments: "Being" is "but an Ear" and mourners, "Boots of lead." Similarly, in "Fly" those gathered around the speaker's deathbed are "Eyes" and "Breaths." By using synethesia (a strategy she uses often) in the line, "Then Space – began to toll," Dickinson increases the feeling of desolation. As in the line, "I could not see – to see" in "Fly," in "I felt a Funeral," all existence coalesces into one heightened yet, paradoxically, failing sense. The aural is persistent throughout the poem, with its mourners "treading – treading," its drum "beating – beating," and the creaking of "those same Boots of / Lead." This acoustic overload culminates when "Being" is "but an Ear" and the speaker "and Silence" are "some / strange Race." Though the speaker reports what she knows through hearing, she is aligned with silence; together they are "some / strange Race." She can sense that the bell of heaven is tolling, but she can't hear it. Excluded from hearing the bell of Heaven, even though her whole "Being" is attuned to "sound," the speaker is utterly alienated: "Wrecked, solitary." The speaker of the poem is alienated because of her necromantic position in relation to others; the result of that position is that her perceptions have broken down the epistemological categories shared in the social universe.

The contradictions of the poem tend to question ways of knowing. To feel a funeral in one's brain is and is not to feel the funeral service, is and is not dying, and is and is not going numb. Space is and is not heaven. Being is but an Ear that can and cannot hear. At the end of the poem it is ambiguous whether the speaker "finishes knowing" or finishes knowing before something else that is unarticulated happens. The end of the poem is and is not the end. It ends with the extinction of being or with the expectation of something else. With its ambiguous last word and an ambiguous dash, the poem ends by launching the reader into the unknown, into the blank page beyond the end of the poem.[11] In that space, which is the next phase of her poetic development, Dickinson tells the story of what happens beyond annihilation, when the self is free to "[a]dventure most unto itself."

The annihilation in "I felt a Funeral" is the particular kind of destruction that is part of the process I call "self-conversion." The poem describes an epistemological process that extinguishes one teleology after another, along with the parts of the self that has internalized them. "Funeral"—and poems like it that appropriate Calvinist conversion—destroys orthodox epistemology and leaves the perceiving "Ear" of the speaker free to hear poetry in the wreck (or to hear the poetry of the wreck). When in her first letters to Higginson in 1862, Dickinson describes her poetics, she often refers to the absence of a ruling authority. In one letter she writes, "You think my gait 'spasmodic'—I am in danger—Sir—You think me 'uncontrolled'—I have no Tribunal" (L 265). In another, the beginning of which I quote for context and for its reversals, she writes:

> Dear Friend—
>   Are these more orderly? I thank you for the Truth—
>   I had no Monarch in my life, and cannot rule myself, and when I try to organize—my little force explodes—and leaves me bare and charred—
>   I think you called me "Wayward." Will you help me improve?
> (L 271)

She "cannot rule" herself once she has destroyed the internal "Monarch," yet in spite of the "danger" and in spite of her posture to Higginson that she seeks in him a "Preceptor," she revels and believes in the unruled territory out of which she creates. In Letter 271 she claims, "I shall observe your precept—though I dont understand it, always," yet later she undercuts her position of obedience and humility. For example, she begins Letter 271 by asking if the two poems she encloses, "I cannot dance upon my Toes" and "Before I got my eye put out" (Fr 336; 1862) are "more orderly" and she thanks Higginson for "the Truth." Yet "I cannot dance upon my Toes" is frequently cited as one of Dickinson's poems of rebellion against the masculine tradition; it is a poem of self-proclamation, one in which she extols her unique vision:

> I cannot dance opon my Toes –
> No Man instructed me –
> But oftentimes, among my mind,
> A Glee possesseth me,
>
> That had I Ballet knowledge –
> Would put itself abroad
> In Pirouette to blanch a Troupe –
> Or lay a Prima, mad,
>
> And though I had no Gown of Gauze –
> No Ringlet, to my Hair,
> Nor hopped for Audiences – like Birds –
> One Claw upon the Air –
>
> Nor tossed my shape in Eider Balls,
> Nor rolled on wheels of snow
> Till I was out of sight, in sound,
> The House encore me so –
>
> Nor any know I know the Art
> I mention – easy – here
> Nor any Placard boast me –
> It's full as Opera
>
> (Fr 381; 1862)

While she asks for instruction in the letter, the poem maintains she "knows the Art." Furthermore, the line, "It's full as Opera," echoes "My little force explodes," implying that whether Higginson and others are capable of ascertaining it, her voice is powerful—"full"—and musical in spite (or perhaps because of) its destructive potential. In the case of "I felt a Funeral," the writing of the poem comes out of the wreck of religious epistemologies; likewise, Dickinson's having "no Monarch" leaves her "bare and charred," but with poems nonetheless.[12]

In the poems of Calvinist revision, then, Dickinson develops a poetics of destitution, which through relinquishing the self paradoxically reestablishes it. Because of her construction of identity through destruction, Dickinson frequently describes her epistemological process in paradoxical terms, as in the first line, "Is Bliss then, such Abyss" (Fr 371; 1862), and these last lines, "Captivity is consciousness— / So's Liberty" (Fr 649; 1863). Similarly, "Images of blindness or thwarted vision," as Evan Carton notes, "abound in Dickinson's poems and usually signify achievement, or its potential, rather than frustration" (48). Dickinson achieves enlighten-ment by abolishing conventional perception, so abyss is bliss, captivity and liberty both are consciousness, blindness is vision, and so on. Fur-thermore, her assertion of identity and personal vision in opposition to the community's theology means not only that she is unsaved and unelect, but that in large measure she excludes herself from the human, affectional world that she was so reluctant to give up in her early religious dilemma.

The World beyond Emerson

Emerson was her rock in the shelter of which she had built her church with its congregation of one.

—Hyatt Waggoner, *American Poets*

Throughout her poems, Dickinson calls her unelect status her "poverty." In the third phase of her development, her adventure of the self, rather than achieving literary election through ritual self-extinction, she sees her ex-clusion from the society of the elect as an opportunity for self-exploration. "Want," she writes in one poem, enlightens "so well – / I know not which, Desire, or Grant – / Be wholly beautiful –" (Fr 856; 1864). As Dickinson's poetic focus shifts from Calvinism to transcendentalism, the self thrown back on itself has different results. After the flood of self-conversion poems, the tone in the poems begins to change. From the mid-1860s on, the poetry reveals an understanding that through its own destitution, the self achieves freedom. A self-reliance close to Emerson's develops out of the wreck of "Funeral" and the numbing despair seen in the "Chill – then Stupor – then the letting go" of "After great pain." Dickinson "adhered to a plan of self-reliance in working out her destiny as an artist," writes Judith Farr, who observes:

> In her copy of Emerson's "Self-Reliance," now in the Harvard collection, a page is turned down at the following passage, which is also marked at the right: "My life is for itself and not for a spectacle. I much prefer that it should be of a lower strain, so it be genuine and equal, than that it should be glittering and unsteady." Again, "What I must do concerns me, not what people think." (46)

In this passage from Emerson's "Self-Reliance"—and in the essay as a whole—Emerson proclaims the truth of individual self in opposition to "what people think." He rejects the notion that in order to conform to the truth of society and of organized religion, the self should make itself into a "spectacle." That spectacle, what Emerson famously calls participation in society's "joint-stock company," is seen in terms of money and class; it is a superficial "glittering," not genuine like the "lower strain."

In "This Consciousness that is aware," Dickinson transforms the language of "Self-Reliance." Joanne Feit Diehl points out that Dickinson made a "practice of defining her self against Emerson. . . . Characteristically, a Dickinson poem takes an example that Emerson introduces into an essay and invests it with the strength of a subversive, anti-Emersonian vision" (177). So Dickinson uses Emerson's statement, "My life is for itself," as the springboard for her lines: "How adequate unto itself / Its properties shall be / Itself unto itself" (she repeats "itself" five times in a sixty-eight-word poem):

> This Consciousness that is aware
> Of Neighbors and the Sun
> Will be the one aware of Death
> And that itself alone
>
> Is traversing the interval
> Experience between
> And the most profound experiment
> Appointed unto Men—
>
> How adequate unto itself
> Its properties shall be
> Itself unto itself and None
> Shall make discovery.
>
> Adventure most unto itself
> The Soul condemned to be—
> Attended by a single Hound
> Its own identity.
>
> (Fr 817; 1864)

Like Emerson, Dickinson contrasts consciousness of self with consciousness of society, but the tone is different because Dickinson inserts the fact of death into the equation. From the first three lines of Dickinson's poem, the ultimate aloneness of the self is mitigated by its attachment to the world, to "Neighbors and the Sun." The simple, bright naming of "Neighbors and the Sun" alongside the awareness of death introduces loss into Emerson's exalted notion of self-reliance as the path to truth. As so many of Dickinson's poems and letters show, the expression of loss—whether it is the loss of a loved one or the loss of one's own loved self—is close to the center to which her work "Converges" (Fr 724). So her work reveals esteem for the affectional world "Of Neighbors and Sun" and respect for the inevitable loss of that world. Those others nearby, who will be lost and will be affected by death, shape the tone of "This consciousness that is aware," Dickinson's "adventure" in self-reliance.

Dickinson shares with Emerson a regard for the world and each human soul as good. She elevates the human soul through her language, a language that (except satirically) excludes the language of sin. Emerson contrasts the goodness he sees with the shame of Calvinist sin when in "Self-Reliance" he writes, "We but half express ourselves, and are ashamed of that divine idea which each of us represents" (*Complete Writings* 138). He replaces original sin, central to Calvinism, with original virtue, which he calls, "the aboriginal self, on which a universal reliance may be grounded" (144). In Emerson's thinking the self is exalted because the truth lies within each person who cares to see it and is willing to give up the security of orthodoxy. Emerson strives to bring together diversitarian ideas with a belief that all things are drawn inevitably toward unity. He asserts that "[p]ower ceases in the instant of repose; it resides in the movement of transition from a past to a new state, in the shooting of the gulf, in the darting to an aim. This is one fact the world hates, that the soul *becomes*" (146; Emerson's emphasis). In all aspects of human existence, Emerson proclaims, "a greater self-reliance must work a revolution" (148).[13] Stasis is the antithesis of revolutionary self-reliance; it is adherence to the past and to received ideas. As Lang understands it, "the man who lives truly according to the dictates of his heart is completely idiosyncratic and utterly representative." (125). Human selfhood is good; the self engaged in creation is the ideal to which all should strive, as the ultimate expression of self-reliance. So in Emerson, change is virtue, as is idiosyncrasy, and idiosyncrasy is the appropriate outcome of change—even as the unique soul moves toward unity.

Yet Emerson resembles the Calvinists whom he rejects in at least three respects. First, he believes each person can connect directly with God (or the supernatural) without clerical mediation. Second, he suggests that attachment to the human emotional (or social) realm obstructs the light of truth, which divinely resides within the self; he claims, "I shun father and mother and wife and brother, when my genius calls me" (140).[14] And he asks "Why drag about this corpse of your memory?" (141). Third, in addition to relinquishing attachment to others, Emerson's self-reliance paradoxically involves self-annihilation. "Ultimately the transcendent self . . . is no self at all but God," Lang writes, "Self-assertion is defined as obliteration of the self. Man at the moment when he sees himself and the universe most clearly—at the moment of 'grace'—sees himself no more." (119). The self is overwhelmed by the "universal mind" as in the following passage from "The Over-Soul":

> The soul gives itself original and pure, to the Lonely, Original and Pure, who, on that condition, gladly inhabits, leads, and speaks through it. . . . Behold, it saith, I am born in the great, the universal mind. . . . More and more the surges of everlasting nature enter into me, and I become public and human in my regards and actions. . . . So come I to live in thoughts and act with energies which are immortal. . . . [Man] will weave no longer a spotted life of shreds and patch, but he will live with a divine unity. (215)

In delineating the transcendentalist paradigm in which individual innovation creates a bridge to a unified understanding of the divine, Emerson renounces the past and, with it, filial attachments. The truth can only be known according to individual "genius," not according to those others, however powerful and distracting the tie. However, for all his delight in diversity, as Greenberg maintains, Emerson was not, "prepared to sacrifice the belief in the underlying universality in each man. . . . The doctrine of correspondence explains how a succession of perspectives, while ostensibly creating a fragmentary experience, actually reveals the universal interrelatedness between man and world" (72). Yet by asserting the doctrine of correspondence, Emerson also asserts aspects of the doctrine of his Calvinist inheritance, in the ways I have enumerated above (individual and unmediated connection to God, the rejection of emotional and social attachment in favor of the divine, and the annihilation of the self at the moment of spiritual unity). Emerson's greatest digressions from Calvinism lie in his eliminating original sin as a crucial theological category and, by extension, in his expansion of human capacity to apprehend the cosmos. According to Calvinist doctrine, the Fall blinds humanity. Emerson's dignification of human virtue and vision was blasphemous because it shifted the vertical arrangement of the universe: it allowed humanity to raise itself up toward God rather imagining the Lord coming down to save the sinful.

In this third phase of her development, her "adventure of the self," Dickinson, like Emerson, sees visionary possibilities for the soul in solitude. But she mitigates those possibilities with ironic distance and skepticism. For her, self-reliant consciousness may mean creative expression but it also means an existential aloneness coupled with the kind of doubt Emerson would not want to admit. Though the tone of "This consciousness that is aware" is promising in comparison to the despair of "I felt a funeral," the sense that death casts the self solitary into the incomprehensible extends from the earlier poem into the later: "itself *alone* / Is traversing . . . the most profound experiment / Appointed unto Men." In both poems the self must find a way to apprehend the unknown, yet the poems differ in emphasis: "Funeral" envisions destruction while "Consciousness" envisions creative possibility, since death is "the most profound experiment." In that "Consciousness" employs the language of innovation — that is, the self "adequate unto itself" is "appointed" to "experiment" and "adventure" — the poem resembles Emerson's "Self-Reliance." The voice of such a self might be, as Emerson says, one of the idiosyncratic "voices we hear in solitude . . . [that] grows faint and inaudible as we enter the world" (139). In other words, the social world drowns out the essential voice of the self. Yet even as it exalts its own particularity, the voice of the poem is "aware" of its grave aloneness, that it is "*condemned*" to "identity," an identity whose isolation at the end of the poem (and at death) contrasts with the beginning, with earthly attachment, with "Neighbors and the Sun." Dickinson sees that the gap — or the abyss — in Emersonian self-reliance is the awareness of death and loss (perhaps because, unlike Emerson, she lived out extreme self-reliance by more completely removing herself from society, which gawks and seeks spectacles).

For Dickinson the cost of self-reliance is loneliness, as in the lines:

> I fear me this – is loneliness –
> The maker of the soul
> It's Caverns and it's Corridors
> Illuminate – or Seal –
> (Fr 877; 1864)

In contrast, because Emerson sees himself in the company of God, of "Truth and Right," he feels less urgency to address the problem of loneliness. (Also, of course, Emerson did not withdraw as Dickinson did.) "All things go well" for the soul at one with the Universal:

> The soul raised over passion beholds identity and eternal causation, perceives the self-existence of Truth and Right, and calms itself with knowing that all things go well. Vast spaces of nature, the Atlantic Ocean, the South Sea; long intervals of time, years, centuries, are of no account. This which I think and feel underlay every former state of life and circumstances, as it does underlie my present, and what is called life, and what is called death. ("Self-Reliance" 145–46)

Here the self encompasses all "long intervals of time" and all "vast spaces," life and "what is called death" with certainty and sanguine calm because, as Emerson says, the foundation of the self, what "underlies" the soul is connection with God. The Emersonian self "beholds identity and eternal causation" *at once*; it understands itself and God's will as a unity. In contrast, because Dickinson doubts that God will recognize her or that she can be in concord with Him, she chooses her way, while God stays aloof in heaven.

In some poems, Dickinson likens the perceptive power of the poet to God's. For example, she "reckons" that poets come first before God, the summer, and the sun. The poem brings heaven down to earth, fourth on the list after poets, sun, and summer. And she impiously puts God's heaven last on the list. Typically, she elevates the human and the earthly, and in so doing, counters the idea of heaven as compensation:

> I reckon – When I count at all –
> First – Poets – Then the Sun –
> Then Summer – Then the Heaven of God –
> And then – the List is done –
>
> But, looking back – the First so seems
> To comprehend the Whole –
> The Others look a needless Show –
> So I write – Poets – All –
>
> Their Summer – lasts a Solid Year –
> They can afford a Sun
> The East – would deem extravagant –
> And if the Further Heaven –
>
> .   .   .

> Be Beautiful as they prepare
> For Those who worship Them –
> It is too difficult a Grace –
> To Justify the Dream –
> (Fr 533; 1863)

This poem is characteristic of the poems of self-conversion in that it confronts God as part of an internal poetic process. "Worship" of Him and
the hope of election are "too difficult a Grace – / to Justify the Dream"
of heaven. The poem turns the tables on the notion that human creation
and earthly existence are "vanity." Rather, except for poets, every other
category, including "the Heaven of God," is "a needless Show." So the
poem reverses the conventional Calvinist notion that self-expression is
the height of vanity. In elevating the human creative act over all else, she
excises God and places the poet at the apex of teleology. In spite of the vast
claims this poem makes for the comprehension of the poet, it remains
disconnected from God. The poem is Emersonian in that the poet's role,
according to Emerson, is to attach the things of the world to God, so the
poet "comprehend[s] the whole." But the poem is not transcendent: since
Dickinson seeks to keep its vision of "Sun" and "Summer" on Earth, she
cannot "Justify" giving up the poet's supreme earthly vision in favor of
"the Further Heaven." The self in this poem doesn't presume to apprehend
"eternal causation" or death. Rather, it outrageously asserts its own vision
in the face of God's will, the inevitability of death, and the "Dream" of
heaven.[15]

In "This consciousness that is aware," Dickinson, like Emerson, is concerned with the parameters of consciousness, with, in Emerson's words,
"identity" in relation to "eternal causation." "Consciousness" echoes the
vocabulary of Emerson's "Self-Reliance." In addition to repeating "itself"
and asserting that the self is "adequate unto itself," the self "alone"

> Is traversing the interval
> Experience between
> And the most profound experiment
> Appointed unto Men –

In these lines Dickinson recasts and compresses Emerson's notion that
self-knowledge underlies all "intervals of time" and his belief that "[t]his
which I think and feel underlay every former state of life and circumstances, as it does underlie my present, and what is called life, and what

is called death." In Dickinson's lines one's own life "Experience"[16] is sand-wiched between death and that "long interval of time," which in Emerson includes the centuries.

The poem also echoes Emerson in the lines: "How adequate unto it-self / Its *properties* [my emphasis] shall be." Dickinson plays here on the meaning of properties as the aspects, virtues, or particularities of character. The self relies on its own territories of consciousness; there it will "make discovery" and "adventure." In the ending paragraphs of "Self-Reliance" Emerson maintains that "the reliance on Property . . . is the want of self-reliance. Men have looked away from themselves and at things for so long, that they have come to esteem the religious, learned, and civil institutions as guards of property. . . . They measure their esteem for each other by what each has and not by what each is" (152). Dickinson like Emerson rejects the traps of materialism and conformity. Paula Bennett reads the poem as a declaration of Dickinson's carrying out "the original Puritan in-junction to examine closely the state of one's soul as far as it will go . . . her speaker relies on the 'properties' of the self instead" of those of the church (*Emily Dickinson* 122). This kind of investigation of the soul is part of the transcendental quest as well. Dickinson seems on the brink of setting the self forth with aplomb, yet she undercuts the assurance that consciousness is "adequate" to the task of its "profound experiment" at precisely the mo-ment that she declares it.

Dickinson takes a step back from Emerson's cosmic optimism by pro-testing too much the adequacy of the self "unto itself" and by qualifying the language of visionary romanticism:

> How adequate unto itself
> Its properties shall be
> Itself unto itself and none
> Shall make discovery.

The repetition refers the reader to Emerson's emphasis on the self and, at the same time, creates a kind of tautological exhaustion. The self should see in itself ever-widening vistas, yet grammatically speaking, "itself unto itself" is nonspecific (pronouns and a preposition) and so sounds vague, numb, and closed. Dickinson further diminishes the faith by combin-ing visionary with legalistic language. Words such as "appointed," "ad-equate," "properties," and "condemned" have legal associations. "None / Shall make discovery" could mean that no one but one's self discovers the inner life of the soul. Yet it also refers to the legal procedure in which one is compelled to give evidence, and implies that no one shall make discovery on the judgment day at the gates of heaven. The self at death is once again cast into the vastness of itself, not into the sheltering arms of Christ, not even to face the terrible judgment of the Lord. As Lang points out, self-reliance should reveal the law of the universe, which is God's will: "Trusting oneself . . . is not an act of assertion in the sense that we normally understand. Rather, the perfectly balanced endowments of man, given full expression, reveal the God within and the perfect law that governs God's creation" (123). Consciousness, though it may be panoramic in Dickinson's estimation, fails to encompass Emerson's transcendent version of the natural order.

Dickinson also compromises the transcendental ideal through her use of scientific language in the poem. Death is "the most profound experiment," whose understanding is based on the "experience" of life and the essential "properties" of the self, and out of which some "discovery" might be made. Such language is empiricist and runs counter to Emerson's belief in the imagination as the key to a transcendental vision of correspondence. Although Emerson did not reject scientific inquiry, he did reject it as a path to spiritual truth. Philip E. Gura explains that Emerson was profoundly interested in finding an alternative to Lockean empiricism, which would allow the human mind free interpretation of the natural order: "[M]an could be sincerely religious without being a mere 'sensationalist' in philosophy. . . . Nature did not exist merely to be absorbed by man's multiple nerve endings but was to be interpreted by his Reason, in acts that allowed him to move—to transcend, if you will—to a higher spiritual plane" (89). Emerson wished to make an infinite space for the imagination, and to allow it ubiquity. Dickinson also wishes to enlarge the circumference of the imagination, but she lacks absolute faith in the transcendent vision and expresses her skepticism through gentle irony. Through her wordplay, by making words *hinges* that open into other epistemological perspectives—legal or rationalist, scientific or empiricist— she engages fully in Emerson's delight in diversity. Yet her diversity tends toward fragmentation rather than unity. This is one of many instances in which Dickinson anticipates the modernist aesthetic, since she uses irony and the double-entendre as a way of questioning the ultimate unity of the universe. Her language is a force of fragmentation.

The last stanza of the poem disperses Emerson's ideal of correspondence through such juxtapositions. "Adventure most unto itself" uses the language of the Romantic quest. The line, "The Soul condemned to be," appropriates the Calvinist belief that the soul may be condemned to damnation and ironically transforms it into the anti-Calvinist notion that self, however exalted its exploratory capacities, is condemned to its own lonely and uncertain search at death.

The melding of the Romantic quest and Calvinist condemnation is further complicated by the addition of classical mythology, which Emily Dickinson knew and frequently referred to in her poetry as an alternative to Christian cosmology. In the lines, "Attended by a single Hound / Its own identity," the "single Hound" alludes to Cerberus, the many-headed hound guarding the underworld. It is Cerberus who keeps the boundary between the living and the dead secure, preventing either the shades from leaving or the living from crossing over into Hades. That Cerberus is imagined as many-headed undoes the notion of single-mindedness, and points to a multifaceted identity, though he is a "single Hound." This figure might be seen to represent Emerson's notion of unity in diversity, but is mitigated by the fact that in the poem connection with God is not achieved through death, that union of "identity" and "eternal causation" does not "underlie" the soul's apprehension of the universe. Rather, the self confronts the multiplicity of its own adventure with *itself.*

"This conscious that is aware" also takes a subtly ironic stance in regard to the judgment of the pious and of God. Dickinson combines the humor in the poem with an excitement and awe. "Consciousness" is not dire in its critique, in the manner of "I felt a Funeral." So, when Dickinson writes that the soul is "condemned," it is condemned ironically to the positive, to that experiment and adventure of a quite "captivating" self traversing the unknown. In another reading of the line "None shall make discovery," because the self is "adequate unto itself," no other being shall give evidence for a judgment against or in favor of it.[17] Furthermore, though Cerberus is depicted in mythology as a monster, he does not lend a Gothic or despairing tone to the poem, as Dickinson makes him her "Hound," and domesticates him. While she names the Hound identity, she does not associate him with a depraved or corrupt part of the soul. Rather, as in other dog references, the hound is the companion that "attends" the soul, as when the poet wrote to Higginson: "You ask of my Companions Hills—Sir—and a Dog—large as myself . . . They are better than beings—because they know—but do not tell—and the noise in the Pool, at Noon, excels my Piano" (L 261). That dogs (and nature) "know—but do not tell—" is important because in her letter, as well as in the poem, she preserves the unknown as unknown, and makes exploring that mystery positive. The human soul she suggests in "This consciousness that is aware" will not transcend itself and see the divine plan because it is limited to its own subjectivity. So in the last stanza of "Consciousness" the soul at death does not achieve transcendence, but is attended by the Hound, "its own identity." The soul does not, as Emerson would have it, "behold eternal causation." However, human perception is vast. And the presence of God and mystery remain.

In "Four Trees – upon a solitary Acre –" Dickinson observes nature, but maintains that its elements are not emblems of the divine plan:

> Four Trees – upon a solitary Acre –
> Without Design
> Or order, or Apparent Action –
> Maintain –
>
> The Sun – upon a Morning meets them –
> The Wind –No nearer Neighbor – have they –
> But God –
>
> The Acre gave them – Place –
> They – Him – Attention of Passer by –
> Of Shadow, or of Squirrel, haply –
> Or Boy –
>
> What Deed is Their's unto the General Nature –
> What Plan
> They severally – retard – or further –
> Unknown –
>
> (Fr 778; 1863)[18]

This poem seems a direct reply to the formula Emerson puts forward in "Nature" regarding the interaction of words, nature, and the spirit:

1. Words are signs of natural facts.
2. Particular natural facts are signs of particular spiritual facts
3. Nature is the symbol of the spirit. (7)

Dickinson is in accord with Emerson's proposal that nature may be a "symbol of the spirit," since in her scene, "No nearer Neighbor – have they [natural elements] But God." However, what "particular spiritual facts" those elements may symbolize remains not just unclear, but emphatically absent. The trees exist on the acre "without Design / Or order" and "What Plan / They severally – retard – or further – /" is "Unknown." Each element of the scene is "particular," named as a list of nouns nearly without modification: tree, an acre, sun, morning, wind, God, passerby, shadow, squirrel, boy. Yet there is no revelation of what "particular spiritual fact" each one represents, "What Deed is Theirs unto the General Nature," which teleological place they occupy.

Rather, the scene is ordered or—more peculiarly—is disordered by the subjectivity of the speaker (who is also absent) and by the "Attention" of various others: the Passer by, the Boy, or the Squirrel, the Shadow, or perhaps by a "Him," who may be God. Shira Wolosky writes that in spite of the presence of God, "the final stanza declares him dubious company. Instead of serving as first or final cause, tying the disparate units together, the poem closes with such a pattern absent. If God is present, he does not unite the scene" (3–4). Yet Wolosky's reading omits the crucial question of agency. The poem suggests that God may be a near "neighbor" but his presence "does not unite the scene" *for the perceivers*. The scene is not transcendent because it does not reveal how its parts are "signs of particular spiritual facts." "The metaperspective represented by heaven and the physical world it should order," Wolosky observes, "remain removed from each other" (4). Yet the poem does create an atmosphere that reveals the mystery of the world, in spite of the lack of transcendence.[19] Though the scene is fleeting, it is a series of meetings and interrelations between the trees, the acre, the sun, the wind, God, and the rest of the elements in the poem. So the reader is left to imagine, for example, how the morning sun and wind tremulous on the trees might catch the "attention" of a passerby, who might give attention to that inscrutable "Him" without necessarily achieving transcendental knowledge. That each "meeting" in the poem is ephemeral does not negate those interrelations. Rather, Dickinson's depiction deepens the perception of natural change; the sense this might be a scene of disarray is an alternative rendering, intensifying the mystery and movement of nature and the astonishment of the observer.

By insisting upon the lack of order, design, plan, or placement within "the General Nature," Dickinson intentionally swerves away the imperative in which heaven "should order" the physical world for the seer. The syntactical complexity of the poem is a disorienting device both purposeful and fruitful. As Benfey puts it: "To read the poem is to slide from one sentence or phrase to another, with later sentences incorporating words or phrases from earlier ones. . . . But as we grope for the proper placement of periods and colons and dashes, we realize that this poem is *about* placement. . . . the place of the four trees in the general nature, the place of human beings in regard to them" (115). Dickinson departs from Emerson's notion of divine order at the level of language by creating with her mysterious sentence structure a scene that creates natural movement without fixing the natural fact of change into a corresponding spiritual fact (or perhaps it re-creates the spiritual fact and the inscrutability of any divine plan). In "The Poet," in a discussion of the "universality of the symbolic language," Emerson writes, "we are apprised of the divineness of this superior use of things, whereby the world is a temple whose walls are covered with the emblems, pictures, and commandments of the Deity . . . there is no fact in nature which does not carry the whole sense of nature" (*Complete Writings* 243). "Four Trees" does not create such a temple of *readable* sacred emblems. The trees, by Dickinson's lights, resist becoming a pictogram of the Lord's design. If "the poem is about placement," it is not a delineation of God's placement, nor of how the trees "carry the whole sense of nature."

In the third stanza, it is the acre rather than God that gives the trees "Place." Yet Dickinson also calls notice to the possibility of God's handiwork in the lines "The Acre gave them – Place – / They – Him – Attention of Passer by," since the "Him" can refer to that "nearer Neighbor," "God" (who resides in the previous stanza). Although the scene is neither "apparent" nor emblematic of God's design, it might be symbolic of the spirit by reminding a passerby of God, of that God who "works in mysterious ways." Yet Dickinson vexes this reading of these lines in several ways. First, the trees don't catch the attention of a speaker. Second, she doesn't refer to God by his name, but by an ambiguous "Him" that can work grammatically to create several readings. If, for example, the lines read "The Acre gave them – Place – / They – God – attention of Me," the lines would have greater transcendental potential. The poem observes that the passerby and others give attention to an ambiguous "Him" who can be either God or the Acre. (It would not be atypical for Dickinson to personify an acre as "Him.") The observing eye in the poem does not presume to know whether that attention is transcendental. Third, the list of those whose attention may be caught by the scene includes human beings, the Passer by and the Boy, who might be capable of transcendental experience—along with Shadow and Squirrel, neither of which would. Finally, the poem throws into question even the pivotal moment of attention through the words "or" and "haply." Any one of the four on the list might give its attention, and if it does, it is by *chance* not by *design*.

"Four Trees" is crucial for understanding how Dickinson replaces Emerson's transcendent system with a series of interactions that are complex,
difficult to decode, fleeting, and magical. She records a scene in which
chance natural "meetings" and chance "attention" evoke the unknown.
She begins with the barest description ("Four Trees – upon a solitary
Acre") and on the ground of that austerity creates a variety of movement
and attention, play and affection: the play of wind, sun, and shadow on the
trees, of squirrel or boy. (The word "haply" happens to sound like "happily.") The poem asks, as Benfey writes: "What then, is the place of human
agency with respect to the trees and the acre? It is to "attend" to them"
(116–17). Benfey maintains that "Dickinson makes room for relations of
reciprocity between the human being and the world. In this allowance
she joins the company of major Romantic writers" (117). I would add,
however, that there is a crucial difference in the mode of relation because
Dickinson's reciprocity is one that quests into the unknown but does not
achieve a unifying transcendence. This form of attention to the world does
not transcend itself, does not rise to the "temple whose walls are covered
with the emblems, pictures, and commandments of the Deity." Rather, the
horizon of the earth stays in place with the unknown, movement, mutuality, and play maintaining.

Dickinson imagines God on the same plane as the earth, not above it.
In "Four Trees" her acceptance of the unknown makes the human being,
nature, and God "near Neighbors." He is a neighbor, not a monarch.
Gary Stonum points out that "[a]n abandoned variant for the key term
'maintain' is 'do reign.' The variant, in other words, attributes to the trees
a monarchical dominion over the scene, albeit one that is still without
design or order. 'Maintain,' on the other hand suggests a different notion
of control and coherence" (16). Dickinson puts her faith in a horizontal and antihierarchical spiritual world, in which beings and nonbeings
alike "neighbor" each other. In that she imagines a world in which things
"maintain" rather than "reign," the contemporary poet Brenda Hillman
resembles Dickinson. In her book *Death Tractates*, a series of poems deal-
ing with the death of a close friend, Hillman imagines the spirit world
"sideways." Hillman throughout the book rejects patriarchal notions of
a vertical (or hierarchical) cosmos; she writes: "—No, the upper heavens
wouldn't do" ("The Panel"). She replaces those "upper heavens" with a
mysterious, relational, horizontal one: "What lived / lived on both sides.
What lived / went back and forth across the panel" ("The Panel"). This
is a "strange world," "all unzipped, / like meaning" ("First Tractate"). For

Dickinson, too, the world and meaning are "all unzipped," free of unify-ing correspondence, yet corresponding "back and forth across the panel," which might be the hedge, fence, or border between two friendly neigh-bors. The poem "Consciousness" grounds awareness in "Neighbors and the Sun." Likewise, in "Four Trees," "giving attention" means going back and forth across to that "nearest Neighbor" God and, equally, to the trees or a boy.

In this third stage of her development, the anger and despair of the earlier poems inform her; she sees her dilemma clearly and she finds her voice. Her desire for connection—which was thwarted and which caused so much pain in her early career—remains constant throughout. Her rela-tional impulse is the impetus for a passionate, philosophical engagement that, constant (or faithful) as it is, never becomes static. I began this book with Emerson's proclamation that the soul must always be in motion: "the soul *becomes*" through intense internal reflection. Dickinson's soul be-comes, and becomes one that ultimately reaches out. The development of her poetry portrays her process through anger, despair, pain, and numb-ness to self-acceptance and reciprocity.[20] So in 1864 she writes:

> Struck, was I, not yet by Lightning –
> Lightning – lets away
> Power to perceive His process
> With Vitality.
>
> Maimed – was I – yet not by Venture –
> Stone of Stolid boy –
> Nor a Sportsman's Peradventure
> Who mine Enemy?
>
> Robbed – was I – intact to Bandit –
> All my Mansion torn –
> Sun – withdrawn to Recognition –
> Furthest shining – done
>
> Yet was not the foe – of any –
> Not the smallest Bird
> In the nearest Orchard dwelling
> Be of Me – afraid.
>
> Most – I love the Cause that slew Me.
> Often as I die

> Its beloved Recognition
> Holds a Sun on Me –
>
> Best – at Setting – as is Nature's –
> Neither witnessed Rise
> Till the infinite Aurora
> In the Other's eyes.
>
> (Fr 841; 1864)

In this poem Dickinson records her transformation. Out of the death of the self, out of that numbing despair and utter loneliness, comes mutuality. She loves the pain because out of it comes an inner self at peace: "Most – I love the Cause that slew me." The cause is love, whether divine or earthly. The speaker can only be resurrected from the abyss through connection: "Neither witnessed Rise / Till the infinite Aurora / In the other's eyes." Instead of the self divided or at war with itself, the self in this poem looks back on her journey and understands how the journey has transformed her.

In her assertion of creative power through the act of writing poems, in that she ascribes a divine place to the poet, Dickinson retains a crucial piece of Emersonian philosophy. For Dickinson, Emerson must have been one of the "liberating gods" he proclaimed poets to be, as well as an opponent (opposing him was liberating, too).[21] By reclaiming humanity from sinfulness, Emerson's work was generative: it liberated the imagination, made a haven where one could "dwell in possibility," and, in so doing, helped the poet freely explore creativity. This is clearly true of Whitman whose relationship with Emerson is well documented. But it is also true of Dickinson who wrote after Emerson visited Amherst, "It must have been as if he had come from where dreams are born!" (PF 10). Part of Dickinson's genius lies in her appropriation of Calvinism and romanticism and in her transformative power. Because she takes from these theological systems the elements that suit her purposes and that collaborate with her to generate poems, she doesn't succumb to the potentials of Calvinism or romanticism to silence the self. Rather, she makes predominant belief systems resonate in *her voice*, fostering and enriching her subject matter and deepening her philosophical perspectives.

Upon Emerson's death, she wrote to her love, Judge Otis Lord:

> I am told it is only a pair of Sundays since you went from me. I feel
> it many years. Today is April's last — it has been an April of meaning to

me. I have been in your Bosom. My Philadelphia [Charles Wadsworth]
has passed from Earth and the Ralph Waldo Emerson — whose name
my Father's Law Student taught me, has touched the secret Spring.
Which Earth are we in?

> *Heaven,* a Sunday or two ago — but that also has ceased — Momen-
> tousness is ripening. I that all is firm. Could we yield each other to
> the impregnable chances till we had met once more? (L 750).

Here, as ever, Dickinson plays on both her skepticism and Emerson's emblems. Death she calls "the secret Spring," and so she names natural fact
and a spiritual fact at once. Her question, "Which Earth are we in?" has
both transcendent and skeptical implications. That is, which earth is this
a sign for? And which earth is our imagination perceiving? Interestingly,
the question leads to her ultimate destination, which is love; she answers:
"*Heaven,* a Sunday or two ago." For Dickinson, an answer to the question
"Which Earth?" is that she and Lord are on earth, which is made heaven
through their love, and, ultimately, through the act of writing. And when
she writes, rather than transcending, she sees "sideways" and touches
Lord (a funny, lucky accident of names).

Dickinson never accepts death, and she never accepts the idea that
God expects her to give Him her loved ones with equanimity. Through
writing she makes an alternative cosmology, one grounded on earth,
with loved "nearest Neighbors." She tells her reader that the soul is "condemned" to its "identity." Out of her loneliness, her sense of exclusion,
Dickinson turns to the self and finds it "adequate." In her adventure of the
self, she turns condemnation into blessing, for it is the beginning of the
mutual journey. Because in her estimation the soul is not sinful, the "consciousness that is aware / Of Neighbors and the sun" is worthy of sharing,
of witnessing "the infinite Aurora / In the other's eyes." She writes to Lord:
"To write you, not knowing where you are, is an unfinished pleasure —
Sweeter of course than not writing, because it has a wandering Aim, of
which you are the goal" (L 750).

In the last phase of her development, after her "adventure of the self,"
Dickinson stops copying her poems into her fascicles, and copies them
instead into letters. The line between letters and poems blurs, and writing
becomes relation. On December 3, 1882, she writes to Lord:

> What if you are writing! Oh, for the power to look, yet were I there,
> I would not, except you invited me — reverence for each other being
> the sweet aim. I have written you, Dear, so many Notes since receiving

one, it seems like writing a note to the Sky—yearning and replyless—
but Prayer has not answer and yet how many pray! While others go to
Church, I go to mine, for are you not my Church, and have we not a
hymn that no one knows but us? (L 790)

So Dickinson returns to her early desire for earthly affection, and her un-
willingness to give up the earth for heaven. In these words to Lord, she
shows that at the end of her life she transforms prayer to writing, church
to "the other's eyes," hymn into the words exchanged between loved ones.
Furthermore, writing for "the other's eyes" is a form of immortality. She
writes, "A Letter always seemed to me like Immortality, for is it not the
Mind alone, without corporeal friend" (L 330; L 788).[22] In her last work,
Dickinson writes with a specific "you" as the "goal" and, by making the
epistolary both immortal and poetic, creates her earthly paradise.

~4~

"They Shut Me up in Prose"

Late Letter-Poems

℮

They shut me up in Prose –
As when a little Girl
They put me in the Closet –
Because they liked me "still" –

(Fr 445)

Poems will be called letters and letters will be called poems.

—Susan Howe

The brief, final scene of Dickinson's writing is played out beyond the asylum of the book on single sheets of fine stationary and on the torn leaves of household leavings. Ink dissolves into lead's transience, and the scripted forms, drifting across loose pages in fantastic designs, possess a telos of their own. Not poems, not letters, never a "masterpiece," these private documents are the "fragments of a lover's discourse" written across night antinomian, some pieces of a trial record challenging our old ideas about authorship, authority, genealogy, and genre—or a series of line drawings. They require of us a new nomenclature.

—Marta Werner

Of that other genius, Walt Whitman, Dickinson wrote that she had heard his poems were "disgraceful." She knew her own were unacceptable by her world's standards of poetic convention, of what was appropriate, in particular, for a woman poet. Seven were published in her lifetime, all edited by other hands; more than a thousand were laid away in her bedroom chest, to be discovered after her death. When her sister discovered them, there were decades of struggle over the manuscripts, the manner of their presentation to the world, their suitability for publication, the poet's own final intentions. Narrowed down by her early editors and anthologists, reduced to quaintness or spinsterish oddity by many of her commentators, sentimentalized, fallen-in-love with like some gnomic Garbo, still unread in the breadth and depth of her full range of work, she was, and is, a wonder when I imagine myself into that mind.

—Adrienne Rich

A Disruptive Discovery

When I was researching the last phase of Emily Dickinson's development, I went to the Robert Frost Library at Amherst College to study the manuscripts. There in the quiet, below ground archives, I made a wonderful yet disturbing discovery:

> The withdrawal of the Fuel of Rapture
> Does not withdraw the Rapture itself
> Like Powder in a Drawer,
> We pass it with a prayer,
> It's Thunders only dormant.

The "poem" above was written by Emily Dickinson, but it is not in the canon of her poetry. It is "shut up in prose." I have lineated these words that were found among the poet's papers and are now published in *The Letters* and labeled "fragment fair copy." Like Thomas H. Johnson's (and now R. W. Franklin's) typographical translations of Dickinson's poems, my lineation follows premodern conventions of line breaks determined by meter and rhyme. And like Johnson and Franklin, by printing Dickinson's words and lineating them according to a conventional premodern model, I have used criteria that were not hers but those derived from voices of authority whom Dickinson did not necessarily heed. In fact, the letter-poem above, typographically translated, looks more like this on the page:

> The withdrawal
> of the Fuel of
> Rapture does not
> withdraw the rap-
> ture itself –
> Like Powder in
> a Drawer, we
> pass it with a
> Prayer, it's Thunders
> only dormant.

We know from her manuscripts that Dickinson scripted her "letters" not at all in conventional paragraphs, but in short lines as in the rest of her poetical canon.[1] I have used Johnson's and Franklin's measure for the line, not because I believe their lineation of Dickinson's poems is necessarily correct, but because I wish to show that many texts that we call letters are indistinguishable from her poetry in subject, structure, meter and rhyme patterns, and line lengths on the original written document. In keeping with this observation, as early as 1956 Jack Spicer wrote:

> The reason for the difficulty of drawing a line between the poetry and prose of Emily Dickinson is that she did not wish such a line to be drawn. If large portions of her correspondence are considered not as mere letters — and indeed, they seldom communicate information, or have much to do with the person to whom they were written — but as experiments in a heightened prose combined with poetry, a new approach to her letters opens up. (quoted in Howe, *Birth-mark* 152 n)

A new approach to her poems opens up as well. Beyond their being "mere letters" or even, as the revolutionary Spicer asserts, "heightened prose combined with poetry," I propose that many of the letters *are* poems, and that regardless of their genre category — poem, letter, letter-poem, or fragment — they are among the fine examples of her art; so regarded, they expand the size and range of the Dickinson canon.

This discovery leads me to disrupt the sequence of this book. In order to discuss the late work, I must simultaneously consider the whole body. So I break the form of this book just as Dickinson made a break in artistic practice at this juncture in her development: she stopped copying her work and preserving it in the fascicles. I knew the work of Susan Howe, and, as many readers of Dickinson do, I resisted her questions about the manuscripts and the authenticity of their published transcriptions. As is true of many others, Emily Dickinson haunts me; her lines name the un-nameable. She is my master, I her student. To consider the idea that the printed canon of her work is untrustworthy, that her lines may not be her lines is, at first, devastating (until one sees the "possibility" that lies in this devastation). Significantly — deeply so — Adrienne Rich in 1975 pro-phetically outlined the issues that would impel later readers to question not just the way Dickinson's life and poetry have been interpreted, but the way the texts themselves were translated into print. Her early editors, who "reduced [her] to quaintness or spinsterish oddity," who "sentimen-talized" her, who made her work fit the "standard of poetic convention" of the 1890s, influenced Johnson, despite his good intentions. The combined power of the mythology of Emily Dickinson and the vexing question of her final intentions could not help but shape his work. Nor, in all humility, can these two questions help but influence any of us who are devoted to the poet, no matter how many revisions come before us.

Nonetheless, I have come to believe that in the early 1990s, I par-ticipated in a serendipitous group coming-into-consciousness about the Dickinson manuscripts, which emanated from Susan Howe's beautiful and urgent imperative that devoted readers study the poet's manuscripts. Out of that revelation came several revolutionary books and essays, most notably, Martha Nell Smith's *Rowing in Eden: Rereading Emily Dickinson*, which argues that the poet eschewed print publication in favor of letter publication; the book that Smith edited and introduced in collaboration with by Ellen Louise Hart, *Open Me Carefully: Emily Dickinson's Letters to Susan Huntington Dickinson*; and Marta L. Werner's *Emily Dickinson's Open Folios: Scenes of Reading, Surfaces of Writing*, which presents fac-similes of the "Lord Letters" with typescript translations, accompanied by her innovative scholarly commentary. The work of these scholars has radicalized the way we read Emily Dickinson. (Even those who disagree with their arguments cannot ignore the questions they have raised.) In the sections that follow — in which I discuss the manuscripts, editing, and publication — my purpose is not to engage in the kind of textual criticism that these scholars have. Rather, I wish to provide a meditative framework in which to consider the late work in the context of the poet's develop-ment. The sections that follow culminate in "The Artist of the Beautiful, a Possibility," which addresses this question: In the last phase of her life, why did Emily Dickinson enclose her art in letters?

Erasing the Line between Poetry and Prose

Don't believe anything you read in print.

—James E. B. Breslin, comment
made to his first-year Ph.D.
students, 1985.

The line between Dickinson's poetry and her prose is, as Spicer proposes, one the poet did not observe. That distinction is often a question of who sees the lines and who has preserved them. How Emily Dickinson's lines have been determined is the work of her editors, not the poet herself. This point has been argued by Susan Howe, who calls for an edition of the poems in which the fascicle manuscripts are transcribed into typographical replicas that maintain Dickinson's placement of line breaks, dashes, plusses, and what Johnson calls "variants" — and Howe (unlike Franklin) holds to be "artistic structures" (*Birth-mark* 146). Just as editors (from Thomas Wentworth Higginson and Mabel Loomis Todd in the nineteenth century, to Johnson and R. W. Franklin in the twentieth) have determined line breaks, so have they fixed the distinction between Dickinson's poetry and prose. The failure of her editors to see the poems in the letters is, ironically, the same weakness that led the much-maligned Higginson and Todd to bowdlerize the first editions of Dickinson's poetry. When faced with tricky textual problems, all her editors found their solutions in nineteenth-century poetic conventions. When Dickinson's poetry failed to meet those conventions and was therefore unacceptable to the publishers, Higginson and Todd altered the poems to fit the obligatory mold. In the case of Johnson and Franklin, the material that failed to meet their criteria was omitted from the poetic canon. I wish to show through my conservative lineation of "The withdrawal of the Fuel of Rapture" that there are poems confined to the labels of "letters" and "prose fragments" because Dickinson's modern editors have not recognized them as poems. They are — right down to the way they are laid out on the page — too modern to be the poems of a nineteenth-century poet. Somewhat paradoxically, my lineation also shows that whole letters or parts of letters conform to the prosody of poems included in the Dickinson canon.

It can be argued that the letters written while Dickinson copied her work into fascicles and sets should not be considered part of the poetical works because her methodical copying of her poems indicates her judgment and intention. This argument would exclude from the canon the "Master Letters," which are clearly drafts since they contain words and phrases that are crossed out. Yet the Master Letters figure among her most breathtaking, daring, and masterly poems or letter-poems. They are her most extended meditations and presage the most accomplished experiments of the modernists. Here are some "lines" from the facsimile edition of the Master Letters:

> I am older – tonight, Master –
> But the love is the same –
> so are the moon and the
> crescent – If it had been
> God's will that I might
> breathe where you breathed –
> and find the place – myself –
> at night – if I can never forget
> that I am not with you –
> and that sorrow and frost
> are nearer than I – if I wish
> with a might I cannot
> repress – that mine were the
> Queen's place – the love of
> the Plantagenet is my only
> apology – to come nearer
> than Presbyteries – and nearer than
> the new coat – that the Tailor
> made – the Prank of the Heart
> at play on the Heart – in holy
> Holiday – is forbidden me –
>
> (ML Letter 3)

With regard to their verve and overheard monologue, these lines recall another precursor of modernity, Robert Browning. Formally, her elliptical symbols and sensitive, radical line breaks bring Dickinson fully into the twentieth century: the line breaks and religious appropriations anticipate Marianne Moore and H.D. In her galloping alliterations, she rides in the company of Dylan Thomas and Sylvia Plath: "the Prank of the Heart / at play on the Heart – in holy / Holiday – is forbidden me."

"These lines," Howe writes, "traced by pencil or in ink on paper were formed by an innovator" (*Birth-mark* 136). Howe's understanding of Dickinson as a modernist precursor led her into the following confrontation:

> In 1986 Ralph Franklin sent me a copy of *The Master Letters of Emily Dickinson*, published by the Amherst College Press. Along with *The Manuscript Books*, this is the most important contribution to Dickinson scholarship that I know of. In this edition Franklin decided on a correct order for the letters, showed facsimiles, and had them set in type on each facing page, with the line breaks as she made them. I wrote him a letter again suggesting that if he broke the lines here, according to the original texts, he might consider doing the same for the poems. He thanked me for my "immodest" compliments and said he had broken the letters line-for-physical line only to make reference to the facsimiles easier; if he were editing a book of letters, he would use run-on treatment as there is no expected genre form for prose. He told me there is such a form for poetry and he intended to follow it, rather than accidents of physical line breaks on paper. (*Birth-mark* 145)

Franklin's belief that there is an expected genre form for poetry that he intends to follow, were he to edit a book of letters, would indicate an ideological and methodological rejection of Dickinson's innovations. It leads me to believe that he would have a reason *not* to see the lines of poetry in the "letters."

This ambiguous distinction between the poetry and the prose is greater in the late poetry, which Dickinson did not sew into fascicles or gather together in sets. When Dickinson made the fascicles, she was like a printer formalizing and finalizing the writing process. Though the fascicle poems include "variants" (she put plus marks above words or phrases and wrote alternatives at the bottom of the page), it is clear the texts are poems. By contrast, the canon of late poems is difficult to determine because the poems were gathered from scraps of paper and letters. Work that has been deemed "prose" scans and rhymes. She sent poems as prose to some friends; sometimes she sent the same pieces as poems to others. So much correspondence was destroyed or is missing. These facts, in addition to the often questionable criteria used by her editor to decide what constitutes a line, a poem, a letter, raise questions about poems shut up in the prose that has been classified as letters. In the extant letters, there could be many unlineated poems that in other letters — now missing — Dickinson sent as lineated poems.

The Question of Publication

Her talk and writing were like no one else's, and although she never published a line, now and then some enthusiastic friend would turn love to larceny, and cause a few verses surreptitiously obtained to be printed. Thus, and through other natural ways, many saw and admired her verses, and in consequence frequently notable persons paid her visits, hoping to overcome the protest of her own nature and gain a promise of occasional contributions at least, to various literary magazines.

> —Susan Dickinson, in an
> unsigned obituary, printed in
> the *Springfield Republication*,
> May 18, 1886

I suspect we ought to think of the obtuseness and conventionalism that kept Higginson from recognizing the quality of her work as fortunate, for if he had been able to understand her and help her to get published, she might have been drawn to his kind of vapid idealism and bland moralism. As it was, she had no temptation to write in any way other than to please herself and her ideal reader. Higginson was incapable of corrupting her by drawing her out of her isolation into his own world of borrowed feelings and second-rate ideas.

> —Hyatt Waggoner, *American Poets*

How Dickinson wanted her verse to be read is one of the most perplexing questions about this mysterious poet. She is known to have sent poems to forty-two different correspondents. As we have only a small fraction of her correspondence, we can only imagine the extent of it. If, for example, she sent out six copies of "A Route of Evanescence" that we know of, she most probably sent the poem to other correspondents as well. She devoted a great deal of time to writing letters and copying poems. In this way, Dickinson could carry on what Jerome Loving calls her "secret career":

> She would not publish, of course, but she would expose enough of her work to become *known* as a poet. . . . This she accomplished through Higginson, for though he was no outspoken champion of Dickinson's, he was bewildered enough to speak of her work to others, including that most public of poets, Helen Hunt Jackson.

Dickinson launched her secret career wisely, and before long had
Jackson and others begging to publish her work. (60)

Yet even as she privately copied and circulated her verse, Dickinson
responded ambivalently to the prospect of publication. Jackson (who was
known as "H.H.") was so convinced of Dickinson's talent that in 1884 she
asked to be her literary executor. (As it turned out Dickinson outlived
her friend.) H.H. chastised Dickinson for withholding her poetry from
the world: "I have a little manuscript volume with a few of your verses
in it. You are a great poet — and it is a wrong to the day you live in, that
you will not sing out loud. When you are what men call dead, you will be
sorry you were so stingy" (Leyda 2:245). Jackson, one of the few people
Dickinson consented to see after her withdrawal, managed to get one
poem (ironically and perhaps tellingly, it was "Success is counted sweetest") for a collection of anonymous poems, A Masque of Poets, edited by
Thomas Niles.

Richard Sewall believes that early on Dickinson made overtures toward
the public, but found that the world would only read her if it first violated
her word. Her good friend Samuel Bowles, editor of the Springfield Republican, published six of her poems. But, as Sewall informs us, they were
printed "all anonymously, all with manufactured titles, most with petty
alterations toward conventionality, and in the final instance, 'The Snake,'
not only altered but 'robbed'" (476). In contrast to Sewall's view (which
is representative of many others) are those of Karen Dandurand, JoAnne
Dobson, Susan Howe, and Martha Nell Smith. Dandurand discovered
that during the Civil War, to help in the war effort, Dickinson published
her poems anonymously in the Drum Beat, a fund-raising paper. Dandurand maintains that these publications, which were unaltered and well
received, disprove the assumption that the poet "gave up hope of being
published because her poems, too advanced for the time, were rejected by
editors" (17). Dandurand concludes that Dickinson "was not deliberately
seeking publication and did not take advantage of the editorial interest in
her poems by offering more of them" (27). Dobson asserts that these publications prove that "Dickinson, had she chosen, could have had as much
control over her publications as any writer" (49). Dobson points out that
in the nineteenth century "only two motives for publication were seen as
viable for women: the desire to be 'an instrument of good' and 'a pressing
need for money'" (50). Since Dickinson had neither the didactic imperative nor the economic need, she "wrote for herself and a small circle of

friends and acquaintances, and in the role of the feminine literary ama-
teur she would find herself recognized and appreciated" (51). This kind of
intimate notoriety better fit the social mores, and Sue's "love to larceny"
statement regarding the poems that were printed while Emily lived may
be seen as a way of protecting her beloved friend from any negative judgment on the part of the public.

Publication of women writers was even more difficult because of the
common nineteenth-century fear that the world of the spirit would be
erased by the market and by the rise of industrialism and commercialism. Harriet Beecher Stowe and her sister Catharine Beecher preached a
"woman's sphere," a virtuous and spiritual realm that, even as it sought to
influence the soul, stood apart from men and their utilitarian and unethi-
cal marketplace. Dickinson, who used monetary metaphors throughout
her career, articulates the dialectic between the market and the spirit. She
writes in "A Light exists in Spring," a poem from her third period, that
when the sublime experience of light passes, we are left with

> A quality of loss
> Affecting our Content
> As Trade had suddenly encroached
> Upon a Sacrament.
>
> (Fr 962; 1865)

As Dickinson asserts in her well-known and frequently discussed
poem, "Publication is the Auction / Of the Mind of Man" (Fr 788), to
publish poetry is to appropriate the spirit for trade, akin to selling human
beings as slaves. Howe reads this poem as evidence that "Use value is blasphemy. Form and content collapse the assumption of Project and Masterpiece. Free from limitations of genre Language finds true knowledge
estranged in it-self" (Birth-mark 137). Publication fixes words on the page,
commodifies them, and limits language. (This idea of fixing and limiting
for the market is borne out by Franklin's notion that there is an expected
form for poetry that must be followed.) For Dickinson this commodifica-
tion is a blasphemy because to limit the possibilities of language limits
the human spirit as well. Howe states that Dickinson is an antinomian,
by definition at odds with authority: "'Authoritative readings' confuse her
nonconformity," while the indeterminacy of the fascicles by "continually
interweaving expectation and categories . . . checkmate inscription to become what a reader offers them" (Birth-mark 136). In contrast to the fascicles, whose multiplicity creates "a halo of wilderness" (Birth-mark 136),

publication means that the "production of meaning will be brought under the control of social authority" (*Birth-mark* 140).

In *Rowing in Eden*, Martha Nell Smith builds her thesis on the foundation of Howe's work, stating that "print reproductions often erase significant textual experimentations directed toward prospective readers and their performances" (13). Smith's book tells the story of the ways in which editors have prepared the Dickinson texts in order to expel from literary record the homoerotic and collaborative relationship Emily had with her sister-in-law, Sue. She argues that the two women made a distinction "between the often synonymously used terms *publish* and *print*. . . . Surrounded by lawyers, these women are somewhat legalistic in their differentiations, using *publish* in the especial sense 'to tell or noise abroad' (OED)" (15).[2] Dickinson's intimate literary and personal relationship with Sue formed the basis of Emily's alternative kind of publication in the form of letters. Smith proposes that Dickinson rejected print publication with the intention to bring the reader into the creative process and that that intention is the result of the shared values she developed in her relationship with Sue. Her book asks us to revise the notion the artist as a creator of "closed artifacts," and to consider the possibility that the "enterprise is generative, turning every reader into a coproducer or coauthor"(76).

I believe that the evidence regarding Dickinson's desire for or resistance to publication is always equivocal. Several factors belie Sue's account that Dickinson's poems were only printed when friends "turned love to larceny." When poems by both women were anonymously published in the *Springfield Republican*, Sue herself eagerly wrote to Emily in March 1962: "*Has girl read Republican?* It takes as long to start our Fleet as the Burnside" (Leyda 2:48).[3] As previously noted, Dickinson willingly made contributions to *Drum Beat* to aid in the Civil War effort, which was certainly an acceptable reason for a woman to publish. But there are other instances in which there was no moral or didactic purpose in her publishing. When her poem, "Success is counted sweetest," was published in *A Masque of Poets*, H.H. writes her in gratitude for her *willing* contribution: "I suppose by this time you have seen the Masque of Poets. I hope you have not regretted giving me that choice bit of verse for it." Furthermore, when Dickinson thanks the editor of the volume for sending her a copy, she encloses two more poems, as "a base return indeed, for the delightful book" (Leyda 2:307), yet nonetheless a method of making more of her poems known to an editor. Perhaps the most revealing example of Dickinson's ambivalence is her well-known first letter in 1862 to Thomas Wentworth Higginson, editor of the *Atlantic Monthly*, asking, "Are you too deeply occupied to say if my Verse is alive?" (L 260). His response disappointed her. When she writes back, "I smile when you suggest that I delay 'to publish' — that being as foreign to my thought as Firmament to Fin —," her renunciation is not entirely credible, especially since in the next sentence she writes ruefully: "If fame belonged to me I could not escape her — if she did not the longest day would pass me on the chase" (L 265). Under veils of modesty, there is an edge of witty defiance: even if Higginson can't hear her genius, if she is truly worthy, the world inevitably will.

Editors

> Printed in the 1890s to promote the poet, the small, ladylike, white leather gilt-edged volumes with suitable subject categories like "Life," "Love," "Nature," and "Time and Eternity" and the essays by Higginson and Loomis Todd touting Dickinson's reclusion present an image which American audiences were prepared to like. These little books present a woman writer, who, though rather eccentric, was not doing anything especially radical with her poems. These first editors of Dickinson, then, perceived unusual techniques of her poetry as quirks to be amended.
>
> —Martha Nell Smith,
> *Rowing in Eden*

If Dickinson resisted publication because she feared editors would tamper with her work, her concern proved to be justified. When the few poems that were published while she lived were altered, she was clearly dismayed. Her "Snake," she complained to Higginson in 1886, was "defeated . . . of the third line by the punctuation. The third and fourth were one." Dickinson was also worried that Higginson might feel she "deceived" him by printing a poem. Out of this anxiety, she pleads for his preceptorship: "If I still entreat you to teach me, are you much displeased?" (L 316). As this letter reveals, Dickinson did fear, as Dobson asserts, that publication would dishonor her. Yet because Dickinson worried that her spirit would be polluted by publication, does not mean that she did not also worry that her poems would be defaced by editors' hands.

The incontestable fact is that the editions of the poems published posthumously *were* bowdlerized, and they remained uncorrected until Johnson's 1955 edition of the complete poems. Johnson's purpose was to make an exact transcription of the original Dickinson manuscripts. Yet interpretative problems arose. For the readers' edition he had to choose which text to use (though for the fascicle poems this question rarely arose), which variant within a single text to use, and how the poems would be presented typographically. (Franklin and Howe have both questioned Johnson's decisions.) In contrast to Johnson, who made decisions about the texts that interpreted Dickinson's intentions, Higginson and Todd changed the verse and knowingly revised her meaning and prosody.

In addition to Higginson and Todd's bowdlerizing of the texts for publication, the manuscripts themselves were also disfigured in order to create the myth of a socially acceptable Emily Dickinson. Smith writes, "according to his lover, Mabel Loomis Todd—Dickinson's brother, 'Austin,' changed his sister's epistolary record by scissoring and erasing passages about his wife that he regarded as private" (*Rowing in Eden* 16). The focal point of these excisions are references to Emily's love for Sue.[4] "So many gaps in her texts," Smith contends, "have been created by efforts to hide Dickinson's blasphemy, be it lesbian or disrespectful of the patriarchal bastion of marriage" (33). Todd (with Higginson's help) essentially created an Emily Dickinson who would not only be acceptable to the public at large but whose life and work would sanitize her own questionable role in the Dickinson family.

Dickinson's first editors transformed her poetry into more conventional verse because they perceived it was necessary if the work were to be published for an audience whose expectations for women writers were extremely restrictive. A symptom of this imperative can be seen in the words of Thomas Niles, who at Jackson's urging published "Success" and who after H.H.'s death wrote to Dickinson, expressing interest in publishing a volume of her poems. Yet after his initial enthusiasm, Niles reversed his opinion; he wrote Higginson: "It has always seemed to me that it would be unwise to perpetuate Miss Dickinson's poems. They are quite as remarkable for defects as for beauties & are generally devoid of true poetical qualities" (quoted in Johnson 176). Johnson warns that Niles's negative assessment may have been "a shrewd bargaining proposal . . . to compel Lavinia Dickinson to pay for the plates" (176) when the poems were published. However, Niles's unappreciative response to the poetry had persuasive power because it was the standard one—and Emily knew it, as did her posthumous literary promoters, Lavinia, Higginson, and Todd. Arlo Bates, one of the readers for Roberts Brothers, the firm that published the first edition of Dickinson's poems, insisted that editorial changes in the poems were "absolutely necessary" (quoted in R. W. Franklin 24).

After the publication of the poems many reviewers reiterated Niles's criticism, declaring the poetry the work of an untutored genius, who had "a startling disregard for poetic laws" (quoted in R. W. Franklin 26). One of the dissenting opinions, happily, came from the powerful William Dean Howells, who praised the poetry for its innovation: "If nothing else should come out of our life but this strange poetry we should feel that in the work of Emily Dickinson America, or New England rather, had made a distinctive addition to the literature of the world, and could not be left out of any record of it" (quoted in R. W. Franklin 27). Howells's high praise disproves those who justify the defacement of Dickinson's texts: even in the nineteenth century, there were those who could see the poet's vision.

From Fascicles to Letters, from Fixed to Flux

> To entertain as fact that she devised her own method of publication by sending her poems out in letters moves the locus of study to the manuscripts themselves.
>
> —Martha Nell Smith,
> *Rowing in Eden*

Certainly, even without publication in printed form, Dickinson made efforts to ensure that her poems could be read, if there were a receptive audience. To this end, she preserved her work, sewing her final drafts into fascicles. Johnson's description of the manuscripts reveal the serious and meticulous work that Dickinson undertook to order her poetry and put it in fair copy:[5]

> sometime during 1858 Emily Dickinson began assembling her poems into packets. Always written in ink, they are gatherings of four, five, or six sheets of letter stationary usually folded once but occasionally single. They are loosely held together by thread looped through them at the spine at two points equidistant from top and bottom. When opened up they may be read like a small book, a fact that explains why Emily's sister Lavinia, when she discovered them after Emily's death, referred to them as "volumes." All of the packet poems are either fair copies or semifinal drafts, and they constitute two-thirds of the whole. For the most part

the poems in a given packet seem to have been written and assembled as a unit. Since rough drafts of packet poems are almost totally lacking, one concludes that they were systematically discarded. If the poems were in fact composed at the time the copies were made, as all evidence seems to point, then nearly two-thirds of her poems were created in the brief span of eight years, centering on her early thirties. (69)

The other one-third of her work is composed of the "sets," fair copy poems that Dickinson continued to make until 1877, and poems gathered from letters, drafts, and scraps of paper.

Why she stopped copying her work and organizing it into volumes is not known. Johnson attributes it to her waning creativity, yet there is another circumstance to consider: her ceasing work on the fascicles and her withdrawal from society coincided with her mother's invalidism, which as Lavinia Dickinson explains, required that "one of her daughters must be constantly at home; Emily chose this part, and finding the life with her books and nature so congenial, continued to live it" (quoted in Sewall 153). Emily had little time. She writes to her Norcross cousins in 1880:

> I have only a moment, exiles, but you shall have the largest half. Mother's little wants so engross the time, — to read to her, to fan her, to tell her health will come tomorrow, to explain to her *why* the grasshopper is a burden, because he is not so new a grasshopper as he was, — this is so ensuing, I hardly have said "Good morning, mother," when I hear myself saying "Mother, good-night." (L 666)

Dickinson's slower, less voluminous production of poems and her less diligent ordering and copying of them may point to her essentially having given up hope of publication and consequently to her no longer feeling the same urgent commitment to verse. Yet even without the fascicles, she continued to work with words, writing shorter poems, less often, and carrying on an extensive correspondence. Johnson observes:

> In later years almost all poems were intended for enclosure in letters to friends. It was the receiving and sending of letters that now constituted her "estate," and on them she lavished as much care as she had earlier devoted to her poems, writing them in first draft, correcting, polishing, then dispatching the finished copy. In some instances her pleasure in the choice of a phrase was such that she incorporated identical paragraphs in letters to different correspondents. (52)

It is true, as Johnson states, that Dickinson was pleased enough with the music of her letters to sing it again as if it were poetry, to incorporate "identical paragraphs in letters to different correspondents." For example, she incorporates most of the letter to the Norcross cousins quoted above into a letter to her dear friend, Mrs. Josiah Holland. From the beginning the letters were poetic and wide in "circumference." There is in them, as Jean-Paul Sartre says in his description of the language of poetry, "always much more in each phrase, in each verse, as there is more than simple anguish in the yellow sky over Golgotha" (34). There is evidence to back Johnson's belief that in her later years writing letters was as important as writing poems.

I would take Johnson's observation a step further. The poetic language of the letters and the fact that they were used as a kind of self-publication to share her vision with readers suggests that at the end of her life there was no intrusive, generic difference between writing letters and writing poems. The genres had so merged that similarity was more significant than difference. As readers, we must regard the letter-poems not merely as biographical information but as art.

To regard the letter-poems as part of the canon, however, raises problems for our ordinary perception of art as a fixed object, bearing out Howe's argument that the established world of publishers and critics silences Dickinson's most extraordinary innovations or excursions into the modern world of indeterminate meaning. In his *The Editing of Emily Dickinson: A Reconsideration*, R. W. Franklin observes that Dickinson did not feel compelled to fix the art object:

> Multiplicity . . . did not bother this poet, and she would without qualms change a reading in order to make it appropriate for different people and different occasions. Each of these fair copies is "final" for its person or occasion, but that cannot be equated with final intention for publication. Sending a poem to a friend is a type of publishing, but it fixes the poem only for that person on that occasion; sending a poem to a publisher is distinctly different and, in theory, fixes the form of the poem for all people and all time. (132)

Dickinson did not instruct her readers in how to translate her work from the multiplicity of her manuscripts to a printed and fixed art object.

The poem "Take all away from me, but leave me ecstasy" is a good example of the notion that Dickinson did not reject multiplicity. In 1885

Dickinson sent the following poem to Mr. and Mrs. Eben Loomis (Mabel's parents), to Helen Hunt Jackson, and to Samuel Bowles, the younger:

> Take all away from me, but leave me Ecstasy,
> And I am richer then, than all my Fellow Men –
> Is it becoming me, to dwell so wealthily, when at my
> very door
> Are those possessing more, in a boundless poverty?
> (Fr 1671; 1885)

In the version of "Take all away" sent to H.H. there are two variants that transform the poem from a question to a statement: she substitutes "Ill it becometh" for "Is it becoming me" and "abject" for "boundless." We have two drafts of the letter sent to H.H.; the letter also contains "Of God we ask one favor" (Fr 1675).[6] The first two lines of "Of God we ask one favor" are written out as prose. And this was not uncommon. She sends to Bowles the same poem to H.H., as prose: "Take all away from me, but leave me Ecstasy, and I am richer then, than all my fellowmen. Is it becoming me, to dwell so wealthily, when at my very door Are those possessing more, in boundless poverty?" (L 1014). The capitalized "A" of "Are" is most unusual, as Dickinson does not have the practice of capitalizing verbs. Because she capitalized the first letter of every line, she may have considered a line break at that capitalized "Are," so Franklin chooses the "prose" version for his edition, while Johnson chooses the one in leonine hexameters. But Dickinson also drafted a version of the poem in which the lines broke into rhyming trimeter couplets (except the last line, which picks up the rhyme from the penultimate couplet), and the poem scans exactly this way:[7]

> Take all away from me,
> But leave me Ecstasy,
> And I am richer then
> Than all my Fellow Men –
> Ill it becometh me
> To dwell so wealthily
> When at my very Door
> Are those possessing more,
> In abject poverty –

If Dickinson had not left drafts of the poem and her letter to Jackson and if the Loomises had destroyed their letters and poems from Dickinson, then we would not have "Take all away from me" in the canon of Dickinson's poetry; we would have only the "prose" version of the poem.

Because it is clear that this poem is shut up in prose in one letter, I have here tried to release another possible poem from prose. Without changing words or punctuation, I have lineated a portion of this late letter, capitalizing the initial letters of the new lines:

> We want you to wake –
> Easter has come and gone –
> Morning without you
> Is a Dwindled Dawn –
>
> April 1885 (L 981)

I have lineated this "prose" not because I advocate mining the letters to create new poems by Emily Dickinson, as William Shurr did in his *New Poems of Emily Dickinson*.[8] Instead, I wish to show that both formally and thematically many letter-poems are a great deal like other late poems: they are short, epigrammatic, and, with their regularities and irregularities, typically Dickinsonian. The letter-poem I have lineated, "We want you to wake" is formally exactly the same as the late poem, "Morning is due to all," written two years earlier, which is also a quatrain with full rhymes in the second and last lines. The poem, according to Johnson, was written about October 1883 and probably "sent to Miss Elizabeth Hoar upon her engagement to Samuel Bowles the younger":

> Morning is due to all –
> To some – the Night –
> To an imperial few –
> The Auroral light –
>
> (Fr 1621; 1883)

The lines I have extracted from the letter meet exactly the same criteria as the one above, yet one was chosen for the canon of poems, and one was not. If different criteria were used, we might regard the entire letter as an astonishing and beautiful poem. Here is the whole text, reproduced as Dickinson lineated it:

> Dear Friend –
> We want
> You to wake –
> Easter has come

and gone –
Morning without
you is a dwin-
dled Dawn –
Quickened toward
all celestial
things by Crows
I heard this
morning –
Accept a
loving Caw
from a
nameless friend –
"Selah."

Just as the regular rhymes in the letter-poems are consistent with Dickinson's late work, so the irregularities, which so distinguish her work from that of her contemporaries, are common devices in her late verse. The letter-poem, "The withdrawal of the Fuel of Rapture," that initiates this chapter is an entire letter manuscript (L 842), believed to be addressed to Judge Otis Phillips Lord around 1883. Compare "Withdrawal of the Fuel of Rapture" to this late elegy written in February 1885 and enclosed in two letters — one to Mrs. J. S. Cooper and one to Benjamin Kimball, a relative of Judge Lord, who died in March 1884:

Go thy great way!
The Stars thou meetst
Are even as Thyself –
For what are Stars but Asterisks
To point a human Life?
(Fr 1673; 1885)

Both "The withdrawal of the Fuel of Rapture" and "Go thy great way!" use word repetition. If "Rapture" is lineated according to conventional metrics, both poems have an odd number of lines: five. Both are similar in their musical irregularities. "Go thy great way!" has four off-rhymes: "meetst," "Thyself," "Asterisks," and "Life." The off-rhymes in "The withdrawal of the Fuel of Rapture" are "Rapture," "Drawer," "Prayer," and "dormant." The letter-poem is actually the more musically complex and sophisticated of the two pieces. In it Dickinson makes strong use of alliteration: "*Powder*," "*pass*," and "*Prayer.*" In the first sentence, the reader tends to pause at the important words, "withdrawal" and "Fuel," because they are internal rhymes and those rhymes are the stressed beats of anapests. There are also the internal rhymes, "Powder" and "thunders," which chime well with the end rhymes "Rapture," "Drawer," "Prayer," and "Dormant." In her letters, Sewall points out, "as in her verse, she was a poet all the time" (751).

The late letters most often are formally and structurally complete — as poems. The subject matter, for example, in many letters and parts of letters proceeds in a way that is similar to Dickinson's poetry. In contrast to earlier poems that rely on more sustained psychological drama, the late poems frequently create an impact of sudden dynamism by speedily playing out a metaphor. Simply speaking, in the poems and letters quoted above, rapture is gunpowder, the hope of resurrection is dawn, and the human spirit is a star.

Because the late poems were gathered from letters and scraps of paper, Dickinson's canon of poems depends on the extant letters. Herein lies a literary tragedy and a terrible textual problem. Richard Sewall writes that it "has been estimated that we have about a tenth of all the letters Emily Dickinson wrote, and probably about a thousandth of those written to her" (400). Dickinson's Norcross cousins, Fanny and Louise — who corresponded regularly with Dickinson from the 1850s until her death — gave Mabel Loomis Todd heavily censored copies of the poet's letters and destroyed the manuscripts. We are missing her letters to crucial friends, such as Charles Wadsworth, whom Dickinson called her "clergyman" and her "Shepherd" (and with whom some speculate Dickinson was in love in the 1860s), and Judge Otis Phillips Lord, with whom she shared love at the end of her life. Wolff writes of Lord's niece, Abbie Farley:

> [She] was the chief beneficiary of Judge Lord's will, and since he was a man of considerable wealth, she stood to inherit a good deal so long as he did not marry. . . . Farley actively opposed the match [between Emily Dickinson and Otis Lord]; indeed, her hostility toward Emily Dickinson was so great that she destroyed everything that the poet had written to Lord, letters and whatever poetry they may have contained. (403)

The letters we have to Lord are drafts and edited copies that Lavinia gave to Mabel Loomis Todd. Since the handwriting goes back as far as 1878, at least six years of correspondence from the poet to Lord is lost. Only two poems and a two-line fragment have been retrieved from this most intimate correspondence. Given her writing habits, it is, as Sewall asserts, "unthinkable that she did not send him many more poems" (660).

The Lord correspondence highlights how much of Dickinson's work has been lost or has been relegated to the pages of her collected letters. The lines to Jackson and the Loomises were not the only ones she seemingly incorporated in prose. In addition to paragraphs in the letters that scan as poetry, there are letters that contain poems that Dickinson wrote out as prose (or what has been deemed prose). Sewall also points out that the last paragraph from one letter to Lord "is a perfect quatrain of '8s' and '6s'" (659). One of the poems found in a draft of a letter to Lord incorporates the first two lines into the prose part of the fragment, yet Johnson counts all four lines as a poem:

> How fleet – how indiscreet an one –
> how always wrong is Love –
> The joyful little Deity
> We are not scourged to serve –
>
> > (Fr 1557; 1881)

The entire draft of the letter-poem reads as follows:

> My little devices
>
> to live until Monday
>
> would woo your
> > win
> sad attention
>
> fill your eyes with
>
> Dew
>
> Full of plots and little
>
> happinesses the
>
> thought of you
> > derides
> protracts them
>
> all and makes
> them sham and
> cold. How fleet
> how indiscrete an

one how always
wrong is Love
The joyful little
Deity
We are not
scourged to serve

Significantly, Johnson sees the lines, "fill your eyes with / Dew" as variant lines, even though there is no particular indication (such as crossing out or writing between the lines) that would point to this phrase as a variant of "woo your / sad attention." Yet if the phrase "fill your eyes with / Dew" is eliminated, the letter-poem is in completely regular 8s and 6s. With the phrase there is an extra line. Here is the letter-poem lineated according to Johnson's metrical criteria:

My little devices to live
Until Monday would woo
Your sad attention – Full of plots
And little happinesses
The thought of you protracts them all
And makes them sham and cold.
How fleet – how indescreet an one
How always wrong is Love
The joyful little Deity
We are not scourged to serve

The fact that Johnson judged "fill your eyes with / Dew" a variant suggests that he tested this draft against his metrical criteria to determine whether or not it was a poem. Why he decided that the last two sets of 8s and 6s are a poem and the previous six are a letter is open to speculation, but it appears he inconsistently utilized his criteria in determining what was a poem and what prose.

As I have suggested above, whether or not Dickinson intended these letters to be poems, the music of her poetry was always with her. She was in the habit of constantly transposing it, of working for years with the same rhythm and words. Wolff surmises that Dickinson used the letters to work out ideas from early on:

In early June 1854 Dickinson wrote a hasty letter to Austin containing this apology: "This is truly extempore, Austin—I have no notes in my pocket . . ." A few *drafts* of letters were preserved when, after

Emily Dickinson's death, Lavinia burned all of her sister's correspondence — drafts of letters to the "Master" and to Judge Otis Lord. That
is, there seems good reason to take Dickinson at her word here and to
assume that she was making first drafts of much of her correspondence.
. . . [this] suggests that far from working haphazardly, Dickinson had
begun to keep some sort of file or record of her work. . . . She seems also
to have begun looking over her own work to choose effective turns of
phrase for further use. (575 n)

From the beginning, then, the letters were part of the process of writing
poems. At the end of her life the process of writing letters and poems was
apparently virtually the same. Furthermore, since Dickinson was no longer compiling her fascicle volumes, the letters were the main vehicle for
poetry. We know Dickinson drafted the letter-poem "My little devices," at
least twice before sending it to Lord, as there is a second scrap of paper
that reads on one side:

> My little devices
> to live until Monday
> would darken all
> your glee – for you
> have a good deal
>   many a glee
> of glee in your
> nature's corners

And on the other side reads:

> the most lurking
> and never to be
> trusted as Brown said
> of sleep — without
> ones prayers —

Unfortunately — and tantalizingly — we cannot know what the words of
the final piece were. We do have, however, a magnificent fragment, proph-
esied by Sappho's lines, which were fragmented by time.

The case of the poem "The Summer that we did not prize" and the letter-poem "I feel like wasting my Cheek" (L 843) is another example both of
inconsistent criteria and of the difficulty presented in the late work by the
extant worksheets. Johnson tells us in the variorum that the manuscript of

poem 1773 "is a rough draft of a poem on a scrap of paper in an envelope containing messages which in their final draft presumably were sent to Judge Lord." On the other side of that scrap of paper is the letter-poem "I feel like wasting my Cheek." The two pieces are drafted in exactly the same manner. The scrap of paper is long and horizontal, and each side is divided by two vertical lines. The poet drafted both pieces in three columns of short lines. Both pieces are extremely rough, and are devastating examples of the loss that Judge Lord's niece inflicted on Dickinson's readers when she destroyed everything the poet sent him. Although "I feel like wasting my Cheek" is not regular in rhyme and meter as is "The Summer we did not prize," it is well established now that Dickinson did not always write poetry in conventional and regular prosody. Furthermore, Johnson, while favoring as poems the writing that is in hymnal meter, *does* sometimes deem as poems unrhyming and irregular language.

The published poem 1773 looks like this:

> The Summer that we did not prize,
> Her treasure were so easy
> Instructs us by departing now
> And recognition lazy –
>
> Bestirs itself – puts on its Coat
> And scans with fatal promptness
> For Trains that moment out of sight,
> Unconscious of his smartness.

Typographically translated the "poem" "The Summer that we did not prize" looks like this in manuscript:

The summer that	Bestirs itself –	
		moment out
we did not prize	Puts on its Coat,	
		of sight,
Her treasures were	With what a fatal	
	promptness	Unconscious of
so easy		
	and scans with fatal	his smartness
Instructs us by	promptness	disdainful
		of his
departing now	For trains that	severely out
more		of sight –
And recognition		derision
lazy –		

"I feel like wasting my Cheek," which was drafted in much the same way in manuscript, looks like this:

I feel like wasting
my Cheek on your
Hand tonight –
Will you accept
  approve
the squander –
Lay up treasures
immediately – That's

the best Anodyne
for moth and
Rust and the
thief whom the
Bible knew enough
of Banking to
suspect would
break in and steal

Night is my favorite
Day – I love silence
so – I dont mean
halt of sound
stop
but ones that
talk of nought all day
mistaking it for
voice[9] – Forgive you

This letter-poem is printed in the *Letters* as prose. Although "Cheek" appears to be unfinished, particularly at the end, many of the poems written in Dickinson's last couple of years of life have been reconstructed from extremely rough worksheets. Certainly, "The Summer that we did not prize" is as rough as "Cheek," yet "Summer" is considered a poem while "Cheek" is not. "I feel like wasting my Cheek" is a refreshingly erotic letter-poem, for which Dickinson should be known.

The fundamental question here has been, When, precisely, is Dickinson writing out words as prose, and when as poetry? Dickinson's famous "prose fragment," "Nature is a Haunted House – but Art – a House that tries to be haunted," was enclosed in a letter to Higginson. Over and over again, these words are cited, and never as a poem, but as significant prose. Here it is as she laid it out on the page:

Nature is
a Haunted
House – but
Art – a House
that tries
to be
haunted
(Leyda 2:252)

And here is her last note to Higginson, written on her deathbed. These contained, passionate, and questioning lines should be known as among the most profound of any poet; as life closes, she asks if there is a savior with human breath:

> Deity – does
> He live now?
> My friend –
> does he breathe?
> (Leyda 2:470)

While the lineation of these two pieces of "prose" might seem overmodern for Emily Dickinson, she often laid out her poems this way in the manuscripts, as can be seen in the poems I quoted earlier. Johnson often understands a line by virtue of its meter, not by its actual placement on the page. If Dickinson's placement divides the metrical line, he assumes that if there were not enough room on the page for the full line, she wrote the line end below. Yet as Howe points out, "Close examination of the Franklin Manuscripts shows that she could have put words onto a line had she wished to; in some cases she did crowd words onto a line" (*Birthmark* 153 n). Here, for example, is the way Johnson lineates the first stanza of poem 1437:

> A Dew sufficed itself –
> And satisfied a Leaf
> And felt "how vast a destiny" –
> How trivial is Life!"

Here is the way Dickinson placed the words in manuscript:

> A Dew sufficed
> itself
> And satisfied
> a Leaf.
> And thought
> "how vast a
> destiny"!
> "How trivial
> is Life"!
> (MB)

By reading these words according to her placement on the page, a multitude of new ambiguities and off-rhymes emerge, emphasizing rather than diminishing, its formal poetic means. It can be argued that in addition to meter, Dickinson's capitalization of the initial words in lines is a defining clue. Yet poems incorporated in letters as prose don't follow that pattern of capitalization, as in, for example, the lines I quoted above: "How fleet—how indiscreet an one— / how always wrong is Love." In short, clues that lead to changes in Dickinson's placement of words are equivocal at best.

How, then, should we read "Nature is" and "Deity – does"? In what typographical form? To what genre do they belong: poetry, letters, or prose fragment? She had the poetic intuition to put these words down as "modern poems." Why should we not recognize her lineated words as poems? These works represent some of her most dynamic and moving words, and reading them allows us to experience her full artistic power.

A Letter Like Immortality

During the last years of her life, letters were Dickinson's way of finding readers for her poems. This method was more direct than publication of the poems (or preservation of them in the fascicles, which like printed publication might keep them for posthumous readership—and, as it turns out, did). Ironically, friendship—and readership through it—prevailed in the years of Dickinson's most poignant isolation. Friendship was there throughout her withdrawal: in overheard conversations of visitors to the Homestead, which nourished her in spite of the separating door left ajar; in letters that contained poems for her friendly audience; and in the poems themselves, which made friendship a subject.

Perhaps precisely because of her late withdrawal from the society of presence, friendship (and its vehicle, letters) took on a supernatural quality of immortality. Very early, Dickinson had articulated the connection between immortality and poetry, as is seen in poem after poem. Yet in a letter (or a perfectly iambic letter-poem) written to Higginson in 1869, she widens the circumference of "immortal writing" to include letters: "A Letter always feels to me like immortality because it is the mind alone without corporeal friend. Indebted in our talk to attitude and accent, there seems a spectral power in thought that walks alone" (L 330). Dickinson's notion of immortality evolved from the Calvinist doctrine of election. Because she never converted, she considers herself shut out of the company of the saved, as when she complains in these early lines, "Why – do they shut Me out of Heaven?" (Fr 268; 1861) and "'Heaven' – is what I cannot reach!" (Fr 310; 1861). Because a letter for her is immortality, when

Dickinson replaces face-to-face meetings with epistolary exchange, she creates for herself a kind of heavenly community. If letters are immortality, they bring her back, through friendship, into the circle of the elect.

Mabel Loomis Todd and Dickinson shared the kind of interaction the poet describes in her letter to Higginson: "the mind alone without corporeal friend." When Todd writes in her journal that "Emily is called in Amherst 'the myth,'" she reveals that in her community Dickinson had become her own prophetic letter, a pure spirit, "a spectral power in thought that walks alone." Dickinson never met Todd face-to-face, yet over the years they communicated by exchanging music, paintings, flowers, sherry, letters, and poems. When in September 1882 Austin Dickinson had taken her to the Homestead to sing for his sisters and invalid mother, Todd records in her journal that Emily Dickinson stayed hidden during the concert: "It was odd to think as my voice rang out through the big silent house that Miss Emily in her weird white dress was outside in the shadows hearing every word. . . . When I stopped Miss Emily sent me in a glass of rich sherry & a poem written as I sang" (Leyda 2:376). The poem that she gave to Todd shows the high value Dickinson placed on this kind of exchange:

> Elysium is as far as to
> The very nearest Room
> If in that Room a Friend await
> Felicity or Doom –
>
> What fortitude the Soul contains,
> That it can so endure
> The accent of a coming Foot –
> The opening of a Door –
> (Fr 1590; 1882)

Although the poem locates "Elysium," the happy island of the blessed, in "the very nearest Room" where a friend waits, it also expresses ambivalence toward an encounter with another: "the opening of a Door," requires "fortitude" as it can mean either "Felicity or Doom."

Dickinson chose to deal with friendship on her own terms; her famous, mythological withdrawal dictated the form that those relationships would take. She shunned most ways of conventional social interaction, yet maintained communication largely through letters. Sometimes the letters were accompanied by a gift of flowers; sometimes she included poems. Letters, as Johnson observes, "gave her the means of selecting her own society" (52). The society she seems to have preferred was sublime, unfettered by the mundane. When Todd sent her a panel on which she had painted Indian pipes, one of Dickinson's favorite flowers, she thanked her with

Dear Friend,
    That without suspecting it you should send me the preferred flower of life, seems almost supernatural, and the sweet glee that I felt at meeting it, I could confide to none. I still cherish the clutch with which I bore it from the ground when a wondering Child, an earthly booty, and maturity only enhances mystery, never decreases it. To duplicate the Vision is almost more amazing, for God's unique capacity is too surprising to surprise.
    I know not how to thank you. We do not thank the Rainbow although it's [sic] Trophy is a snare.
    To give delight is hallowed — perhaps the toil of Angels, whose avocations are concealed —
    I trust that you are well, and the quaint little Girl with the deep Eyes, ever more fathomless.

                    With joy,
                    E. Dickinson

                        (L 769)

Dickinson writes that "meeting" Todd's painting filled her with such "sweet glee," she "could confide [it] to none," yet shortly after sending her note of gratitude, she writes to Todd, "Dear Friend, / I cannot / make an / Indian Pipe / but please / accept a / Humming Bird" (L 770) and the poem "A Route of Evanescence" follows. Dickinson answers art with art. While she cannot "confide" her "sweet glee" through other means of communication, she does express it in a poem.

        A Route of Evanescence
        With a Revolving Wheel –
        A Resonance of Emerald –
        A Rush of Cochineal –
        And every Blossom on the Bush
        Adjusts its tumbled Head –
        The mail from Tunis, probably,
        An easy Morning's Ride –
            (Fr 1489; 1879)

It is significant that although Dickinson might have written the "Elysium" poem as an instantaneous response to Todd's singing, she did not write "A Route of Evanescence" in a similar moment of inspiration provoked by "Indian Pipes." According to Johnson's variorum, Dickinson wrote "Evanescence" about three years earlier, in 1879, and she sent it to six of her correspondents. Two of them were important literary figures: Higginson and Helen Hunt Jackson. The number of recipients of the poem, Johnson surmises, indicates "the assurance ED felt about its quality." Like "Take all away from me," "A Route of Evanescence" was disseminated among her friends.

The poems were gifts, and she sent them to friends in whom she saw kindred sensibilities. Significantly, there is evidence that her friends understood and valued the poems they received, not just as words (which could be reproduced by hand-copying or by print), but as unique artifacts made by the poet's hand. For example, Dickinson sent Helen Hunt Jackson a poem to commemorate her marriage, H.H., in turn, sent the poem back and asked for an explanation, adding, "This is *mine*, remember. You must send it back to me, or else you will be a robber" (Leyda 2:243). When Dickinson failed to return the poem, H.H. wrote her: "But you did not send it back, though you wrote that you would. Was this an accident, or a late withdrawal of your consent? Remember that it is mine — not yours —, and be honest" (Leyda 2:245). H.H. valued Dickinson's words, as I've shown, but she cherished the original product, made by the poet, in the form of a letter.

In later years her letters to friends carried poems or were poems. Dickinson had established this mode of finding an audience early on, especially in her relationship with Sue, to whom she sent more letters and poems than any other correspondent. The difference is that in the later years the letters became the final product of the creative process, and the fascicles were abandoned. At the end Dickinson devoted herself to her friends, whom early in her career she proclaimed her "estate":

> My friends are my "estate." Forgive me then the avarice to hoard them!
> . . . God is not so wary as we, else he would give us no friends, lest we
> forget him! The Charms of the Heaven in the bush are superseded I fear
> by Heaven in the hand, occasionally. (L 193)

To her the earthly heaven of friends "superseded" God. She left it to them and to their descendants to elect her poetry to immortality, and to choose what form that immortality would take. Her choice was to make her art immediately relational, an art that not only invited its readers to reply, but entreated them, and waited for another voice to speak.

The Artist of the Beautiful, a Possibility

I dwell in Possibility –
A fairer House than Prose –

—Emily Dickinson (Fr 466)

Or Butterflies, off Banks of Noon,
Leap, plashless as they swim.

—Emily Dickinson (Fr 359)

I held it so tight that I lost it
Said the Child of the Butterfly
Of many a vaster Capture
That is the Elegy –

—Emily Dickinson (Fr 1659)

Why did Emily Dickinson stop copying her poems and organizing them in her "little volumes," the fascicles? Why, at the end of her life, did she send fair copies of her poems out in the form of letters? How does this change in her creative process fit into a scheme of development?

A possible answer may lie allegorically in Nathaniel Hawthorne's story, "The Artist of the Beautiful." The story is a brilliant illumination of the relationships between the artist and his or her audience, the maker and the made, a portrait of artistic nature at odds with the practical and unsympathetic social world. The artist of the beautiful is Owen Warland, whose "love of the beautiful" was "completely refined from any utilitarian coarseness" (161). He is a man who remarks, "Strength is an earthly monster. I make no pretentions to it. My force, whatever there may be of it, is altogether spiritual" (163). Owen has been the apprentice of a dismissive Puritan watchmaker, Peter Hovenden, who scoffs at all that is not pragmatic. The artist is in love with Hovenden's daughter, Annie, who, to her father's satisfaction, ends up marrying a man who is the opposite of Owen, the cheerful, brawny blacksmith, Robert Danforth, "who spends his labor on a reality" (160). When Owen achieves financial independence, he is released from working, free to devote himself to creating the beautiful, to "putting spirit into machinery" (166).

At the end of the story, Owen goes to Annie's home to give her "a bridal gift," the product of his artistry, a butterfly of such magnificent beauty, "it is impossible to express by words the glory":

> Nature's ideal butterfly was here realized in all its perfection; not in the pattern of such faded insects as flit among earthly flowers, but of those which hover across meads of paradise for child-angels and the spirits of departed infants to disport themselves with. . . . In its perfect beauty, the consideration of size was entirely lost. Had its wings overarched the firmament, the mind could not have been more filled or satisfied.

In the butterfly, as in a poem, the vastness of the entire spiritual universe is compressed into a small, exquisite object, as when Dickinson writes "the First so seems / to Comprehend the Whole –" of the list, "First – Poets – then the Sun – / Then Summer – then the Heaven of God –" (Fr 533). As in Greek mythology, the butterfly represents the artist's psyche, which, as in Dickinson's poem, "Comprehends the Whole": "Had its wings overarched the firmament, the mind could not have been more filled or satisfied."

Annie asks if the butterfly is alive, in words eerily reminiscent of the famous letter Dickinson wrote to Higginson: "Are you too deeply occupied to say if my Verse is alive?" (L 260). Just as Dickinson waits for the judgment of her reader to determine whether her "Verse is alive," so Owen Warland asks his reader (and audience) to judge for herself whether the butterfly lives:

> "Is it alive?" she repeated, more earnestly than before.
>
> "Judge for yourself," said Owen Warland, who stood gazing at her face with fixed attention. . . .
>
> "But is it alive?" exclaimed she again; and the finger, on which the gorgeous mystery had alighted, was so tremulous that the butterfly was forced to balance himself with his wings. "Tell me if it be alive, or whether you created it?"
>
> "Wherefore ask who created it, so it be beautiful?" replied Owen Warland. "Alive? Yes, Annie; it may well be said to possess life, for it has absorbed my own being into itself; and in the secret of that butterfly, and in its beauty — which is not merely outward, but deep as its whole system — is represented the intellect, the imagination, the sensibility, the soul, of an Artist of the Beautiful! Yes, I created it. But" — and here his countenance somewhat changed — "this butterfly is not now to me what it was when I beheld it afar off, in the day-dreams of my youth."

The *living* spiritual being of the artist is embodied in the butterfly he made. Likewise, the spirit of poet is incarnated in the words on the page, as Dickinson observes in so many of her poems. In Dickinson's case, pulsing with her spirit are perhaps even in the ink, the lead, the paper, the actual materials used to make the manuscripts, to draw words on the page. Because the artist imbues the text with his or her "soul" with the intent to give it to someone else, the text is "alive" when the reader willingly and openly receives it, and re-creates it with his or her imagination. As Robert Scholes puts it: "Reading is a creative process in which we generate, use, and discard our own texts as a way of making sense of the text we are ostensibly 'reading'" (8). Owen has created the butterfly with Annie in mind as his reader (and muse): "he had persisted in connecting all his dreams of artistical success with Annie's image; she was the visible shape in which the spiritual power that he worshipped, and on whose alter he hoped to lay a not unworthy offering, was made manifest to him." As it turns out, Annie accepts the gift of Owen's art, though she doesn't accept his love. She represents the reader who, whether she is known to the artist or not, fulfills the covenant between the artist and the audience: in the moment that she receives the butterfly, she allows a meeting of minds, she allows a union between herself and Owen. Scholes depicts the relationship between the reader and the writer (or artist) this way:

> In reading we find ourselves, to be sure, but only through the language of the Other, whose existence we must respect. . . . because, as human beings, we have a dimension that is irreducibly social. We have been constructed as human subjects by interacting with other people, learning their language and their ways of behaving. Having come to consciousness in this way, we have an absolute need for communication. As human subjects we must exchange meanings with others whom we recognize as subjects like ourselves, in order to confirm our own right to be treated as subjects rather than objects. In every act of reading the irreducible otherness of writer and reader is balanced and opposed by this need for recognition and understanding between the two parties. (50–51)

This process in which the reader finds herself "through the language of the Other" is similar to the process I describe earlier in this book, with respect to Dickinson's artistic appropriation of crisis conversion. Reading is an ecstatic process in which the reader "stands beside herself" in order to allow the text of the Other to enter her consciousness (a consciousness that is filled with the texts of her life and culture). This is a reciprocal kind of ecstasy because, in her desire to communicate, the writer also stands outside herself, imagining the reader who will receive her creation. In Hawthorne's terms, "spiritual power" is "made manifest" in the image of the Other. If the reader finds herself "through the language of the Other," so does the artist find the path to creation by imagining a language that will reach the Other.

But there is another kind of reader, one closed to such a union, and this reader is represented by Annie's father:

> "Let us see," said Peter Hovenden, rising from his chair, with a sneer upon his face that always made people doubt, as he himself did, in everything but a material existence. "Here is my finger for it to alight upon. I shall understand it better when once I have touched it."
>
> But, to the increased astonishment of Annie, when the tip of her father's finger was pressed against that of her husband, on which the butterfly still rested, the insect drooped its wings, and seemed on the point of falling to the floor. Even the bright spots of gold upon its wings and body, unless her eyes deceived her, grew dim, and the glowing purple took a dusky hue, and the starry lustre that gleamed around the blacksmith's hand became faint, and vanished.
>
> "It is dying! it is dying!" cried Annie, in alarm.
>
> "It has been delicately wrought," said the artist, calmly. "As I told you, it has imbibed a spiritual essence — call it magnetism, or what you will. In an atmosphere of doubt and mockery, its exquisite susceptibility suffers torture, as does the soul of him who instilled his own life into it. It has already lost its beauty; in a few moments more, its mechanism would be irreparably injured."

This is the dilemma of the relationship between the artist and the audience. The soul of the artist "suffers torture" in the face of the unsympathetic reader. Yet equally the artist knows that art is not art without an imagined audience. As the representative and product of the artist's creative psyche the butterfly can only live in the presence of an open-minded reader (or audience). Emily Dickinson chose her readers carefully to ensure that her butterfly would not die in "an atmosphere of doubt and mockery."

Hawthorne distinguishes in his allegory between the question of whether the butterfly lives at all and how long its life lasts. Whether the butterfly lives at all is *intimate*, in that it resides in the judgment of the work of art at the moment a single reader receives it (as when Owen says to Annie, "Judge for yourself" when she asks if it is alive). How long the life of a work lasts, whether it is "immortal," resides in a larger social realm, in that immortality is achieved in some measure when the readers who promote the work win the debate about its merits, about whether (as Thomas Niles said of Dickinson's poems) the work should be "perpetuated":

> Had there been no obstruction, it might have soared into the sky, and grown immortal. But its lustre gleamed upon the ceiling; the exquisite texture of its wings brushed against that earthly medium; and a sparkle or two, as if stardust, floated downward and lay glimmering on the carpet. Then the butterfly came fluttering down, and, instead of returning to the infant, was apparently attracted towards the artist's hand.
>
> "Not so, not so!" murmured Owen Warland, as if his handiwork could have understood him. "Thou hast gone forth out of thy master's heart. There is no return for thee!"

Owen understands that once a work of art has left the artist and gone out into the world, it no longer belongs to him or her, it must be given away. If the work is not given over to the audience, it cannot live, as Dickinson observes in one of her early poems:

> A word is dead, when it is said
> Some say –
> I say it just begins to live
> That day
>
> (Fr 278)

The butterfly of the artist's psyche would remain in the realm of the merely material, were it not for the audience's apprehension of it, which allows its spirit to spread wings and fly. Likewise, the body of the text is unliving matter (paper and ink) until the reader breathes life into it. As Owen says to his butterfly, "Thou hast gone forth out of thy master's heart. There is no return for thee!" Once the Artist of the Beautiful has released the embodiment of his psyche, it cannot return to the hand of its maker; it has already been transformed by the reader. If the reader is not an "obstruction," the art can rise to the heavens and grow immortal.

In another sense, once the work has been created, it takes on a life of its own, separate from its maker. So, too, at the end of her life, does Dickinson take the separation between the maker and the made to its logical end. She gives away what she has created—her art enclosed in "letters to the world"—and does not make it a practice to keep fair copy *records* of her art; it belongs now to the (deliberately chosen) reader, who will either pose as an obstruction or send it to celestial immortality. This relinquishing of ownership may seem paradoxical with respect to Dickinson's having so carefully chosen the recipients of her poem-gifts, for by limiting her audience she gave her butterfly the best chance to live. On the one hand, she controls her audience in a way that is impossible in print publication. On the other, she surrenders control of the texts themselves, leaving it to her readers to determine whether her butterfly lives longer than she or her recipients.

> With a wavering movement, and emitting a tremulous radiance, the butterfly struggled, as it were, towards the infant, and was about to alight upon his finger. But, while it still hovered in the air, the little Child of Strength, with his grandsire's sharp and shrewd expression in his face, made a snatch at the marvelous insect, and compressed it in his hand. Annie screamed! Old Peter Hovenden burst into a cold and scornful laugh. The blacksmith, by main force, unclosed the infant's hand, and found within the palm a small heap of glittering fragments, whence the Mystery of Beauty had fled for ever. And as for Owen Warland, he looked placidly at what seemed the ruin of his life's labor, and which yet was no ruin. He had caught a far other butterfly than this. When the artist rose high enough to achieve the Beautiful, the symbol by which he made it perceptible to mortal senses became of little value in his eyes, while his spirit possessed itself in the enjoyment of the Reality.

Hawthorne invokes Plato throughout "The Artist of the Beautiful," as when he refers to the theory of forms in Owen's creation of the butterfly: "Nature's ideal butterfly was here realized in all its perfection; not in the pattern of such faded insects as flit among earthly flowers." The end of the story, in which Owen's spirit "possessed itself in the enjoyment of the Reality," is an uncanny echo of the moment in Plato's *Phaedrus* when Socrates says that before birth "every soul of man has by the law of nature beheld the realities" (249E). Through the divinely mad poet's recollection of the beautiful reality, his soul grows wings and becomes immortal, "which causes him to be regarded as mad, who, when he sees the beauty on earth, remembering true beauty, feels his wings growing and longs to stretch them for an upward flight" (*Phaedrus*, 249D). Emily Dickinson also "rose high enough to achieve the Beautiful," in her spiritual purity. She too caught "a far other butterfly than this," in imagining the ideal and creating art to embody it. In the end, *possibly*, the product, which makes the vision "perceptible to mortal senses," no longer matters to the Artist of the Beautiful. In the act of catching her "far other butterfly," her art turned spirit into words, and she imagined the art that would reach the reader as the animate lines of the beautiful, and in so doing experienced the ecstasy of creation.

> Imitate Jesus and Socrates.
>
> —Benjamin Franklin,
> *Autobiography*

Hawthorne's story, as I have been showing, is an exquisite meditation on the relationship between the artist and his or her reader. Implicit in his story is the notion that the creation of art is engagement in a dialogue. Hawthorne shows that the beauty of art is at its highest spiritual moment when it reaches the reader, especially the reader who allows it to live in the moment of contact, and the reader who enters into a creative dialogue with the artist. With respect to this vibrant connection between the artist and the reader, Willis Barnstone compares the dialogues of Plato with those of Jesus (Yeshua), and shows that it is in the "imitation of convincing speech" that words live:

> The salient virtue of unfixed scripture is its liveliness, its imitation of convincing speech. Plato cast his writings in the form of the *Dialogues*, philosophical talk, precisely to preserve the spontaneous live speech, which, he argued, holds meaning that the written word cannot capture. Speech comes from live persons. Writing becomes dry ink. Through Socrates' voice, Plato said, "to write with pen and ink is to write in water, since the words cannot defend themselves. The spoken word—the living word of knowledge which has a soul—is thus superior to the written work, which is nothing more than its image" (Plato, *Phaedrus*, 278b). So at the heart of the Gospels is the living, heard voice of Yeshua, usually in the form of a platonic dialogue.

Seen through the lens of Plato, Dickinson's fascicles "cannot defend themselves," but the letter-poems are live speech, transported from one person to another. The letter is "the living word of knowledge which has a soul." Her late work is the remnants of one side of a dialogue, even if she sent the same poem to several correspondents. They are not immutable poems locked in print, but live poems, formed, sounded by their presence in a dialogue, which implies a discourse with an intended reader, a response, and a continuation of the dialogue. She writes to Lord "What if you are writing!" (L 790). What if, in other words, you are replying to my writing with writing of your own, if reading my act of creation has sparked your own creation. Dickinson is after the immediacy of ecstatic union with the reader, which is, in Hart Crane's words, "this great wink of eternity," the flash of inspiration, the flash of readership, the living, moving word of the soul. Just as Hawthorne's Owen creates for the woman he loves, Dickinson was always writing for her loved ones. So at the end of this book, I return to where I began: with two quotations that speak of the rapture of the changing soul. Plato states: "Every soul is immortal. For that which is ever moving is immortal" (*Phaedrus* 245C). Emerson moves from Plato to say: "Power ceases in the instant of repose; it resides in the movement of transition from a past to a new state, in the shooting of the gulf, in the darting to an aim. This is one fact the world hates, that the soul *becomes*" (146). If the immortal soul is "ever moving" and "*becomes*," perhaps it is also ever reaching toward the other, the relational, the dialogic, and ultimately the social. Through the act of making art that unites with the reader in dialogue, the soul can achieve immortality without an object or a record of that achievement. Dickinson's poetic soul moved from creation in solitude to creation toward the social. The period at the end of her life, when she was most withdrawn from face-to-face physical contact with society, was paradoxically the period when she moved her art out of the private production of the fascicles and fully into the social production of the letter-poems.

Emily Dickinson knew her Plato, and strangely, for the purposes of this discussion, her girlhood friendship (and correspondence) with Abiah Root involved the taking on of personae in which "Abiah was 'Plato' and Emily was 'Socrates'" (Sewall 372). (And Socrates was the speaker, Plato his scribe.) In his allegory, Hawthorne unwittingly prophesies Emily Dickinson, Artist of the Beautiful. I am not saying that Dickinson's reading of Plato or Hawthorne decided her course. I posit the possibility that Dickinson chose her way, informed by a full consciousness of a complex web of philosophical questions about the nature of the soul, its immortality, and the creation of art. These ideas were in the air, shared and debated by the important writers of her time, including Emerson and Hawthorne, both of whose work deeply affected her.[10] Ultimately these are spiritual or religious questions. The connection between the dialogues of Plato and Jesus brings me full circle to Dickinson's early struggle with Calvinism. In the poems of self-conversion she appropriates crisis conversation, the orthodox vehicle for uniting with Jesus Christ, and unites with poetic consciousness. In her late letter-poems, she appropriates the Gospels' dialogue as a vehicle for uniting with her reader and for making her words live.

In this undated poem Dickinson deals with the immortality of the word (and steals from the first lines of the Gospel of John):

> A word made Flesh is seldom
> And tremblingly partook
> No then perhaps reported
> But have I not mistook
> Each one of us has tasted
> With ecstasies of stealth
> The very food debated
> To our specific strength –
>
> A word that breathes distinctly
> Has not the power to die
> Cohesive as the Spirit
> It may expire if He –
> "Made Flesh and dwelt among us"
> Could condescension be
> Like this consent of Language
> This loved Philology
>
> (Fr 1715)

With respect to the question of what I have called Dickinson's relational poetics, "A word made Flesh" is an example of the living word "that breathes distinctly," that is immortal — it "has not the power to die" — precisely because it is "partook" by the reader. In erotic metaphysical language, she evokes the communion ritual (the Eucharist), the moment when the body of human mortal unites with the body of the immortal Christ. "This consent of Language" like Jesus's "condescension" that brings him down to earth to "[dwell] among us," engages us in dialogue with the distinctly breathing word. Significantly, the "consent of language" is a "*loved* Philology," just as writing poetry, for Dickinson, is an act of love toward another person who consents to be her reader.

So, too, we readers engage in a dialogue with Dickinson's living word. Each reader re-creates Emily Dickinson, as I have, and as Susan Howe suggests that she has in the title of her book, *My Emily Dickinson*. We are like Mark, Matthew, Luke, and John writing the Gospels: we tell our version of Emily Dickinson. But unlike the evangelists of the Bible, rather than assert that our words are the fixed truth, we can only seek truth, knowing that truth is a place we journey toward, but never reach: "Finite – to fail, but – infinite – to Venture" (Fr 952). We cannot know what her final intentions were for her manuscripts; yet our charge as readers is, somehow, to come close to those intentions. "As readers we cannot ignore the intentions of writers without an act of textual violence that threatens our own existence as textual beings," Scholes writes. "But neither can we ever close the communicative gap completely — and in many cases we must acknowledge that the gap is very wide indeed" (51).

How can we read Dickinson in print without committing "an act of textual violence"? Since the poet's texts have been brought into the publishing world, which is not a world purely of print, I propose that we allow the texts to live in their multiplicity, both in print and in script. The texts in Dickinson's own dazzling hand combine the word with the expressive line of the visual artist. They are the antecedent to concrete poems. I know they are poems because they make me feel what Dickinson says I should feel: "If I read a book and it makes my whole body so cold no fire can ever warm me, I know *that* is poetry. If I feel physically as if the top of my head were taken off, I know *that* is poetry" (L 342A). They, too, should "dwell in Possibility – / A fairer House than Prose –" (Fr 466).

Dare I say it? These handwritten texts are beautiful. They are the last distinctly breathing words of a soul in changing rapture, of Emily Dickinson, Artist of the Beautiful, a Possibility.

NOTES

1. Travisano writes: "Looked at in mid career, Bishop's work did not clearly reflect what Anne Stevenson, her first biographer, called 'a sense of growth, of what might be called a development in understanding.' Stevenson's 1966 book was based on the premise that 'Bishop's work, elegant and eloquent as it often is, does not achieve this kind of organic unity.' This assessment was echoed by many others, including Jerome Mazzaro, who, commenting on the separateness of individual poems, concluded in a 1969 review: 'This sense of boundaries, which makes her an ideal poet for anthologies, mitigates against any cumulative effect and keeps her work discrete.' More recently, Kalstone made a contrary observation. Noting that 'she has become known as the author of single, stunning poems,' Kalstone rightly suggests the inadequacy of Stevenson's and Mazzaro's view: 'Wonderful as the anthologized poems may be, they give, even for anthologies, an unusually stunted version of Bishop's variety, of the way her writing has emerged, of her developing concerns.' Unfortunately, Kalstone does not survey Bishop's development himself. This suggests the need for a chronological study of her artistic evolution, a study that outlines and explores the 'developing concerns' of Bishop's career, defining the nature of its 'organic unity'" (6–7).

2. Two excellent studies that explore Dickinson's cultural influences are David S. Reynolds's *Beneath the American Renaissance: The Subversive Imagination in the Age of Emerson and Melville* (1989) and Barton Levi St. Armand's *Emily Dickinson and Her Culture: The Soul's Society* (1984). The biographies by Richard Sewall, Cynthia Griffin Wolff, and Alfred Habegger are also, of course, replete with such cultural considerations.

3. Each of these writers — Emerson, Thoreau, Whitman, and Dickinson — were inspired and influenced by other writers (of course, the work of the latter three is unimaginable without Emerson). Although Emerson names Plato as one of the sages whose light should not blind us to our own, he himself writes in his journal that to inspire writing he has "often used Plato" (*Heart* 311). He also notes that in the university, to be sure "the Imagination [in the scholar] is cared for and cherished," and "that Enthusiasm is not repressed. . . . Teach him Shakespeare. Teach him Plato" (ibid., 314). In another twist of influence and the denial of it, Emerson is unimaginable without Plato.

4. See John Cody's *After Great Pain: The Inner Life of Emily Dickinson*, Vivian R. Pollak's *Dickinson: The Anxiety of Gender*, and Maryanne M. Garbowsky, *The House without the Door: A Study of Emily Dickinson and the Illness of Agoraphobia*.

5. Finch says that Dickinson does use two "hymn-stanza lines" in the last quatrain. My point is that she does not return to a regular hymnal quatrain of alternating 8s and 6s, as an alternative to iambic pentameter.

6. It is not an accident that the poems of 1863 coincide with the Civil War. Eliza-beth Phillips argues that poems in this period, such as "I felt a funeral in my brain," which have been read psychobiographically as evidence of Dickinson's having a mental breakdown, should be read as the poet's taking on personae and performing them in her work. She connects some of these poems to the Civil War and the death of Frazer Sterns, a family friend, and the first soldier from Amherst who was killed in the war. Dickinson wrote that "Austin is chilled" by the death of his friend: "his brain keeps saying Frazer is killed. . . . Two or three words of lead—that dropped so deep, they keep weighing" (L 256). Phillips writes: "'I felt a funeral in my brain' probably has its origins, then, not in the poet's collapse, but in her sympathetic and imaginative participation with those she loved in the rites for the ruddy-faced boy they had all finished knowing. Its 'words of lead' belong . . . to a sequence of four poems that culminate in an elegy expressing grati-tude for the sacrifice he embodied" (50). Though Phillips does not identify "After great pain" as one of the sequence, it would fit into her reading. The question, "'Was it He, that bore,' / And 'Yesterday, or Centuries before'?" could refer to the sacrifice of Frazer—or any soldier—"Yesterday" or Christ "Centuries before." Furthermore, the "Hour of Lead" echoes the "two of three words of lead" in Dickinson's letter and the "Boots of Lead" in "Funeral." The "Lead" may refer to the bullet that wounds the soldier, and the "Hour" to the period of pain "Remembered, if outlived," if the man survives his injury. The numbness of the first stanza describes the body in shock "after great pain." In addition to the physical suffering of the soldier, "After great pain" can be seen also as the failed "deathbed conversion" of the soldier. (See my reading of "I heard a Fly buzz" in "the Ad-venture of the Self" for more about deathbed conversions.) To understand "After great pain" and other poems of the period in the context of the Civil War actually enhances my argument that these poems struggle deeply with questions of salvation, with God's choice to elect a few to heaven and damn the many to hell, and with the evil with which God afflicts the world. In her *Emily Dickinson: A Voice of War*, Shira Wolosky observes: "Dickinson's religious doubts became acute, or at least expressed, at a time of violence in which religion was implicated" (98). At the historical moment when God's malevolence against humanity was most agonizingly visible to her, Dickinson favored self-conversion rather than conversion to Him. Wolosky writes: "the contradictions involved in a be-nevolent and omnipotent God remains preeminent for Dickinson. It extends beyond the fact of war, which finally becomes an instance—and at times a model—for Dickinson's confrontation with evil and suffering. And the theodicy invoked for war, as for suffering in general, becomes less and less satisfactory. The Civil War, as a War of religious rheto-ric, helped undermine that rhetoric as a justification of evil. As a way of God, it helped cast doubt on his ways" (95). Wolosky's study is essential for those interested in an in-depth analysis of Dickinson's poetic and theological response to the war. While my study does not deal extensively with the Civil War, it does deal with the theological issues that were debated and grimly intensified during the war.

7. For further explorations of Emily Dickinson's private mythology, see St. Armand's *Emily Dickinson and Her Culture: The Soul's Society*. St. Armand devises an enlightening chart of Dickinson's "Mystic Day," in which he synthesizes the mythological associa-tions the poet made among the times of day, seasons, directions, flowers, psychological,

spiritual and religious states, and so on. See also Rebecca Patterson's *Emily Dickinson's Imagery*.

8. Here, as in so many poems and letters by Dickinson, one hears the echo of Blake. In *Emily Dickinson's Reading: 1836–1886*, Jack L. Capps writes: "Although she seldom uses quotations from the Romantic poets, her own writing shows a love of natural beauty, a belief in man's innate goodness, and a faith in human intuition typical of the Romantic attitude. There is, for instance, no concrete evidence of her having read Blake, still she realized as completely as he how 'To see a World in a grain of sand, / And a Heaven in a wild flower; / Hold infinity in the palm of your hand, / And eternity in an hour.'" Both Dickinson's "Far from Love the Heavenly Father" and Blake's "The Garden of Love" compare the dictates of religion to "Briars" and the innocence of Edenic love to the flowers of the meadow. Both see the interdictions of orthodoxy as a kind of living death; they see a terrible irony in the idea that in order to secure eternal life one must "bind with briars [one's] joys & desires." The two poems, however, differ significantly on the question of culpability. Dickinson places the blame on "the Heavenly Father," who leads with "the Claw of a Dragon" rather than "the Hand of Friend." Blake, in contrast, blames the priests who disseminate such beliefs:

> I went to the Garden of Love,
> And saw what I never had seen:
> A Chapel was built in the midst,
> Where I used to play on the green.
>
> And the gates of this Chapel were shut,
> And "Thou shalt not" writ over the door;
> So I turn'd to the Garden of Love
> That so many sweet flowers bore;
>
> And I saw it was filled with graves,
> And tombstones where flowers should be;
> And Priests in black gowns were walking their rounds,
> And binding with briars my joys & desires.

9. In my work at the Robert Frost Library at Amherst College, I discovered that Dickinson sent Thomas Niles "Further in Summer" and "It sifts from leaden sieves" (Fr 291) with a note that read "I bring you a chill Gift – my Cricket – and the Snow"; she enclosed a cricket carcass, carefully wrapped in paper.

10. Weisbuch makes the connection between Dickinson's philosophical explorations and those of Kant: "Dickinson cannot take seriously the all-or-nothing question of whether the internal or the external is the source of the other. . . . Dickinson's poetic techniques generally put the question aside to examine things-as-they-are. . . . I do not wish to picture Dickinson poring over the Critique of Pure Reason, but she shares Kant's sense of the futility of the prior debate and reaches toward the same conclusions. Bertrand Russell neatly summarizes Kant's resolution: 'According to Kant, the outer world causes only the matter of sensation, but our own mental apparatus orders this matter in space and time, and supplies the concepts by means of which we understand experience.

Things in themselves, which are the causes of our sensations, are unknowable; they are not in space and time. . . . Space and time are subjective, they are part of our apparatus of perception'" (160–61).

11. How the readers' edition of Dickinson's work was established by Thomas H. Johnson, what the order (or disorder) of the fascicles might mean, how we should read the variants, what reading Dickinson in manuscript might reveal, how the letters were edited, and whether the letters cross genres into poetry are subjects of much critical debate by Ralph W. Franklin (who edited the new variorum edition of Dickinson's poems published in 1998 and the readers' edition published in 1999), Paula Bennett, Sharon Cameron, Ellen Louise Hart, Susan Howe, Dorothy Huff Oberhaus, Erika Scheurer, Martha Nell Smith, William Shurr, Lewis Putnam Turco, and Marta Werner, among others.

12. I use Johnson rather than Franklin in this discussion because in his new editions, Franklin uses essentially the same methodology as does Johnson. Further, it is Johnson who established the Dickinson canon of record; Franklin builds on his work.

13. I have lineated all these pieces as they appear in manuscript.

14. This is a Christmas message written in 1885 to Kendall Emerson. Emerson was a young friend of Dickinson's nephew, Gilbert Dickinson, who died in 1883 at the age of eight.

15. Marta Werner's book, *Emily Dickinson's Open Folios: Scenes of Reading, Surfaces of Writing* gathers together forty facsimiles of the Lord letters, drafts, and fragments, and includes a lengthy scholarly introduction. Werner has also published a digital book, *Radical Scatters: An Electronic Archive of Emily Dickinson's Late Fragments* (University of Michigan Press, 2000), a compilation of Dickinson manuscripts and an essay. *Radical Scatters*, unfortunately, is not readily available, as only institutions may subscribe to it. Furthermore, the copyright restricts use in a way that makes the archive difficult and frustrating to use. Ellen Louise Hart and Martha Nell Smith have gathered the correspondence between Emily and Sue in *Open Me Carefully: Emily Dickinson's Letters to Susan Huntington Dickinson* (Ashfield, Mass.: Paris Press, 1998). In the works is a project to compile a hypermedia archive of all Dickinson's extant written work in print and in manuscript. See Martha Nell Smith's "The Importance of a Hypermedia Archive of Dickinson's Creative Work." That archive, edited by Smith, can be found at "Dickinson Electronic Archives" http://jefferson.village.virginia.edu/dickinson/. Like *Radical Scatters*, the archive has restricted access. Despite the good work of scholars such as Werner and Smith to make the manuscripts easily available, their accessibility remains extremely circumscribed, whether they are in an archive in a physical library at Amherst or Harvard or whether they are in an electronic one at the University of Michigan or the University of Virginia.

16. There are several studies of Dickinson's development. William R. Sherwood bases his book *Circumference and Circumstance: Stages in the Mind and Art of Emily Dickinson* on the "assumption that poetry is a form of autobiography" (vii). To him the Reverend Charles Wadworth is Emily Dickinson's "own god" (230). Dickinson's relationship with the reverend is the focal point of his book; he understands the work and career through it. Dickinson is mastered by her relationship to Wadsworth and likewise must

finally be mastered by Puritanism. At the end of her life, Sherwood maintains, Puritanism became a "conviction"; transcendentalism "was a passing fancy" (231). Sherwood's Emily Dickinson is ladylike, conservative, aristocratic, and ultimately too tidy and formal not to submit to Puritan orthodoxy: "she disliked nature untamed and unsurveyed . . . despised people too stupid to know their place. . . . transcendentalism could never have satisfied her: it was too messy, and too democratic" (233).

In his *The Marriage of Emily Dickinson*, William H. Shurr traces the development of Dickinson's poetry by looking at the order of the fascicles. Like Sherwood, Shurr regards the poems as autobiography. Shurr believes if we don't investigate the autobiographical truth of the fascicles' love story, we must assume that Dickinson never sent the poems to her lover. That assumption sets us "light-years back to . . . 'poor Emily,' talking only to herself" (10). Thus, "[t]he canons of esthetics still apply, but now as secondary to the canons of correspondence and autobiography" (10). According to Shurr, the fascicles reveal a plot in which Dickinson and Wadsworth fall in love and, since he is already married, in 1860 agree to a spiritual marriage. In 1861 they consummate the marriage "with pregnancy or the deep fear of pregnancy as the result. In her later poems Dickinson responds to the events in Wadsworth's life, to a brief renewed intimacy with him, and finally to his death in 1882" (186).

I find it hard to take seriously the autobiographical "facts" that Sherwood and Shurr derive from Dickinson's poems. Lines such as "I heard a Fly buzz – when I died," "My Life had stood – a Loaded Gun," "And Consciousness – is Noon," and "We send the Wave to find the Wave" (which, it is fair to say, are typical of her verse) invite the reader to abandon the search for a literal level in her poetry, much less an autobiographical one. The elusive literal level in her work claims for her, no less than for Whitman, the authority to be an Emersonian representative poet. To this end she instructs her reader Thomas Wentworth Higginson, "When I state myself, as Representative of the Verse—it does not mean—me—but a 'supposed' person" (L 268). This is not to say that biographical information is irrelevant to reading Dickinson's poetry—I base much of my thought about the poetry on the fact that she never converted—but to say that perhaps it is more fruitful to consider *how* she loved in her poetry than *whom* she loved in her life.

Two studies come close to my approach in that they assume that Dickinson's poetic development reflects the development of her style and ideas. These are by David Porter and Timothy Morris. David Porter's *The Art of Emily Dickinson's Early Poetry* concentrates on the poetry through the year 1862. By charting the development of the early poems, Porter hopes to establish "a perspective from which a further search for developmental patterns may be launched" (x). His study explores how Dickinson's early work culminates in the powerful poems of 1863 (then dated 1862): "[T]he early stylistic habits equipped her for the enormous flood of poetry in year 1862 and after" (ix). Porter regards Dickinson as an accomplished artist rather than as a strange spinster. As the title of his concluding chapter—"The Early Achievement"—indicates, his book, published in 1966, seeks to correct some of the more disparaging accounts of Dickinson's work.

In his essay, "The Development of Emily Dickinson's Style," Timothy Morris argues that Dickinson's "book," like Whitman's *Leaves of Grass*, was "very much a work in progress" (172). Using Indian summer as his example, he shows how Dickinson reworks themes in three distinct ways. The early versions are more regular and more conventional; the middle are less regular and more obscure; the last are "haikuizations." Morris concentrates on Dickinson's style and technique, on how her poetry departs from convention. For the most part, form and content are estranged in his account of her development. Perhaps because her reworkings are central to Morris's argument, Dickinson's ideas do not change so much; rather, she grows more adept at expressing them.

Both Porter and Morris maintain that the nature of Dickinson's work is internal. Porter observes: "[S]he had by 1862 developed her unique ability to dissociate feelings from the limitations of specific causal experiences. Her poems exist independent of the confining facts of exterior experience, and become thereby increasingly universal" (175). Morris concludes: "Her work is inward-directed. . . . The most distinctive thing about her poetry is, finally, the intensely problematic nature of her painstaking and often enigmatic adaptation of her private texts" (172). For me, Dickinson's poetry is neither merely internal and private, as Morris would have it, nor simply internal and universal, as Porter would have it. Both authors suggest that almost entirely separated from causal fact or event, the poems reside entirely in the interior. Porter assumes that internal worlds are universal and, since Dickinson is a good poet, the reader will empathize. Because both exclude the external world, neither critic allows Dickinson to rename experience. I do not believe her poetry substitutes one world for another. Rather, the poetry concerns itself with the question of the boundary between internal and external, as Dickinson indicates when she writes to Higginson, "My Business is Circumference" (L 268) The questions that accompany the internal and the external—those of influence, appropriation, and culture, of the public and the private, of representative and universal poetry—reveal a great deal about Dickinson's development, for she negotiates the internal and the external in different ways at different times in her career.

The scholar with whose work on development I feel a strong and grateful kinship is Hyatt Waggoner. In his chapter on Emily Dickinson, "Proud Ephemeral," in his *American Poets, from the Puritans to the Present*, Waggoner asserts that without an assessment of the poet's "growth," "[w]e are left . . . with Dickinson's lack of consistency in belief as a problem" (201). Like me, Waggoner observes her movement from a struggle with Calvinism to one with Emersonian transcendentalism: "She debated with her father on the subject of the validity of his faith, she debated Emerson on the validity of his, and she debated with both of them, her two fathers as it were, on the question of whether there could be any valid faith at all, as they both thought" (205). Unlike me, Waggoner does not delineate four stages of her poetic development. His work on development is part of a chapter that situates Dickinson in the context of three and a half centuries of American poetry; mine is a full-length study. Other scholars, particularly her biographer, Cynthia Griffin Wolff, make Dickinson's development implicit in their work, but development per se is not their explicit subject.

The premise of Alfred Habegger's biography, *My Wars Are Laid Away in Books: The Life of Emily Dickinson*, is that "[t]here is development over time, in other words, and this directional trend becomes a map by which readers steer" (xiii). While he does cite other doctoral theses, he does not cite my 1995 dissertation, "While Rapture Changed its Dress: The Development of Emily Dickinson's Poetry." Nor does he cite my essay, "Mastering the Master: Emily Dickinson's Appropriation of Crisis Conversion" (in *The*

Calvinist Roots of the Modern Era, ed. Barnstone, Manson, and Singley), in which I delineate the first two stages of the Dickinson's development. Habegger's biography differs from Sewall's and Wolff's in that his main objective is to create a chronological narrative of the poet's life. That narrative is a good read, lively and full of historical detail, but there is very little analysis of the poetry. While Habegger's assertions about Dickinson's development are eerily close to mine, his approach is fundamentally different than mine. He, like earlier scholars whose methods I criticize above, uses the poems as evidence for events that he postulates occurred in the poet's life. For example, the poem "The Soul selects her own Society" (Fr 409A) is used to back up the statement that "[Samuel] Bowles no longer had the key to Dickinson's attention" (450). In this book I put Dickinson's work in a philosophical and cultural context of ideas, and show ways to read the poems closely within the framework of development. Her biography is important to me insofar as it provides the reader with an understanding of the major intellectual currents of the day as well as the issues vexing or fascinating the poet. I am not concerned with using the poems to show what may or — just as probably — may not have happened in her real life; I am interested in what transpired in the life of Dickinson's imagination.

17. In discussing the reigning critical assumptions about Dickinson's work, Sharon Cameron writes in a note: "Certainly the history of Dickinson criticism from the 1890's to the present . . . has preserved a consistent account of the poet. . . . Specifically, as the chronology of the poems is not seen to signal development, critics are deprived of one conventional way of discussing the poetry, and this deprivation is often countered by certain primitive groupings of poems, according to thematic similarities, formal properties, evaluative assessments which discriminate poems that are successful from those that are not — with the constant implication that there is no inherent way of understanding relations among poems. The taxonomies advanced for Dickinson's poems are different from those advanced for other poets, because when the poems are sorted it is precisely to emphasize idiosyncrasies and repetitions, as if what Dickinson had to teach us were that there is no way to comprehend the alien except by the most critically reductive strategies of categorizing and comparison" (*Choosing Not Choosing* 1–2 n). Although I am not sure that there is ever an "inherent way of understanding relations among poems," I am sure that reading poems in the context of development serves as a most plausible method of understanding the relations among Dickinson's poems.

18. Dickinson's first extant letter is dated April 18, 1942; she was eleven. A study of the earliest letters could reveal much about how Dickinson developed into a poet. I begin my study, however, with her first transcriptions of poems into fair copy.

19. Sandra M. Gilbert writes of the poet's self-mythologizing: Dickinson used "all the materials of daily reality, and most especially the details of domesticity, as if they were not facts but metaphors" in order to "recreate herself-and-her-life as a single, emblematic test" (23).

1. "BURGLAR! BANKER – FATHER!" RENAMING GOD THROUGH SATIRE (PP. 30–53)

1. This idea came from a conversation with my colleague Michael Payne.

2. In *Comic Power in Emily Dickinson*, Suzanne Juhasz, Cristanne Miller, and

Martha Nell Smith argue that "a feminist critical approach to Dickinson's comedy reveals a poet whose topic and audience are larger than herself." They argue, as I do, that comedy is subversive and is a way of critiquing prevailing social conventions. They also argue against critics (specifically John Cody, Paula Bennett, and Vivian Pollak) who see Dickinson as a tragic figure whose "audience is herself" (2). These critics, Juhasz, Miller, and Smith contend, demean Dickinson's poetry because it is as seen merely as self-therapy and self-expression, with a limited "circumference": "Without reference, then, to the performative aspect of the literary act, that is, to the complex function of any poem, such critics end by simplifying not only the affective purpose of the poem but its content as well" (2).

Comic Power owes a debt to Elizabeth Phillips's book Emily Dickinson: Personae and Performance (University Park: Penn State Press, 1988), though the authors do not cite Phillips. Phillips, like Juhazs, Miller, and Smith, argues that "readings in which the daring innovative qualities of the poems yield to psychobiography and the belief that the subject is always Dickinson herself tend also to be reductive in relation to much that interested her. She is, moreover, nearly dispossessed of the magnitude of the work of a single woman whose sense of creative freedom was consonant with the virtuosity of the 'performance'" (2–3). Phillips traces the ways in which Dickinson transformed her readings of Shakespeare, the Brownings, Charlotte Brontë, and others in order to create her own personae and dramatic monologues, elements that should not necessarily be traced to events (that may or may not have taken place) in Dickinson's own life.

3. Both Cynthia Griffin Wolff and Paula Bennett have chapters in their books entitled "Pugilist and Poet." The title comes from a letter to Higginson in which Dickinson writes, "Audacity of Bliss, said Jacob to the Angel 'I will not let thee go except I bless thee'—Pugilist and Poet, Jacob was correct" (L 1042).

4. Wolff maintains that the poet "pursue[s] the heroic quest by wrestling with the word and creating even as God had created, by sowing Logos. . . . Jacob's struggle was a starting point for Dickinson as artist" (151). Richard S. Ellis has written a fascinating essay, "'A little East of Jordan': Human-Divine Encounter in Dickinson and the Hebrew Bible." He writes: "As in the Hebrew Bible, in this poem Dickinson's use of such devices as paradox, wordplay, and shifts of perspective reflects her understanding of the hierarchical/intimate relationship offered by God to Jacob and to her. Like God, the poem invites the reader into a hierarchical/intimate relationship with itself, in which the reader must imaginatively coordinate multiple perspectives, synthesizing the poet's desire both to control meaning and to engender open-endedness and multiplicity of meaning. Relax, the poem urges. Play with me, wrestle with me, as God did with Jacob at Peniel" (46). Ellis observes that "the human-divine encounter is unportrayable because finite human awareness, mediated by the finitude of language, cannot grasp the infinitude of God" (51). Both Dickinson and the Torah "crafted their dazzling panoplies of literary artifice so that this unportrayable encounter could be portrayed" (52).

5. In "In the Waiting Room" Bishop's child speaker wonders "What similarities— / . . . / held us all together / or made us all just one? / How—I didn't know any / word for it—how 'unlikely.'"

6. Two other examples are the poems beginning "Talk with prudence to a Beggar / of 'Potosi,' and the mines!" (Fr 118; 1859) and "As Watchers hang upon the East— / As Beggars revel at a feast" (Fr 120; 1859).

7. Dickinson has been accused of not being concerned about the outer social universe. In her essay, "Emily Dickinson and Class," Betsy Erkkila makes some of the most egregious charges against the poet (while also arguing that her sentimental sisters did more for society than the poet). Dickinson did have a social conscience and was aware and took to heart the suffering of others. In her essay, "New Dickinson Civil War Publications," Karen Dandurand shows that Dickinson published poems in *Drum Beat*, a paper devoted to raising funds for the Civil War, and asks "us to reconsider [her] . . . supposed indifference to the catastrophic events of the Civil War" (17). Shira Wolosky thoroughly examines the poet's response to the Civil War in her *Emily Dickinson: A Voice of War*. In *Comic Power*, Smith takes Erkkila to task for her claim in *Wicked Sisters: Women Poets, Literary History, and Discord* that Dickinson "set herself against the abolitionist, reformist, and democratizing energies of the times" (7). Erkkila, Smith asserts, "ignores many of Dickinson's direct commentaries about politics, the most significant of which are her lifelong complaints about her disenfranchised status as a woman. When the poet was twenty-one, she opined, "Why I can't I be a Delegate to the great Whig Convention? — don't I know all about Daniel Webster and the Tariff and the Law? (L 94), then three decades later sardonically observed that "Little Boys are commemorating the advent of their Country (L 650)" (146 n).

8. Charles Dickens was one of Edward Dickinson's favorite authors, and it is clear from references in her letters and poems that Emily was thoroughly familiar with the novelist, appropriating and playing upon his work. In *Comic Power*, Smith argues that the poem "A poor – torn heart – a tattered heart" is an ironic take on "the one-dimensional, cartoon-like quality of nineteenth-century notions regulating women to a 'separate sexual caste' " (77). Because when Dickinson sent the poem to Sue, she attached two pictures of Dickens's Little Nell, Smith asserts the poem is satirical: "In this context calling attention to her appropriations of Dickens' work and the poem's hyperbolic overstatement, a lyric that might be either disregarded or read earnestly as religious or romantic sentiment becomes the cartooning play of one writer responding to another. The fact that her own surname christened her 'Dicken's son' was surely not lost on this writer so given to puns and verbal play. What is also clear from Dickinson making this poem in direct response to Dickens and then sending it to Sue is the women's communion and mutual play as readers, kinds of interpretive interaction common among America's literate classes" (78).

9. Pascal Covici writes that "humor that has concerned itself with confounding itself with easy assumptions about the transparency of God's will, of the real world, of the human psyche, does indeed offer something 'solid' to put on the place of the genteel tradition [which attempts to evade the questions and ambiguity such humor raises, and for which Covici uses Dickinson's friend, Josiah Holland as the exemplar]. Such humor may not—of course it cannot—remove those doubts 'too profound to bear.' It did, it does, function to help readers to cope with mystery as well as with pain. Both abound when we cut the ties to what we have known, culturally or psychologically" (173). So

Dickinson's satirical humor serves as a first step to later poems that unblinkingly expose those doubts "too profound to bear."

10. For more on Dickinson and Moore see Cynthia Hogue's "'The Plucked String': Emily Dickinson, Marianne Moore and the Poetics of Select Defects."

11. Eleanor Heginbotham associates these lines with Milton: "Satan and the Dickinson of many poems maneuver by way of angled roads. Dickinson's slant ways to truth suggest the poet's visualization of Milton's 'oblique route of Satan down to Eden. . . . Perhaps she noted Raphael's counsel to Adam to take the plain path" (64).

12. In *Comic Power*, Juhazs writes of the child persona: "The perspective of ingenuousness in Dickinson's poetry is a tease from the word go, because it is a role assumed by an educated, adult, cultured woman. It is a way to play at innocence, to imagine a condition beyond the full constraints of culture, and then to use it as a position from which to critique the culture. A sophisticated person pretends to be an unsophisticated person in order to make a sophisticated point" (29).

13. I do not rule out the possibility that Dickinson plays on other texts, as well. Heginbotham's tracing the first stanza of this poem to Milton is certainly valid. For my purpose, which is to show the ways in which Dickinson satirizes conventional thought, it is important to consider that the Bible and Emerson's "Self-Reliance" would be thoroughly familiar to Dickinson's peers.

14. Erkkila writes that "the language of Dickinson's poems slips between the old and the new, between an aristocratic language of rank, royalty, and hereditary privilege, and a Calvinist language of spiritual grace, personal sanctity, and divine election, in which the aristocratic ideals of hierarchy and social subordination are displaced from the secular to the divine arena. . . . For her, as for other conservative New England Whigs, the notion of a divinely elected spiritual aristocracy predestined to power served ultimately to support a hierarchical social order against the more public, egalitarian rhetoric of the time" (9). As I have been arguing, Dickinson's poems satirize just such displacements of social hierarchy onto the question of divine redemption.

15. The poem also serves as a critique of a watered-down Calvinism, for Calvinism rejects the doctrine of good works. It is the will of God to choose who is and is not predestined for election, and the will of God is inscrutable to humanity.

16. Dickinson may also have been thinking of Thoreau's "Resistance to Civil Government" (published 1849), which owes a tremendous debt to Emerson's thought: "I think we should be men first, and subjects afterward. It is not desirable to cultivate a respect for the law, so much as for the right. The only obligation which I have a right to assume is to do at any time what I think right. . . . Law never made men a whit more just; and, by means of their respect for it, even the well-disposed are daily made the agents of injustice."

17. This poem is in dialogue with Emerson's idea in "The Over-Soul": "A certain tendency to insanity has always attended the opening of the religious sense in men, as if they had been 'blasted with excess of light'" (210). Significantly, Plato, to whom Emerson is deeply indebted, discusses exactly this conundrum of the artist as the divine seer who is deemed mad. Dickinson's poem is a remarkable echo of Plato's language and ideas: "And a third kind of possession and madness comes from the Muses. This takes hold

upon a gentle and pure soul, arouses it and inspires it to songs and other poetry. . . . But he who without the divine madness comes to the door of the Muses, confident that he will be a good poet by art, meets with no success, and the poetry of the sane man vanishes into nothingness before that of the inspired madmen" (*Phaedrus* 245A).

18. In *Comic Power*, Juhasz sees this strategy as the tease of the bad girl: "The poet as tease: this is voice of the bad girl, who will not be silenced, who will come out in words before the world. Simply by speaking, this poet puts into question all laws and rules. Consequently, the world of the poem, that space between the inside and outside, safety and danger becomes an alternative world, standing in critical relation to its readers and the culture in which they reside and read" (58).

19. See Emerson's essay of the same name.

20. In his study on the way in which the establishment of democracy in the United States affected religious ethics and influenced literature, Richard Forrer explains that "such factors as the more democratic climate of the latter 1700s and early 1800s, the emergence of deism, and an increasing skepticism in religious matters prompted many to reject the Puritan theodicy and its synthesis of world view and ethos. Such representative liberal theologians as Jonathan Mayhew, Charles Chauncy, and William Ellery Channing argued that the sovereign God of Puritan orthodoxy was an amoral deity, an unjust tyrant, whose arbitrary disposition of human destinies denies people any reliable foundation for the moral life. Such seeming capriciousness on God's part represented to these theologians not only an unwarranted abuse of divine power but also the same gross disrespect for human life against which they struggled in earthly authorities. Their orientation toward the increasingly democratic ethos of American culture led them to reject the Puritan theodicy as ethically unacceptable and to replace it with a theodicy which was its opposite, a theodicy which expressed the rationalistic and egalitarian values shaping the emerging American Republic" (5).

21. St. Armand enumerates the types of thought that influenced Dickinson: "Her use of a common Calvinist rhetoric, already reeling from the redefinitions of gradualists like Horace Bushnell and sentimentalists like Harriet Beecher Stowe, confirmed the tight logic of its grammar while ironically narrowing the syntax and personalizing the meanings . . . . Calvinism was not the only language that Dickinson spoke with an individual accent. There were the competing dialects of Transcendentalism, Gothicism, primitivism, occultism, and Ruskinism" (17).

22. See St. Armand, who establishes some of the ways in which Dickinson's work is informed by the Sentimental Love Religion. St. Armand takes his cue from Leslie Fiedler, who coined the term, "Sentimental Love Religion," in *Love and Death in the American Novel*.

23. Elizabeth A. Petrino writes: "Emily Dickinson's assurance of God's love was deeply troubled by the deaths of children. Ravaged by tuberculosis and childhood diseases, most children born in the nineteenth century died before reaching adolescence; of those, more than half died before they reached the age of five. Neither the severe Calvinist God of Jonathan Edwards nor the merciful 'Everlasting All' of Isaac Watts's hymns could rationalize adequately the death of an innocent child" (53–54). Petrino also suggests that Dickinson derides the sentimental view of childhood death, at the same time

that she appropriates its tropes: "In the child elegy, Dickinson expresses her dissatisfaction with the contemporary consolation myth that the child enjoys a blissful existence after death. Like [Lydia] Sygourney's tribute volume, her poems frequently empower the child, who revenges himself for his early death on those who are left behind. Rather than offering the grieving family reasons to let the child go, she reverses the standard consolation format by depicting a dead child who himself mourns for his family. She thus undercuts the consolation offered to the mourner by openly portraying the pain and anxiety that the child goes through in life and death. Even in poems that do not specifically commemorate the death of an actual child, she suggests that the promise of an untroubled reunion between parents and child in heaven is ultimately delusive" (56).

24. Martha Dickinson Bianchi puts Lavinia's letter into perspective. Bianchi was taught as a child that questions about Aunt Emily should not be answered. Of Lavinia she writes: "Lavinia was a New Englander of New Englanders. To her it was a sacriledge for any outsider to suppose her idolized sister could have had a 'disappointment' in love. To the curious she denied it fiercely" (52).

25. Though Martha Dickinson Bianchi, in keeping with the "Dickinson reserve" (50) does not mention his name, she indicates that Emily fell in love with Charles Wadsworth, the Philadephia minister: "The testimony of her closest contemporary leaves no doubt that during her visit to Philadelphia, following her stay in Washington, my aunt met the man who was henceforth to stand to her for the Power and the Glory, and with whom, in the phrase of the day, she 'fell in love.' These contemporaries were agreed that any further development of what was stated to be their mutual recognition of each other was impossible, owing to the fact that he was already married. According to them, the definite renunciation followed a brief interview in her father's house, and left a permanent effect upon my aunt's life and vision (50 n).

26. "Dickinson employs the conventional terms of male power and female powerlessness," Paula Bennett writes in her discussion of the poet's relationship to the masculine: "So closely does Dickinson identify the male lover with the male governing principle that in some poems it is impossible to tell whom the speaker is addressing: a lover or God" (*Emily Dickinson* 158).

27. For a thorough exploration of woman's sphere see Cott's *The Bonds of Womanhood: "Woman's Sphere" in New England, 1780–1835.*

28. In her argument for a traditional Marxism and against the French feminist "emphasis on language as a site for political transformation," Erkkila writes: "If on the level of language Dickinson might be celebrated as a kind of literary terrorist—a 'loaded gun' and dancing 'Bomb'—who blew up the social and symbolic orders of patriarchal language, it is also important that we recognize that her poetic revolution was grounded in the privilege of her class position in a conservative Whig household whose elitist, antidemocratic values were at the very center of her work" (22–23). Perhaps we should imagine God sent Emily Dickinson to Purgatory Camp to be reeducated with the rest of the world's persecuted writers?

29. Barbara Antonina Clarke Mossberg writes of "Over the fence": "Dickinson presents her relationship with God, and the moral dilemma she experiences as a woman poet in her society, as daughter-father conflict. . . . The little girl . . . is torn between her

desire for berries . . . and her sense that going 'over the fence' is a defiance of God's will. . . . The real 'fence' is God or society's forbidding her to 'climb.' . . . going over the fence is a sin" (117–18). In *Comic Power*, Juhasz writes that the poem emphasizes "the speaker's gendered distance from her God": "God may once have been a boy (a climber), but this speaker is clearly a girl. Her boyish desire to climb, therefore, makes her a bad girl because she would make a good boy. She is prohibited from her natural bent by gender rules that inhibit childish behavior in girls, who are therefore negated as children as well as adults. . . . [God's] rules make her an altogether different species: entirely marginal" (36).

30. William Merrill Decker, in *Epistolary Practices: Letter Writing in America before Telecommunications*, writes: "In early letters Dickinson resorts to satire in general and sacrilege in particular in an effort to assert her own subjective space, to formulate her emphatic, even her eternal, difference from others, and to propose to her correspondents the terms of such intense, dangerous, and exclusive bonds as she then sought" (149–50).

2. MASTERING THE MASTER: APPROPRIATIONS OF CRISIS CONVERSION IN THE POEMS OF 1863 (PP. 54–75)

1. While this poem is dated late in Dickinson's life, she retains her wit and her penchant for satire throughout her career. Because a poet develops does not mean that she completely abandons the old devices. Frequently, poets imitate themselves late in life. There is also the possibility that she copied this poem in 1882 from an early draft, now destroyed.

2. Traditionally, Dickinson's annus mirabilis has been set at 1862, based on Johnson's dating, but Franklin's 1998 Variorum sets the date at 1863.

3. When I describe the self in pain, I do not wish to engage in the kind of psychobiography — correctly refuted by Juhasz, Miller, and Smith in *Comic Power* and by Elizabeth Phillips in *Emily Dickinson: Personae and Performance* — that one-dimensionally portrays Dickinson as a tragic figure. From my perspective, Phillips makes an excellent point when she observes that the poems from this period are intense dramatic monologues and literary performances: "She writes 'as the Representative' of the verse and the 'supposed person' to claim the privilege to draw upon whatever resources are available to her for writing. . . . the dramatic monologue is a genre by which to move beyond 'me, myself' into a relationship with them. The view that she wrote almost exclusively about herself, however, pervades Dickinson studies" (81). As all writers must, Dickinson drew on her own experiences in order to dramatize the "supposed person." I am depicting a process in this chapter, as well as the ways in which, through her writing, the poet traversed the theological and relational realms.

4. These words in letter 271 scan perfectly in iambic tetrameters and trimeters, Dickinson's characteristic hymnal meter. Her letters carry the same poetics as her identified verse, as well as the same spiritual battle for liberation.

5. "Omissions are not accidents," written by Moore, is the epigraph of *The Complete Poems of Marianne Moore*.

6. The manuscript (ML3) was written in ink, corrected in pencil; words Dickinson crossed out I have indicated by striking through. I have reproduced the line breaks of the letter in my transcription.

7. James McIntosh writes that one of "Dickinson's key principles . . . is the idea that belief and thought and feeling are transient, that one's mental life is continually in flux. Mostly, Dickinson prefers it that way. . . . she cherishes evanescence and makes poetry out of 'internal difference'" (2).

8. St. Armand calls this poem "a negative crisis conversion to unbelief" (239).

9. As Wolff sees it, God still refuses to loosen the Seal of Revelation; instead he inflicts the "Seal Despair."

10. St. Armand sees the "air" as different pun, one that augments my argument: "This cold Pentecost that numbs rather than inflames decends upon her not from the Father or the Holy Ghost but the 'the Air,' a lofty pun signifying the complete vaporization of the Son, 'heir' to the kingdom, the power, and the glory" (239–40).

3. THE ADVENTURE OF THE SELF: ON TRANSFORMING CALVINISM AND EMERSON'S TRANSCENDENTALISM (PP. 76–110)

1. Sue's reporting to Emily her experience of Emerson's visit indicates the depth of intimate, literary friendship the two women shared. For thorough explorations of the literary relationship between the two women, see Smith's essay in Juhasz, Miller, and Smith, *Comic Power* and her book, *Rowing in Eden: Rereading Emily Dickinson*. Smith and Ellen Louise Hart have edited and written the introduction to *Open Me Carefully: Emily Dickinson's Intimate Letters to Susan Huntington Dickinson*.

2. Wolff calls poems written from the grave, Dickinson's "proleptic voice" (219–38).

3. I have put side-by-side Franklin's version and a version transcribed from the fascicle manuscript.

4. Plato writes: "For a human being must understand a general conception formed by collecting into a unity by means of reason the many perceptions of the senses; and this is a recollection of those things which our soul once beheld, when it journeyed with God and, lifting its vision above the things which we now say exist, rose up into real being" (*Phaedrus* 249C).

5. Hagenbuchle writes: "Puritan concepts such as 'Heaven' and 'Grace' frequently trigger open conflicts in Dickinson between a religious and a poetic world view; the Christian heaven as a posthumous otherworldly reality, for example, clashes with her poetic heaven of symbolic potentiality. . . . Knowledge for her cannot be fixed in terms of some definite truth. . . . Therefore, her definitions are dynamic and open-ended explorations rather than assertions. In contrast to the Bible's apodictic 'Center,' Dickinson's poetry—to use her own term—is a poetry of 'Circumference' (L950); it pursues the movement of the very spirit of knowing, a process which is inseparably bound up with movement of language" (139).

6. Jane Donahue Eberwein sees this poem in terms of Calvinist theology or what conversion might be like had Dickinson actually experienced it: "Read in the light of

Calvinistic sacramental theology, the poem can be identified as a proclamation of grace achieved and immortality promised. Whether it celebrates an actual experience of assurance or is simply an imaginative rendering of what conversion would feel like to the saved, it shows the poet working brilliantly with an enduring Puritan system for language" ("Emily Dickinson and the Calvinist Sacramental" 94).

7. For a full discussion of Dickinson's funeral, see St. Armand (73–77), who observes that Dickinson planned every detail of her funeral. She "insisted on an all white funeral. Dickinson, who adjured the 'Dark Parade' of ebony hearse, tasseled horses, and muffled undertaker — 'the man / of Appalling Trade' (P 389) — anticipated royalty by commanding her own dazzling 'White Exploit' (P 922). . . . Every detail of the ritual had as many allegorical resonances as did the emblems in a Rossetti painting. In effect it was not only an innovative late Victorian 'happening' but Dickinson's last poem, a living witness to her symbolic intent to go 'White Unto the White Creator' (P 709), as well as to approach her heavenly lover in the spotless draperies of a spiritual virgin" (74). Dickinson's funeral, like her poems, plays on the conventions of nineteenth-century American culture. Dickinson at once appropriates the emblems of these conventions for her own empowerment and laughs at them. So in planning her funeral, Dickinson appropriates the symbols of spiritual purity while taking the path of the outsider. St. Armand notes that diarist Eudocia Flynt recorded "these startling facts: 'Emily Dickinson's funeral observed, private, no flowers, taken to the Cemetery by Irishmen, out of the back door, across the Fields!! her request.' . . . Not only was Dickinson as elusive in death as she had been in life, but she slipped out the back way of the family homestead, an exit traditionally reserved only for murderers, reprobates, and outcasts" (75). For a personal account of Emily Dickinson's funeral, see the description by her niece, Martha Dickinson Bianchi, in *Emily Dickinson Face to Face* (61–62 n).

8. In her essay, "Emily Dickinson and Class," Betsy Erkkila claims that this poem is racist: "Setting the speaker's own right to possession against the claims of some unnamed antagonist, the poem inscribes the social and territorial as well as racial imperatives of New England's ruling class. Although the poet speaks the language of Revelations, here as in 'A solemn thing – it was – I said / A woman – white – to be –' and other poems, the language of the 'Right' of 'White Election' cannot finally be separated from nineteenth-century debates about the racial hegemony of the white race and of New Englanders in particular" (9). This claim seems patently unfair or at the very least not warranted by the evidence. The resonance of white as mythology is greater; Mark Twain also dressed in white, and he clearly opposed slavery. Dickinson's choice of friends would indicate her sympathy lay with the abolitionists, not with maintaining "the hegemony of the white race." She, for example, befriended Thomas Wentworth Higginson, who was, according to Richard Sewall, a well-known "revolutionary abolitionist and reformer who, during the Civil War commanded a black regiment. Sewall notes that Dickinson "must have known Higginson's leanings since he was 'editorially applauded' in the Springfield Republican (540). Yet the poet sought him out and made him her 'preceptor.'"

9. In 1854, Dickinson wrote to the Reverend Edward Everett Hale to inquire about the last hours of her "Tutor" (who introduced her to Emerson), Benjamin Franklin Newton: "He talked often of God, but I do not know certainly if he was his Father in

Heaven — Please Sir, to tell me if he was willing to die, and if you think him at Home, I should love to know certainly that he was today in Heaven" (L 153) In 1878, when her dear friend Samuel Bowles died, she wrote to Higginson: "Mr. Bowles was not willing to die" (L 553).

10. St. Armand explains that the Sentimental Love Religion transformed Puritan death rituals, which stressed the horrors of death as a warning to the sinner: "The strategies of consolation developed by the Sentimental Love Religion stressed peaceful rest, aesthetic pleasure, and pious preservation over stern judgment, harsh utilitarianism, and physical decay. As Washington Irving admitted in 'Rural Funerals' in *The Sketch Book*: 'there is a dismal process going on in the grave, ere dust can return to its kindred dust, which the imagination sinks from contemplating.' Airtight caskets, marble mausoleums and garden cemeteries were surely one way to 'soften the horrors of the tomb, to beguile the mind from brooding over the disgraces of perishing mortality, and to associate the memory of the deceased with the most delicate and beautiful objects in nature'" (68).

11. About Emily Dickinson's dashes, see Paul Crumbley's *Inflections of the Pen: Dash and Voice in Emily Dickinson*. Crumbley writes that Dickinson's dash "can be read as an indication that Dickinson has rejected the myth of wholeness implied by the possibility of rending. Rather than being a painful symbol of loss and division, the dash suggests that disjunction, to Dickinson, is one of the defining characteristics of the self in language" (15).

12. In *Comic Power*, Juhasz uses poem 381 as an example of Dickinson in her teasing mode: "This turns out to be a poem about poetry, not about ballet, because the ballet performance takes place here in words, not en pointe. It's a glorious performance precisely because it does foreground its linguistic status. . . . watching her write about dancing helps us to see that she can indeed write" (57). Phillips, who sees both poems as literary performances (one of which performs glee, the other of which performs despair) writes of Dickinson's selection of the two poems to enclose in her letter: "The poet's choosing to pair the two poems was deliberate. They represent her confidence in herself and her art, whether or not any recognized it" (208). Eberwein writes that in this "delightfully ironic work . . . she deftly demonstrated her insight into the unfamiliar arts of ballet and opera and represented herself as deploying exuberant energy with graceful ease. The poem gives clear evidence of technical control, skill, and playfulness from its ostensibly humble beginning to its expansive conclusion" (*Dickinson Strategies* 130). Mossberg sees this poem as a declaration of independence, a refusal to conform to nineteenth-century conventions for poetry or women: "The poem champions self-reliance for a poet" (158).

13. Robert M. Greenberg observes: "That immediate individual experience is the medium by which the world is known and that consciousness is a ceaseless stream are the double doorway into Emerson's sense of experience; and they lead us to his ideal of innovation" (65).

14. There is an echo here of Plato, who says that before its birth every soul has beheld the original "beauty" or "realities." Once the soul unites with beauty (which Emerson translates into "Truth" or union with self-reliant "genius"), "the soul will not, if it can help it, be left alone by the beautiful one, but esteems him above all others, forgets for

him mother and brothers and all friends, neglects property and cares not for its loss, and despising all customs and proprieties in which it formerly took pride" (*Phaedrus*, 252). In the New Testament, too, there are echoes of this idea. In Matthew 10.33–36 Jesus says: "But whosoever shall deny me before men, him will I also deny before my Father which is in heaven. Think not that I am come to send peace on earth: I came not to send peace, but a sword. For I am come to set a man at variance against his father, and the daughter against her mother, and the daughter in law against her mother in law. And a man's foes shall be they of his own household." Also in Matthew 12.46–50 is the following: "While he yet talked to the people, behold, his mother and his brethren stood without, desiring to speak with him. Then one said unto him, Behold, thy mother and thy brethren stand without, desiring to speak with thee. But he answered and said unto him that told him, Who is my mother? and who are my brethren? And he stretched forth his hand toward his disciples, and said, Behold my mother and my brethren! For whosoever shall do the will of my Father which is in heaven, the same is my brother, and sister, and mother."

15. Wolosky argues that this poem shows that the "interest in language for its own sake is a function of lost proximity to the divine. . . . Emily Dickinson ultimately rejects poetry and language as a religious sphere in the church's stead. Instead of embracing language as an independent and self-sustaining power, she considers it in these terms and denies its efficacy" (154–55). I agree that the interest in language may be the result of "lost proximity to the divine." However, I have been arguing that Dickinson *does* replace the church with poetry.

16. "Experience" here may play on Emerson's "Experience," the despondent essay in which the death of his son puts his idealism to the test: "Grief too will make us idealists" (*Complete Writings* 253). Yet in the essay, grief makes Emerson a cynic (at least temporarily) as he struggles with the problem of subjectivity: "Dream delivers us to dream, and there is no end to illusion. . . . Nature and books belong to the eyes that see them" (253). And he laments: "We have learned that we do not see directly but mediately, and that we have no means of correcting these colored and distorted lenses which we are, or of computing the amount of their errors. Perhaps these subject lenses have a creative power; perhaps there are no objects" (261). Emerson expresses his fear that perception is pure projection, and that the "creative power" that he believes comes from self-reliance and idiosyncrasy may result in fragmentation rather than unity: "I know better than to claim any completeness for my picture. I am a fragment and this is a fragment of me" (264). Yet in the end Emerson reasserts that the individual needs to see subjectively and "[t]hat need makes in morals the capital virtue of self-trust" (263). And he ends by retracting his skepticism: "I know that the world I converse with in the city and in the farms is not the world I think. I observe that difference, and shall observe it. . . . in the solitude to which every man is always returning, he has a sanity and revelations which in his passage into new worlds he will carry with him. . . . there is victory yet for all justice; and the true romance which the world exists to realize will be the transformation of genius into practical power" (264). Dickinson asks similar questions in "her passage into new worlds" from solitude; unlike Emerson, however, she does not return to a self-reliant vision of correspondence. For a fuller discussion of "Experience," see the introduction.

17. Wendy Martin writes: "In this poem, consciousness replaces Christ and self-awareness supersedes salvation. Critics have traditionally focused on Dickinson as a religious poet and have failed to see that, for her, temporal life is not extended after death but becomes an 'experiment' or 'adventure.' No longer framed by a divine plan, the drama of the poet focuses on what happens between birth and death, not on the ultimate destiny of heaven or hell" (118).

18. Although the date of this poem is 1863, I maintain that it falls into the third phase of Dickinson's development. Dickinson's concerns are consistent throughout her life, yet in each stage of her development, her focus changes. In 1863, she was most concerned with "self-conversion." This poem indicates that in 1863 she is looking forward to her challenge of Emersonian transcendentalism.

19. McIntosh maintains the opposite: that "Four trees" "is apparently not concerned with a spiritual mystery" (156).

20. Diehl argues that Dickinson never achieves either the kind of acceptance of the self's relationship to the world or the acceptance of the self that I have been describing. She writes that "the salves Emerson applies to heal the wound between 'I and the abyss' remain temperamentally unavailable to Dickinson" (171). As Diehl goes on to explain, for Emerson, even his later period, in which, as in "Experience," his earlier idealism is tempered by his confrontation with the abyss, he finds human consciousness a "salve": "The eye of the observer is the gift of the poet and offers him imaginative freedom from the circumstances of life, the pain of existence. . . . The human mind provides the consciousness that lends meaning to an otherwise un-self-conscious, hence powerless nature. Man is the vital, necessary force that unites God to his works. Moreover, if one goes deep enough into the self, he discovers the truth is applicable to all men; the Other for Emerson is the Self, whereas for Dickinson the self can and most often does become the demonic Other" (172). Diehl's analysis of Dickinson's relationship to the Romantics and to issues of gender is an excellent and crucial contribution. And I agree with her assertion that the "degree to which Dickinson risks all, her quality of radical experimentation, is . . . intimately connected to her sense of herself as estranged from the tradition" (1). However, I argue that Dickinson's response to her "estrangement from the tradition" changes over time. The self figured as "demonic Other" is the part of the self that has internalized cultural imperatives. The struggle with the demon virtually disappears after the early 1860s because, as I have been showing, Dickinson develops a different, relational way of seeing. Like Benfey, I believe Diehl's claims that Dickinson was utterly estranged from an Emersonian connectedness with nature to be too extreme. In response to Diehl's assertion that Dickinson "perceives a damning division between herself and the surrounding landscape" (36), Benfey modifies the schism by complicating the notion that the poems that deal with romantic concerns are not merely "expressions of Dickinson's skepticism with regard to the natural world," but are more complex perceptions about the problem of relation: "these poems are, in fact, investigations of what prevents our access to the world (and to other people), and what might allow for it" (110).

21. Diehl writes, "Each of us hold a particular, if hidden, resentment towards the voice that first liberates us" (162).

22. Dickinson incorporated these words into two letters, one to Higginson (L 330) and one to James D. Clark (L 788). Because I believe that many of her "letters" are poems (or challenge what we think a poem is) and because these words scan, I argue they should be looked upon as literary language and would categorize them as a poem.

4. "THEY SHUT ME UP IN PROSE": LATE LETTER-POEMS (PP. 111–150)

1. We have R. W. Franklin's *The Manuscript Books of Emily Dickinson*, which provides facsimiles of the fascicles. However, to date, except in the archives in libraries, very few of the manuscripts that were not included in the fascicles are available. There is also little available in which the reader can see, typographically translated, how the letter-poems were lineated by Dickinson. Marta L. Werner has published *Emily Dickinson's Open Folios: Scenes of Reading, Surfaces of Writing*, which includes forty facsimiles of the "Lord letters" and commentary by Werner. Werner has also published a site-licensed electronic archive that includes her commentary, *Radical Scatters: Emily Dickinson's Fragments, 1870–1886*.

2. Smith writes that her book "distinguishes itself from other Dickinson studies in two primary and vital ways: first, by arguing that Dickinson 'published' herself, thereupon comparing and contrasting her various presentations to different audiences accordingly; and second, by placing Dickinson's thirty-five-year literary relationship with Susan Huntington Gilbert Dickinson at the center of the inquiry. Throughout the book, all interpretations of Dickinson's texts will be illuminated by relevant comments to, from, and about her most influential audience, "Dear Sue," upon whom the poet lavished more attention and more poetic and epistolary works than any other contemporary" (*Rowing in Eden* 4).

3. In *Open Me Carefully*, Ellen Louise Hart and Martha Nell Smith comment: "In one of the few surviving letters from Susan to Emily, Susan excitedly inscribes the greeting, 'All's well' in one corner of the fold, and then compares their mutual enterprise — making their poetry known to the public — to the Civil War general Burnside's siege and the capture of Roanoke Island in February 1862 (96–97).

4. "Sue Dickinson's importance has been downplayed. We are indebted to one of husband Austin's other women, Loomis Todd, for initially editing and translating Emily Dickinson's texts into mass reproducible texts. That the adulterous editor would want to deemphasize the importance of her lover's wife to the poet whom Loomis Todd commodified but never met face to face is not at all surprising" (*Rowing in Eden* 40).

5. There is also this beautiful and loving description by Smith: "To see the quiet weave of the fine stationary, and the pinholes those leaves had been so carefully threaded together to make the fascicles, the manuscript books she folded and tucked and left in her drawer (or chest) for posterity, and to see the poems written and rewritten, sometimes even revised after they had been carefully copied onto these pages sometimes edged with gold lead, sometimes embossed (with a capitol building or a queen's head or flower), enables one to see more clearly the writer for whom the choice of each word mattered, the woman who diligently recorded her words on exquisite paper, then

lovingly laid the little books of lyric away in a place where they were sure to be discovered by those willing away that portion of her belongings 'Assignable' (F 26; P 465)" (*Rowing in Eden* 16).

6. Johnson chooses the version of the poem that reads in leonine hexameters, a hexameter line consisting of two rhyming trimeters:

> Take all away from me, but leave me Ecstasy,
> And I am richer then than all my Fellow Men –
> Ill it becometh me to dwell so wealthily
> When at my very Door are those possessing more,
> In abject poverty –
>
> (J 1640)

7. Perhaps in her drafts, Dickinson first wrote her words out in prose, then worked them into form, as the late Thom Gunn said he did.

8. Shurr extracted parts of the letters which seemed to him to be poems, without consulting the manuscripts. Such a process is, to say the least, an act of revision, and is subject to idiosyncrasies of the editor. Shurr's "new poem" 330 reads "Morning without you is a dwindled dawn – / Quickened toward celestial things / by Crows I heard this Morning." If one is mining the letters for poems, the only criteria for determining what is a poem are the editor's ear and taste. Shurr heard poetry in letter 981, as I did. But we created different poems out of what we heard.

9. In *Emily Dickinson's Open Folios*, Werner notes: "The illegible word, here transcribed as voice, is transcribed by Johnson as [racy?]." I think Werner's transcription makes more sense in the context of the letter-poem, and the script certainly could read "voice."

10. Emerson's ideas about creation of the soul are indebted to Plato, as I have noted throughout this book.

WORKS CITED

Anderson, Charles R. *Emily Dickinson's Poetry: Stairway of Surprise*. New York: Holt, 1960; Garden City, N.Y.: Anchor/Doubleday, 1966.

Barnstone, Aliki. "Mastering the Master: Emily Dickinson's Appropriations of Crisis Conversion." In *The Calvinist Roots of the Modern Era*, edited by Aliki Barnstone, Michael Tomasek Manson, and Carol J. Singley. Hanover, N.H.: University Press of New England, 1997.

———. "While Rapture Changed its Dress: The Development of Emily Dickinson's Poetry." Ph.D. diss., University of California Berkeley, UMI, 1995.

Barnstone, Willis. *The New Covenant*. New York: Penguin-Putnam, 2001.

Benfey, Christopher E. G. *Emily Dickinson and the Problem of Others*. Amherst: University of Massachusetts Press, 1984.

Bennett, Fordyce R. *A Reference Guide to the Bible in Emily Dickinson's Poetry*. Lanham, Md.: Scarecrow, 1997.

Bennett, Paula. "'By a Mouth That Cannot Speak': Spectral Presence in Emily Dickinson's Letters." *The Emily Dickinson Journal* 1, no. 2 (1992): 76–99.

———. *Emily Dickinson: Woman Poet*. Iowa City: University of Iowa Press, 1990.

Bianchi, Martha Dickinson. *Emily Dickinson Face to Face*. Boston: Houghton Mifflin, 1932.

Bishop, Elizabeth. *Geography III*. New York: Farrar, Straus and Giroux, 1976.

Blackmur, R. P. "Emily Dickinson: Notes on Prejudice and Fact." In *Selected Essays of R. P. Blackmur*, edited and introduced by Denis Donaghue. New York: Ecco, 1985.

Blake, William. *The Complete Poetry and Selected Prose of John Donne & The Complete Poetry of William Blake*. With an introduction by Robert Silliman Hillyer. New York: Modern Library, 1941.

Blasing, Mutlu Konuk. *American Poetry: The Rhetoric of its Forms*. New Haven: Yale University Press, 1987.

Bradstreet, Anne. "Prologue." http://www.annebradstreet.com/prologue.htm

———. "Verses upon the Burning of our House, July 10th, 1666." http://www.annebradstreet.com/verses_upon_the_burning_of_our_house.htm

Breitwieser, Mitchell Robert. *Cotton Mather and Benjamin Franklin: The Price of Representative Personality*. Cambridge: Cambridge University Press, 1984.

Bulfinch, Thomas. *Myths of Greece and Rome*. with an introduction by Joseph Campbell. Compiled by Bryan Holme. New York: Penguin, 1981.

Burke, Kenneth. "I, Eye, Ay—Emerson's Early Essay on Nature: Thoughts on the Machinery of Transcendence." In *Romanticism: Critical Essays in American Literature*, edited by James Barbour and Thomas Quirk. New York: Garland, 1986.

Cameron, Sharon. *Choosing Not Choosing: Dickinson's Fascicles*. Chicago: University of Chicago Press, 1992.

———. *Lyric Time: Emily Dickinson and the Limits of Genre*. Baltimore: Johns Hopkins University Press, 1979.

Capps, Jack L. *Emily Dickinson's Reading: 1836–1886*. Cambridge, Mass.: Harvard University Press, 1966.

Carton, Evan. *The Rhetoric of American Romance: Dialectic and Identity in Emerson, Dickinson, Poe, and Hawthorne*. Baltimore: Johns Hopkins University Press, 1985.

Cixous, Hélène. "The Laugh of Medusa." In *New French Feminisms: An Anthology*. Edited and with an introduction by Elaine Marks and Isabelle de Courtivon. New York: Schocken, 1980.

Cody, John. *After Great Pain: The Inner Life of Emiy Dickinson*. Cambridge, Mass.: Harvard University Press, 1971.

Cott, Nancy F. *The Bonds of Womanhood: "Women's Sphere" in New England, 1780–1835*. New Haven: Yale University Press, 1977.

Covici, Pascal. *Humor and Revelation in American Literature: The Puritan Connection*. Columbia: University of Missouri Press, 1997.

Crumbley, Paul. *Inflections of the Pen: Dash and Voice in Emily Dickinson*. Lexington: University Press of Kentucky, 1997.

Dandurand, Karen. "New Dickinson Civil War Publications." *American Literature* 56, no. 1 (March 1984): 17–27.

Decker, William Merrill. *Epistolary Practices: Letter Writing in America before Telecommunications*. Chapel Hill: University of North Carolina Press, 1998.

Dickinson, Emily. *The Letters of Emily Dickinson*. Edited by Thomas H. Johnson and Theodora Ward. 3 vols. Cambridge, Mass.: Harvard University Press, 1958.

———. *The Manuscript Books of Emily Dickinson*. Edited by R. W. Franklin. 2 vols. Cambridge, Mass.: Harvard University Press, 1981.

———. *The Master Letters of Emily Dickinson*. Edited by R. W. Franklin. Amherst, Mass.: Amherst College Press, 1986.

———. *The Poems of Emily Dickinson*. Edited by Thomas H. Johnson. 3 vols. Cambridge, Mass.: Harvard University Press, 1951, 1955.

———. *The Poems of Emily Dickinson: Variorum Edition*. Edited by R. W. Franklin. 3 vols. Cambridge, Mass.: Harvard University Press, 1998.

Diehl, Joanne Feit. *Dickinson and the Romantic Imagination*. Princeton: Princeton University Press, 1981.

Dobson, Joanne. *Dickinson and the Strategies of Reticence: The Woman Writer in Nineteenth-Century America*. Bloomington: Indiana University Press, 1989.

Douglas, Ann. *The Feminization of American Culture*. New York: Avon, 1977.

Eberwein, Jane Donahue. *Dickinson: Strategies of Limitation*. Amherst: University of Massachusetts Press, 1985.

———. "Emily Dickinson and the Calvinist Sacramental Tradition." In *Emily Dickinson: A Collection of Critical Essays*, edited by Judith Farr. Upper Saddle River, N.J.: Prentice-Hall, 1996.

Edwards, Jonathan. "Personal Narrative." http://www.jonathanedwards.com/text/
Personal/PNarrative.htm.
———. "Sinners in the Hands of an Angry God." http://www.jonathanedwards
.com/sermons/Warnings/sinners.htm.
Ellis, Richard S. "'A little East of Jordan': Human-Divine Encounter in Dickinson
and the Hebrew Bible." *Emily Dickinson Journal* 8, no. 1 (1999): 36–58.
Emerson, Ralph Waldo. *The Complete Writings of Ralph Waldo Emerson*. New York:
Wm. H. Wise, 1929.
———. *The Heart of Emerson's Journals*. Edited by Bliss Perry. Boston: Houghton
Mifflin, 1926.
Erkkila, Betsy. "Emily Dickinson and Class." *American Literary History* 4 (Spring
1992): 1–27.
———. *The Wicked Sisters: Women Poets, Literary History, and Discord*. New York:
Oxford University Press, 1992.
Farr, Judith. *The Passion of Emily Dickinson*. Cambridge, Mass.: Harvard University
Press, 1992.
Fiedler, Leslie. *Love and Death in the American Novel*. New York: Dell, 1966.
Finch, A. R. C. "Dickinson and Patriarchal Meter: A Theory of Metrical Codes."
PMLA 102, no. 2 (March 1987): 166–76.
Forrer, Richard. *Theodices in Conflict: A Dilemma in Puritan Ethics and Nineteenth-
Century American Literature*. New York: Greenwood, 1986.
Franklin, Benjamin. *The Autobiography of Benjamin Franklin*. In Archiving Early
America: Historic Documents from 18th Century America. http://earlyamerica
.com/lives/franklin/.
Franklin, R. W. *The Editing of Emily Dickinson: A Reconsideration*. Madison: Uni-
versity of Wisconsin Press, 1967.
Garbowsky, Maryanne M. *The House without the Door: A Study of Emily Dickinson
and the Illness of Agoraphobia*. Rutherford, N.J.: Fairleigh Dickinson University
Press, 1989.
Gelpi, Albert J. *The Tenth Muse: The Psyche of the American Poet*. Cambridge, Mass.:
Harvard University Press, 1965.
Gilbert, Sandra M. "The Wayward Nun beneath the Hill: Emily Dickinson and the
Mysteries of Womanhood." In *Feminist Critics Read Emily Dickinson*, edited by
Suzanne Juhasz. Bloomington: Indiana University Press, 1983.
Greenberg, Robert M. *Splintered Worlds: Fragmentation and the Ideal of Diversity in
the Work of Emerson, Melville, Whitman, and Dickinson*. Boston: Northeastern
University Press, 1993.
Gura, Philip E. *The Wisdom of Words: Language, Theology, and Literature in the
New England Renaissance*. Middletown, Conn.: Wesleyan University Press,
1981.
Habegger, Alfred. *My Wars Are Laid Away in Books: The Life of Emily Dickinson*.
New York: Random House, 2001.
Hagenbuchle, Roland. "Sign and Process: The Concept of Language in Emerson
and Dickinson." *Journal of the American Renaissance* 25 (1979): 137–55.

Haltteunen, Karen. *Confidence Men and Painted Women: A Study of Middle-Class Culture in America, 1830–1870.* New Haven: Yale University Press, 1982.

Hart, Ellen Louise. "The Elizabeth Putnam Whitney Manuscripts and New Strategies for Editing Emily Dickinson's Letters." *The Emily Dickinson Journal: Special Issue on Editing and the Letters* 4, no. 1 (1995): 44–75.

———. *Open Me Carefully: Emily Dickinson's Letters to Susan Huntington Dickinson.* Edited by Ellen Louise Hart and Martha Nell Smith. Ashfield, Mass.: Paris Press, 1998.

Hawthorne, Nathaniel. "The Artist of the Beautiful." In The Writings of Nathaniel Hawthorne. http://www.eldritchpress.org/nh/nhwrit.html.

Heginbotham, Eleanor. "'Paradise Fictitious': Dickinson's Milton." *The Emily Dickinson Journal* 7, no. 1 (1998): 55–74.

Hillman, Brenda. *Death Tractates.* Hanover, N.H.: University Press of New England/ Wesleyan University Press, 1992.

Hogue, Cynthia. "'The Plucked String': Emily Dickinson, Marianne Moore and the Poetics of Select Defects." *The Emily Dickinson Journal* 7, no. 1 (1998): 89–109.

Homans, Margaret. *Women Writers and Poetic Identity: Dorothy Wordsworth, Emily Brontë, and Emily Dickinson.* Princeton: Princeton University Press, 1980.

Howe, Susan. *The Birth-mark: Unsettling the Wilderness in American Literary History.* Hanover, N.H.: University Press of New England/Wesleyan University Press, 1993.

———. *My Emily Dickinson.* Berkeley, Calif.: North Atlantic Books, 1985.

Jack, Dana Crowley. *Silencing the Self: Women and Depression.* New York: Harper-Collins, 1991.

Johnson, Thomas H. *Emily Dickinson: An Interpretive Biography.* Cambridge, Mass.: Harvard University Press, 1955.

Juhasz, Suzanne, Cristanne Miller, and Martha Nell Smith. *Comic Power in Emily Dickinson.* Austin: University of Texas Press, 1993.

Keller, Karl. *The Only Kangaroo Among the Beauty: Emily Dickinson and America.* Baltimore: Johns Hopkins University Press, 1979.

Kermode, Frank. *The Genesis of Secrecy: On the Interpretation of Narrative.* Cambridge, Mass.: Harvard University Press, 1979.

King, John Owen. *The Iron of Melancholy: Structures of Spiritual Conversion in America from the Puritan Conscience to Victorian Neurosis.* Middletown, Conn.: Wesleyan University Press, 1983.

Lang, Amy Schrager. *Prophetic Woman: Anne Hutchinson and the Problem of Dissent in the Literature of New England.* Berkeley and Los Angeles: University of California Press, 1987.

Leyda, Jay. *The Years and Hours of Emily Dickinson.* 2 vols. New Haven: Yale University Press, 1960.

Longsworth, Polly. *Austin and Mabel: The Amherst Affair and Love Letters of Austin Dickinson and Mabel Loomis Todd.* With an introduction by Richard Sewall. New York: Holt, 1984.

Loving, Jerome. *Emily Dickinson: The Poet on the Second Story*. Cambridge: Cambridge University Press, 1986.

Martin, Wendy. *An American Triptych: Anne Bradstreeet, Emily Dickinson, Adrienne Rich*. Chapel Hill: University of North Carolina Press, 1984.

McIntosh, James. *Nimble Believing: Dickinson and the Unknown*. Ann Arbor: University of Michigan Press, 2000.

Miller, Perry. *The New England Mind: The Seventeenth Century*. Cambridge, Mass.: Harvard University Press, 1954.

Milton, John. *The Complete Poetry of John Milton*. Edited by John T. Shawcross. Garden City, N.Y.: Anchor/Doubleday, 1971.

Moore, Marianne. *The Complete Poems of Marianne Moore*. New York: Macmillan/Viking, 1967.

Morgan, Edmund S. *Visible Saints: The History of a Puritan Idea*. Ithaca, N.Y.: Cornell University Press, 1965.

Morris, Timothy. "The Development of Emily Dickinson's Style." In *On Dickinson: The Best from American Literature*, edited by Edwin H. Cady and Louis J. Budd. Durham, N.C.: Duke University Press, 1990.

Mossberg, Barbara Antonina Clarke. *Emily Dickinson: When a Writer is a Daughter*. Bloomington: Indiana University Press, 1982.

Oberhaus, Dorothy Huff. *Emily Dickinson's Fascicles: Method and Meaning*. University Park: Penn State Press, 1995.

Patterson, Rebecca. *Emily Dickinson's Imagery*. Edited and with an introduction by Margaret H. Freeman. Amherst: University of Massachusetts Press, 1979.

Petrino, Elizabeth A. *Emily Dickinson and Her Contemporaries: Women's Verse in America, 1820–1995*. Hanover, N.H.: University Press of New England, 1998.

Pettit, Norman. *The Heart Prepared*. New Haven: Yale University Press, 1966; reprint, Middletown, Conn.: Wesleyan University Press, 1989.

Phillips, Elizabeth. *Emily Dickinson: Personae and Performance*. University Park: Penn State Press, 1988.

Plato. *Plato: Euthyphro, Apology, Crito, Phaedo, Phaedrus*. Translated by Harold North Fowler. Cambridge, Mass.: Harvard University Press, 1914.

Pollak, Vivian R. *Dickinson: The Anxiety of Gender*. Ithaca, N.Y.: Cornell University Press, 1984.

Porter, David. *The Art of Emily Dickinson's Early Poetry*. Cambridge, Mass.: Harvard University Press, 1966.

———. "Emily Dickinson: The Poetics of Doubt." *Emerson Society Quarterly* 60 (Summer 1970): 86–93.

Reynolds, David S. *Beneath the American Renaissance: The Subersive Imagination in the Age of Emerson and Melville*. Cambridge, Mass.: Harvard University Press, 1989.

Rich, Adrienne. "Vesuvius at Home: The Power of Emily Dickinson." In *Lies, Secrets, and Silence: Selected Prose, 1966–1978*. New York: Norton, 1979.

Rowlandson, Mary. "A Narrative of the Captivity and Restoration of Mary Rowlandson." In *So Dreadful a Judgment: Puritan Responses to King Philip's War,*

1676–1677, edited by Richard Slotkin and James K. Folsom, 315–366. Middletown, Conn.: Wesleyan University Press, 1978.

St. Armand, Barton Levi. *Emily Dickinson and Her Culture: The Soul's Society.* New York: Cambridge University Press, 1984.

Sartre, Jean-Paul. *"What is Literature?" and Other Essays.* With an introduction by Steven Ungar. Cambridge, Mass.: Harvard University Press, 1988.

Scholes, Robert. *Protocols of Reading.* New Haven: Yale University Press, 1989.

Sewall, Richard B. *The Life of Emily Dickinson.* New York: Farrar Straus, 1974.

Sherwood, William R. *Circumference and Circumstance: Stages in the Mind and Art of Emily Dickinson.* New York: Columbia University Press, 1968.

Sheurer, Erika. "'Near, but remote': Emily Dickinon's Epistolary Voice." *The Emily Dickinson Journal* (Special Issue on Editing and the Letters) 4, no. 1 (1995): 86–107.

Shurr, William H. "Editing *New Poems of Emily Dickinson.*" *The Emily Dickinson Journal* (Special Issue on Editing and the Letters) 4, no. 1 (1995): 118–25.

———. *The Marriage of Emily Dickinson.* Lexington: University Press of Kentucky, 1983.

———, ed., with Anna Dunlap and Emily Grey Shurr. *New Poems of Emily Dickinson.* Chapel Hill: University of North Carolina Press, 1993.

Slotkin, Richard. *Regeneration Through Violence: The Mythology of the American Frontier, 1600–1860.* Middletown, Conn.: Wesleyan University Press, 1973.

Smith, Martha Nell. "The Importance of a Hypermedia Archive of Dickinson's Creative Work." *The Emily Dickinson Journal* (Special Issue on Editing and the Letters) 4, no. 1 (1995): 75–85.

———. *Rowing in Eden: Rereading Emily Dickinson.* Austin: University of Texas Press, 1992.

Stonum, Gary Lee. *The Dickinson Sublime.* Madison: University of Wisconsin Press, 1990.

Thoreau, Henry David. "Resistance to Civil Government, or Civil Disobedience." Webtext by Jessica Gordon. http://www.vcu.edu/engweb/transweb/civil/.

Tompkins, Jane. "Sentimental Power: *Uncle Tom's Cabin* and the Politics of Literary History." In *Feminisms: An Anthology of Literary Theory and Criticism,* edited by Robyn R. Warhol and Diane Price Herndl. New Brunswick, N.J.: Rutgers University Press, 1991.

Travisano, Thomas J. *Elizabeth Bishop: Her Artistic Development.* Charlottesville: University Press of Virginia, 1988.

Turco, Lewis Putnam. *Emily Dickinson: Woman of Letters.* Albany: State University of New York Press, 1993.

———. "Iron Pyrites in the Dickinson Mine." *The Emily Dickinson Journal* (Special Issue on Editing and the Letters) 4, no. 1 (1995): 108–17.

Waggoner, Hyatt. *American Poets, from the Puritans to the Present.* Baton Rouge: Louisiana State University Press, 1968; rev. ed., 1984.

Walker, Nancy A. *A Very Serious Thing: Women's Humor and American Culture.* Minneapolis: University of Minnesota Press, 1988.

Wallace, Ronald. *God Be With the Clown: Humor in American Poetry.* Columbia: University of Missouri Press, 1984.

Weisbuch, Robert. *Emily Dickinson's Poetry.* Chicago: University of Chicago Press, 1975.

Werner, Marta L. *Emily Dickinson's Open Folios: Scenes of Reading, Surfaces of Writing.* Ann Arbor: University of Michigan Press, 1995.

——. *Radical Scatters: Emily Dickinson's Fragments, 1870–1886.* Ann Arbor: University of Michigan Press, 2000.

——. "The Shot Bird's Progress: Emily Dickinson's Master Letters." In *Emily Dickinson: Woman of Letters,* edited by Lewis Putnam Turco. Albany: State University of New York Press, 1993.

Whitman, Walt. *Leaves of Grass.* First (1955) edition, eidted and with an introduction by Malcolm Cowley. New York: Viking, 1959; reprint, Penguin, 1986.

Wilson, R. Jackson. *Figures of Speech: American Writers and the Literary Marketplace, from Benjamin Franklin to Emily Dickinson.* Baltimore: Johns Hopkins University Press, 1989.

Wolff, Cynthia Griffin. *Emily Dickinson.* New York: Knopf, 1986.

Wolosky, Shira. *Emily Dickinson: A Voice of War.* New Haven: Yale University Press, 1984.

INDEX OF FIRST LINES

SUBJECT INDEX

Abolitionism, 159n6, 165n8. *See also*
reformers.
affections. *See* earthly attachment; friends;
the relational; vanity
Affliction, 13, 72–75, 152n6
afterlife, 48, 57, 73, 77, 86. *See also* damnation; grace; heaven; hell; redemption
alienation, 10, 33–35, 77, 81, 90. *See also*
exclusion
ambiguity, 55, 75, 78, 81, 86, 159n9. *See also*
indeterminacy; whiteness
Amherst, 1, 10–11, 33–34, 69, 76, 108, 138,
152n6
anger, 9, 45–46, 51, 107
antinomianism, 37, 111, 120
appropriation, 13, 41, 44–45, 85–86, 102, 108,
116, 120, 156n16, 159n8, 162n23, 165n7; of
crisis conversion, 54–75, 77, 91, 143, 148
annis mirabilis, 8; characteristics of, 8–10.
See also self-conversion
attachment. *See* earthly attachment
audience, 49, 122–24, 137–141, 143–146,
157n2. *See also* reading
Authentic Self, the, 39–40, 47, 49, 51. *See also*
the Over-Eye
autobiography, 44–45, 154–155n16. *See also*
psychobiography

Beecher, Catharine, 120. *See also* Harriet
Beecher Stowe; woman's sphere
Bianchi, Martha Dickinson (ED's niece), 54,
162nn24, 25
Bible, the, 55, 72–73, 80, 85, 135, 150, 160n13,
164n5; David and Goliath, 59; Gospels
and dialogue, 147–150; Hebrew, 158n4;
Jacob, biblical story of, 31–33, 158nn3,
4; Mark 4.12, 61, 75; Mark 15.17–20, 38;
Matthew 7.14, 36; parables, 61; Paul
in 2 Corinthians, 41; Torah, the, 158n.
See also dialogue; Plato

Bishop, Elizabeth, 2–3, 151n3, 158n5
Blake, William, 53; and child persona, 7,
43–44; "Chimney Sweeper, The," 7,
43–44; "I went to the Garden of Love,"
153n8; "Poems of Innocence," 7. *See also*
child persona; suffering
blankness, 58, 64, 71, 74–75, 78; of the page,
81, 91. *See also* numbness; white
boundaries of the self. *See* the self
Browning, Robert, 116, 158n2
Browning, Elizabeth Barrett, 45, 158n2
Brontë, Charlotte, 158n2
Bushnell, Horace, 47, 48, 52, 161n21

Calvinism, 6, 8–21, 41–45, 54–75, 77–93,
95–97, 99, 102, 108, 137–38, 148–149,
154–157n16, 160nn14, 15, 161n20, 21,
23, 164n5, 164–165n6, 166n10. *See also*
conversion; death; election; heaven
Cerberus, 102
change vs. stasis. *See* stasis
Channing, William Ellery, 161n20. *See also*
democracy; reformers
Chauncy, Charles, 161n20. *See also* democracy; reformers
child persona, 7–8, 27, 33–38, 43–44, 51–52,
158n5, 160n12, 162–63n29. *See also*
William Blake; death; sentimentality;
suffering
circumference, 40, 59, 83, 101, 126, 137, 158n2,
164n5
Civil War, the, 152n6, 159n7, 165n8; ED's
Civil War publications, 119–121, 159n7
Cixous, Hélène, 30, 38–39, 49, 53. *See also*
feminist criticism
Clemens, Samuel (Mark Twain). *See* Twain,
Mark; white
Coleridge, Samuel Taylor, 80. *See also*
reason
comedy, 158n2. *See also* humor; satire